Just Violence

Stanford Studies in Human Rights

Just Violence

Torture and Human Rights in the Eyes of the Police

Rachel Wahl

Stanford University Press
Stanford, California

Stanford University Press
Stanford, California

Printed in the United States of America on acid-free, archival-quality paper.

Library of Congress Cataloging-in-Publication Data

Names: Wahl, Rachel, author.
Title: Just violence : torture and human rights in the eyes of the police / Rachel Wahl.
Other titles: Stanford studies in human rights.
Description: Stanford, California : Stanford University Press, 2017. | Series: Stanford studies in human rights | Includes bibliographical references and index.
Identifiers: LCCN 2016020138 (print) | LCCN 2016020970 (ebook) | ISBN 9780804794718 (cloth : alk. paper) | ISBN 9781503601017 (pbk. : alk. paper) | ISBN 9781503601024 (electronic)
Subjects: LCSH: Police--India--Attitudes. | Police brutality--India--Public opinion. | Torture--India--Public opinion. | Violence--India--Public opinion. | Human rights--India--Public opinion. | Public opinion--India.
Classification: LCC HV8247 .W34 2017 (print) | LCC HV8247 (ebook) | DDC 364.6/7--dc23
LC record available at https://lccn.loc.gov/2016020138

Typeset by Dovetail Publishing Services in 10/14 Minion Pro

For Jeff

Contents

Foreword

IN HER MULTILAYERED, PROVOCATIVE, AND DEEPLY REASONED STUDY of perceptions of human rights practices among police officers in contemporary India, Rachel Wahl forces us to consider "human rights from the other side." In leading us into her interlocutors' morally complex worldviews and then in showing us how and why these worldviews are as much a part of the "culture of human rights" as the more immediately recognizable forms of human rights advocacy and education, Wahl brings us right up against the lines that separate understanding from resignation, ethical creativity from sheer corruption, and cultural context from the impossibility of translocal normative action. In the process, her ethnographic and critical research demonstrates the ways in which the most basic of moral questions—What do my beliefs demand of me? Is justice compatible with certain kinds of practical compromises? Must I act on behalf of something bigger than myself to be a good person? Am I prepared to use violence to defend my beliefs?—shape and even define the micro-normative vernacularizations of human rights well beyond the shining light of naming and shaming, country reports to national and international monitoring bodies, and the "justice cascades" that flow from human rights prosecutions.

Wahl's book provides yet more compelling evidence for precisely why scholarship that combines ethnographic accounts of human rights practices with bold theorizing about what these practices have to teach us form a kind of urgent rejoinder to the recent lamentations over human rights having entered their historic "endtimes" on the one hand, and, on the other, those enduringly seductive critiques of human rights that traffic in the simplifying (and often ideological) rhetorics of postcolonial resistance. In the course of Wahl's analysis, the master narratives of "Global North," "Global South," "postcolony," "the West," and many others wither on the vine of abstraction as the practice of human rights from the perspective of intimate levels of moral accommodation and personal struggle reveals interpretation, negotiation, and reframing that defy comfortable categorical slotting.

Wahl began her research on human rights education and police tactics in India with an *apparent* paradox: Why would individual police officers admit to torturing suspects when they both knew that such treatment violated human rights and they had nothing to gain by making such admissions? Yet understanding why this paradox was apparent is the key to understanding why the implications of Wahl's study are so far reaching. As other ethnographers of human rights have shown, the experience of human rights training, appropriation, and performance is largely intransitive. Although the possibility of purposive and collective action based on human rights is always kept in the distance, in fact, the most immediate effects take place at the level of moral identity. As scholars have demonstrated, people encounter the strong message of human rights as a call to think of themselves as different kinds of moral actors.

But when this shifting and unstable moral consciousness eventually comes to shape action, not through the grand gestures of social change or in historic struggles for justice, but through the minute, everyday ethical decisions whose consequences are ultimately limited, even banal, the results appear confounding only when read against the foundational metaphors of human rights. Yet when seen as the result of new moral thinking put to use in a world marked by Taylorian "cross-purposes" (and here is where the paradox disappears), one comes to understand how the torture of suspects can be seen by police officers as a legitimate—even necessary—connection in a moral and cultural chain on which human rights, compassion, duty to community, and the wisdom of sacrifice (*kuch paane ke liye kuch khona parta hai*) are also links.

Like all education, human rights education is not a technical blueprint, in which moral choice A requires moral action A1. Instead, as Wahl's study shows us, the practice of human rights takes place in terms of what she calls the "plasticity of moral vocabularies." This is not, however, a model of analysis that leads to the relativistic justification of violence in the name of cultural authenticity. Rather, in Wahl's deft rendering, we come to appreciate the fact that empathetic understanding, grounded in the methodologies of close observation and thick description, is a precondition for lasting change in a world in which there "can be no perfect way to advocate for equality, liberty, and protection from harm."

Mark Goodale
Series Editor
Stanford Studies in Human Rights

Preface

IT IS ALWAYS DIFFICULT TO KNOW precisely how the questions that drive research first emerge. But two early experiences stand out as formative for this project. The first was my visit as a child to Yad Vashem, Jerusalem's Holocaust Museum. It was around then that I became preoccupied with understanding how it is possible for people to do others so much harm. The stories I heard there still haunt me, as does the question of how people who brutalize others understand and live with what they do.

The second experience came years later, when I worked with educational NGOs in the United States, Peru, and China. In different ways, these organizations sought to change what other groups believe and how they live. The American organization hoped to model particular ways of parenting for families whose children had been incarcerated. The Peruvian NGO worked to convince impoverished parents to value education for their children. In China, the aim was to change how children use their minds and relate to authorities as well as peers, encouraging "critical thinking" by urging them to question their teachers and debate with one another. I came to wonder how the targets of these efforts perceive them. What values do these parents and children hold that may be displaced by these new ideals? What do these already existing values mean to the people who live by them, and how do such concerns inform the way they respond to educators' and activists' efforts to change what they believe?

My attention ultimately turned to one of the most visible education and advocacy efforts of our era: the human rights movement. In Michael Ignatieff's words in his book, *Human Rights as Politics and Idolatry*, human rights have become the "lingua franca of global moral thought," spreading around the globe and winning the endorsement of almost every state. But how state officials respond to this international effort to change them remains even more opaque than how children and parents respond to the prodding of NGOs.

This book then is inspired by the two questions that arose from my early experiences. The first question probes how people—in this case, police officers—understand their own violence. The second examines the implications of their self-understanding and the values that accompany it for how police respond to human rights campaigns to prevent this violence.

There could be many possible settings for a book on police violence. National outrage over police killings of unarmed people of color in the United States makes the problem impossible to ignore there; indeed, there are few if any countries where the coercive power of the police has not created problems for the promises of democracy and the protection of human rights.

I turned to India for this study because of the contradiction and therefore the puzzle it offered. Even more so than the United States, the country embraces the institutions and language of international human rights. While the U.S. government tends to be vocal about human rights beyond its borders, it is notoriously hesitant to scrutinize domestic concerns in such terms. Hence, while India boasts a National Human Rights Commission and requires all police officers to be trained in human rights, neither are the case in the United States. India is also home to dynamic local movements for social justice. Rooted in national history such as the Independence movement and in the response to the State of Emergency under Indira Gandhi, civil society in India is no mere response to international norms. Yet as I'll discuss, torture, extrajudicial executions, arbitrary arrest and detention, and related abuses of power on the part of the police and military are pervasive. The formal national embrace of human rights seems to mean little in police stations around the country. This freights with importance the question of how Indian officers understand and respond to the messages they receive about human rights protection.

Answering this question depended upon the help of innumerable people. The twelve months of fieldwork I conducted in India were made possible by the assistance of many, and the same is true of the years of preparation leading up to the fieldwork as well as the years since then spent analyzing, reflecting, and writing.

The project began while I was lucky enough to be a doctoral student in New York University's Department of Humanities and Social Sciences in the International Education Program, and I have so many reasons to thank the people there. Rene Arcilla made this book possible. He has for years been an ideal conversation partner, pushing me to go deeper and further in my work while at the same time giving me reason to trust my discernment. Rene creates around him a utopian environment of genuine intellectual engagement, a place where the real questions can be asked. The ideas in this book owe much to our discussions. I remain ever grateful for his relentless encouragement to center my work on what really matters to me, and to his patient and insightful responses to my ideas and their translation on the page.

Dana Burde read this work in its entirely from its earliest stages with incredible patience and attention. I benefited greatly from her exacting and generous mind. She was precise in her feedback and always encouraged me to explore new territory. From the beginning of the project, she inspired me with her boldness about what my fieldwork could be and where it could take me. Cynthia Miller-Idriss, now at American University, Jon Zimmerman, now at the University of Pennsylvania, and Niobe Way offered consistently sharp and thought-provoking comments that regularly reignited my own excitement about the project. I am grateful for their insight and support. Ritty Lukose helped illuminate the complexity of India's social and cultural landscape. My cherished writing group, consisting of Amy Kapit, Naomi Moland, Karen Ross, Jennifer Auerbach, and Elizabeth Knauer, along with other close colleagues such as Christian Bracho and Alexandra Wood, provided invaluable comments on drafts as well as phenomenal support.

I also benefited greatly from the insights of faculty at Columbia University. Jack Snyder's sound advice and sharp but open-minded perspective continue to enrich my work. Sudipta Kaviraj was invaluable in shaping my thinking on Indian politics and connecting me with scholars in India. Al Stepan also contributed to the project early on through his lively intellect and discussions of the politics of secularism in India and elsewhere. Monisha Bajaj, now at theUniversity of San Francisco, has been integral to the project from the very beginning, giving much to this work both practically and intellectually.

Moreover, I owe a great deal to the members of the monthly seminar at the Columbia University Institute for the Study of Human Rights. In particular, I am grateful to Zehra Arat, George Andreopoulos, and Yasmine Ergas. They gave especially careful comments on an early chapter draft and served as valued conversation partners on a wide range of human rights issues.

I am indebted, too, to colleagues who have commented on this research at conferences, colloquia, and in private conversations. Mahmoud Monshipouri, Amitav Acharya, Kathryn Sikkink, Martha Finnemore, Michael Goodheart, Shareen Hertel, Michelle Jerkovich, John Wallach, Tim Dunne, Stephen

Hopgood, Benjamin Gregg, Wendy Wong, Clifford Bob, Hun Joon Kim, Jinee Lokaneeta, Anil Kalhan, Francisco Ramirez, Oren Pizmony-Levy, James Williams, Christine Monaghan, Paula McAvoy, David Hansen, Megan Laverty, and Sally Merry have provided valuable comments on this work. I am grateful for their time and thoughtfulness. My conversations with Danielle Celermajer, Kiran Grewal, and Jack Saul on their research to understand and prevent torture were especially helpful. I wish to thank James Dawes not only for a helpful conversation but also for inspiring me with his own stunning writing on violence.

At Stanford University Press, I have been lucky to work with Michelle Lipinski and Mark Goodale, whose support and suggestions have improved this work. Two blind reviewers provided comments that proved exceptionally helpful in revising the manuscript.

At the University of Virginia, I have many colleagues to thank for sharpening my thinking about this book in its later stages. I am grateful to Derrick Alridge, Nancy Deutsch, Brian Pusser, Stephen K. White, Jeffrey Legro, Lawrie Balfour, Jennifer Rubenstein, John Echeverri-Gent, Josipa Roksa, Allison Pugh, David Eddy-Spicer, Caitlin Donahue Wylie, Sarah Mosseri, Diane Hoffman, Joanna Lee Williams, Carol Tomlinson, David Edmunds, Johann Neem, Liya Yu, Robin Kimbrough-Melton, Jeffrey Guhin, Lisa Messeri, and China Scherz for their valuable comments. I am grateful to Jieun Sung for her careful, astute proofreading. Moreover, Derrick Alridge and Diane Hoffman have made Social Foundations a supportive and intellectually alive place to work and write, and did much to contribute to the book by supporting my commitment to it.

In India, I was fortunate to be a Visiting Fellow for a year at the Centre for the Study of Law and Governance at Jewaharlal Nehru University. My discussions with Niranja Gopal-Jayal, Amit Prakash, and Pratiksha Baxi were particularly illuminating, as were the Centre's weekly seminars.

I am also grateful to the many devoted human rights workers in India who spoke with me for this study, including the staff of the Human Rights Law Network, Commonwealth Human Rights Initiative, Asian Centre for Human Rights, Indian Social Institute, Indian Institute of Human Rights, Centre for Social Research, and the South Asian Human Rights Documentation Centre. I would especially like to thank Nawaz Kotwal, Colin Gonsalves, Ravi Nair, Suhas Chakma, and Rahul Rai for their illuminating discussions and support for this research. I am in awe of the tireless efforts of these advocates and of their deep commitment to reducing suffering.

It may go without saying that I was able to write this book only because so many law enforcement officers were willing to speak with me. But it should not go without note. Not only did they speak with me, but they devoted hours of their precious time off of work to explaining themselves in great detail. They sat patiently through what likely seemed like endless questions. I believe they did so out of a commitment to broadening public understanding of their experience and perspective. I am grateful for their time and openness.

Many people not directly associated with this book also made it possible. To name just a few, I am grateful to James Corrick for years of encouragement as well as patient and sound advice. Amy Arani and Linda Wahl were supportive and enthusiastic. Mythri Jayaraman was one of the first people to cause me to think differently about justice. Her analytical prowess and originality of thought are matched by her commitment to upholding her ideals in her daily work. Cara Blouin was the reason I first traveled for educational work and has helped me to think through the complex questions such work inspires. At home in Virginia, Veronica Lowry and Julie O'Brien made it possible for me to concentrate on writing through the incredible support they provide. In India, Sunetra Lala is the reason that New Delhi became for me a home.

Finally, I am absurdly lucky to have a family that has cared about my ideas as well as about me during these years of fieldwork and writing. I have been speaking to my father, Richard Wahl, and mother, Margaret Wahl, about my questions for as long as I can remember. It is because of them that I developed a fascination with the world around me. My husband, Jeffrey Brewer, has made everything possible by providing ceaseless support and a love that includes but is not limited to intellectual companionship.

The years of writing this book also included death and birth. My grandparents, who supported this work in spite of the absence from them it required, passed away in its later stages. My son Oliver came along as I wrote the final drafts and burst everything open with joy.

Rachel Wahl
University of Virginia

Introduction

Human Rights from the Other Side

ON DECEMBER 13, 2006, a man named Ajay arrived at a police station in West Bengal, India. He had come to report that his wife, Namita, had gone missing. According to a report by a local human rights organization, the police illegally detained Ajay and brutally tortured him.

What happened at that police station in West Bengal, and why? The case is described in a report[1] by the Asian Human Rights Commission, a regional nongovernmental organization (NGO). It was reports such as this that impelled me to conduct twelve months of research in India to understand how police make sense of their violence and how they respond to education and activism to prevent it. As part of this research, I gave the report to human rights activists and law enforcement officers, and asked them what they believe occurred and why they think the police acted in this way.

Human rights advocates in India respond quickly to this question. "This is such a common case," one human rights educator asserts. He explains that this is an "open and shut case" in which it is obvious that "the police got some money. They were bribed. Otherwise, they normally would not take interest." Echoing this, another human rights educator reads the report and concludes, "This is a typical case of police brutality for extorting money." Across the interviews, human rights professionals point to the "pecuniary motive" as one put it, as the reason the police tortured Ajay.

How might police officers in India explain the alleged torture? There are several plausible responses. They could condemn the torture, distinguishing themselves as supporters of human rights compared to the faraway police officers who violate rights in a small town in West Bengal. The officers I interviewed have no connection to the police officers described in the report, so they could easily distance themselves from them. And they have a motivation to do so. These officers chose to enroll in a human rights course in the hopes that it would help them advance professionally. As such, they could be expected to see it as in their interest to condemn torture. They might assume such statements to be "safer," especially for an interviewer such as myself who has contacted them through the institution in which they are learning human rights.

Alternately, they may wish to defend the honor of the police as well as preserve their own standing in the eyes of the interviewer. In this case, they could question the validity of the report, arguing that the human rights organization may have false information and doubting that the torture occurred. Or they could try to make the interviewer sympathetic to the plight of the police, pointing out that the officers in the report likely have little training, few resources, and abysmally low salaries, making torture for bribe money regrettable but inevitable.

All of these explanatory options are available to the police in this study. After all, nobody is accusing these particular officers. They have no reason to defend the torture described in the report. Their self-interest, furthermore, seems squarely on the side of distancing themselves from allegations of human rights violations.

None of the above possible responses, however, constitute law enforcement officers' primary reaction to the alleged torture of Ajay. Instead, over and over in interviews, police defend not only the torture but also the ethical motivations behind it. The commander of a paramilitary police force from Sikkim asserts:

> In this case, Mr. Ajay is fighting for his rights only. The police officer is fighting for the human value of the missing lady, of Miss Namita, to restore the liberty of Miss Namita. You ask me, 'What are police doing?' They are trying to restore the rights of Miss Namita. There is a Hindi saying, *kuch paane ke liye kuch khona parta hai.* [This means] for some water, something is lost. Something must be sacrificed.

The police officer is clear. This is not a matter of excusing an immoral act. On the contrary, the act is justice itself. Across ranks and police organizations, officers are consistent and effusive in their response to the report. A low-ranking police officer in Haryana asserts, "Using torture doesn't mean the police are violating human rights. The police are also trying to deliver justice to someone." In the officers' explanations, torture is an act of justice.

On the surface, it seems as if someone must be deeply mistaken. Are human rights workers wrong to deny officers' understanding of themselves as moral actors? Do they see corruption where police are motivated by a sense of justice, however misguided it may be? Or are the police simply lying about their motivations? This raises the question, though, of why they would not simply condemn the torture and distance themselves from it if they are going to lie for the sake of appearances.

An answer begins to emerge as my interviews with both human rights advocates and police officers progress. When I ask a human rights educator for his opinion about who would have bribed the police to torture Ajay, he replies:

> The woman's parents, the woman. 100 percent. It's very clear. Why would they brutally torture him? At best they would normally register the FIR[2] and start an investigation. The only reason they would brutally torture is for money. That's for sure.

This maintains the picture of police as motivated by monetary self-interest. In unexpected ways, however, this narrative begins to merge with the story the police provide. As the paramilitary commander from Sikkim continues to explain the position of the officers in the report, he is so ready to defend their actions that he speaks in the first person, placing himself in the position of the police who allegedly tortured Ajay. He asserts:

> I need to convince Miss Namita's family . . . because they have confidence in us that we will find their daughter. And the police is answerable to society also. They expect police to be effective, to be their guardian.

This explanation emerges repeatedly. When I ask a high-ranking Indian Police Service officer in Punjab why the police used torture in the reported case, he theorizes:

> I think the police and the parents of the girl suspect the husband. That's the crux of the matter. Maybe the husband is trying to play smart. But it is a matter of study what is the reality on the ground. It becomes an emotional issue. The parents of the girl coming to the police saying, 'Where is my daughter?' If they suspect the husband, it is serious. There is no magic wand held by the police. They must follow some path. The police must go into the nuts and bolts of the case. What is the background? What is the relationship between husband and wife? Emotional honesty is very important. Who is at fault?

In the explanations of both human rights advocates and police officers, a similar story begins to emerge. A girl is reported missing. The parents of the girl suspect the husband. They urge the police to torture the husband. Human rights advocates note that this urging takes the form of a bribe, while police describe it as emotional persuasion. The police accept the parents' request, or as human rights advocates describe it, the police accept the parents' bribe and torture Ajay.

The similarity in the assumptions that human rights advocates and officers make about what happened suggests that both may be accurate to some degree. Considering the pervasiveness of police corruption that has been reported throughout India, and the nearly ubiquitous assertions of human rights professionals in interviews, it is reasonable to suppose that the police did receive a bribe to torture Ajay. And yet given that police passionately defend the justice of the torture when they could have simply condemned and distanced themselves from it, it is likely that police also believe that torture was the right thing to do.

One might imagine the story now by piecing together the narrations of human rights advocates and police. A man comes to the police station to report that his wife is missing. The parents of the girl suspect the husband and offer the police a bribe to torture him. The police want the money and also see it as their job to recover the missing girl. They believe that both the easiest and the most reliable way to find out where the girl has gone is to torture her husband. Doing so serves both their self-interest and their sense of justice and duty.

This violence may also increase their legitimacy in the eyes of the public. In a country where the police and elected officials enjoy little public respect, direct action that sidesteps what is viewed as a corrupt and inefficient legal bureaucracy can increase officers' standing in the community. The high-ranking Indian Police Service officer from Punjab continues to narrate his perception of what occurred in the case of Ajay's torture:

> The girl's parents go to the police and say, 'This man is torturing my daughter.' They find that the law is lacking in that situation. The law cannot give [teach] a lesson. The parents say, 'Do something that will teach him a lesson.' If the case goes to court, it will take months. There will be intimidation or bribery of witnesses. They want extra-legal methods. Parents become very insecure [and say], 'What has this man done to my daughter?' The parents become reactive and lose faith in the system and sometimes tell the police, 'Do it [torture] in front of me.' It is wrong, but it is a mindset. They will bribe a lower officer to beat the man

> in front of them. The fellow is being tortured at the behest of the parents. The lower officer gets a bribe and becomes a hero in the mind of the parents, so he is happy. It is a great challenge for those of us who are sensitive. So why torture? If he is accused, you book him. But for the parents, it won't matter because if you just book him, he will be back in the house torturing the girl again.

This officer's portrayal of torture suggests that law enforcers' beliefs, their self-interest, and their desire for public respect intersect and reinforce one another. Acknowledging all of these factors, this officer still foregrounds the positive principled beliefs that might motivate the police in the report: he emphasizes the desire to help the parents and be seen as a "hero."

Police leaders echo this interpretation of events. When I give the report to the director of investigation at the National Human Rights Commission, his first response matches that of the lower-ranking officers. He theorizes, "The wife's family must be pressurizing the police, saying 'You have not done anything; he won't tell you anything if you don't torture him.' " At the Bureau of Police Research and Development, a high-ranking official recalls the public pressure he experienced when working as a police officer in the field, remembering how "the public wants us to beat up the criminal." Even though these leaders do not argue that law enforcers should torture as a result of public pressure, they do support the consensus that the police in the report were responding to the public—in this case, the wife's family—by choosing to torture.

When human rights advocates read the story, they focus on the acceptance of the bribe. They assume this can explain the police officers' actions in their entirety. When police read the story, they emphasize the motivation to help the missing woman and her family, not denying but also not wishing to stress the likelihood that money was exchanged.

The gap between these explanations causes problems for both the practice and the study of human rights. Assuming that police use torture due to deficiencies such as a lack of training and ignorance of the law and to improper motivations such as to extract a bribe, human rights educators typically provide information and try to convince the officers that what they do is wrong. The officers, who know that torture is illegal but believe that what they do is right, reject these messages.

Talking to Perpetrators

The difference in interpretations of one case of torture reveals a chasm between how human rights workers and police understand violence. But before delving into the moral universe police inhabit and its meaning for human rights protection, it is worth considering why it is worth bridging this divide. The political theorist Danielle Allen insists that speaking with and thereby understanding those who are most different from ourselves creates the cooperative spirit necessary for democracy.[3] But can and should this willingness to interact and understand be extended to the people who violate the fundamental protections of democracy—the police who support or even commit torture? What good could understanding them bring? Moreover, why write a book that examines torture and human rights from the perspective of perpetrators? Many robust studies attempt to isolate the causes of violations. Why focus instead on officers' reasons?

At least four benefits can derive from speaking with and attempting to understand state officials who support or engage in extrajudicial violence. The first positive result is pragmatic: understanding the meaning police give the violence they commit has important implications for the most effective ways to prevent this violence. As I discuss throughout the book, my interviews with police suggest that interventions based on faulty assumptions about officers' motivations often fail to accomplish their aims.

The second gain is intellectual. Speaking to these officers reveals what happens to ideas as they circulate around the world. There have been many valuable macro-level studies regarding how and why ideas or "norms"[4] spread. International relations theorists have provided rigorous analyses of when national governments comply with human rights treaties by studying state behavior.[5] Philosophers and other theorists have offered rich intellectual histories of the emergence and spread of liberalism.[6] Sociologists have also examined how liberal ideas disseminate, with a focus on providing quantitative evidence of their impact worldwide.[7] In many studies of nongovernmental actors such as activists and the communities in which they work, anthropologists have provided in-depth examinations of how global ideas, particularly human rights, translate into local contexts.[8] But far less is known about what happens to such global ideas when they are taken up and used by the state officials whose power they are meant to constrain.

The next two benefits of this inquiry fit less easily into the canon of human rights scholarship and are primarily ethical in the sense that they inform reflection on right action more than provide clear-cut directions for it. Human rights advocates and other reformers are engaged in a crucial effort, and to highlight the ethical complexity of that effort is in no way to condemn it or to suggest that there are simple solutions that are free from such dilemmas. But once we see these perpetrators as real people who believe they are doing good things in complex circumstances, questions arise not only about the most effective way to deter their violence but also about the most ethical way to treat them. The police become subjects whom we address rather than only barriers to justice.

The fourth reason to understand people who play the villains to contemporary liberalism is that this can clarify what is at stake. As I'll discuss, it is sometimes expedient to frame the rights movement in technical rather than ethical terms. Yet it is important to recognize the struggle against torture as a contested rather than universal moral ideal. In theory, scholars likely recognize that movements to eradicate torture are moral in nature and contested. But when researchers assume that people use such violence only for immoral or amoral reasons, the implication is that the antitorture struggle represents a universal conception of the good from which there is no genuine dissension. In so doing, researchers avoid the moral nature of the commitment upon which much research on violence is premised by cloaking it in terms of rational and neutral principles from which all disagreement is a mere rationalization. I suggest instead that the struggle against torture is a crucial effort to promote a particular, contested conception of the good. The consistency and passion with which police and military officers argue against this conception reveal its vulnerability. The understanding of this vulnerability can deepen rather than weaken the efforts of those who are committed to the eradication of torture.

Aims and Considerations

To realize these goods, this book reveals what happens when law enforcement officers—the "foot soldiers" of state governments—interpret and respond to educators' and activists' attempts to teach what the philosopher Charles Taylor calls the "modern moral order." In this order, "human beings are rational, sociable agents who are meant to collaborate in peace to their mutual benefit." The existence of natural rights that precede political arrangements is a key element: the "underlying idea of moral order stresses the rights and obligations we have as individuals in regard to each other, even prior to or outside of the political bond."[9] Taylor traces its development to the seventeenth century, particularly to the philosophy of Grotius, but it has come to dominate our thinking about what societies are and should be. This is especially evident in the human rights movement, which is premised on an understanding of people as rights-bearing individuals with the potential to live together in mutual benefit.

It is clear that this "modern moral order" has spread around the globe. It is, however, less clear what occurs when the people who are at the front lines of its protection respond to efforts to teach it, such as through human rights education and activism. Ethnographic studies reveal how rights concepts change as human rights educators and activists "vernacularize" them.[10] These studies typically focus on the translation efforts of committed rights supporters. Many more people are in a position to vernacularize rights, however; in a sense, everyone who learns these concepts may do so. The interpretations of state agents who learn rights concepts carry particular weight because they are responsible for implementation.

And there is much to suggest that how state agents use rights concepts is quite different from how educators and activists intend. International relations theorists have shown that state endorsement of a human rights treaty has an inconsistent relationship to rights protection.[11] Scholars usually explain this by examining international factors, such as the strength of transnational networks, or national characteristics, such as the structure of domestic politics and state institutions.[12] But human rights ultimately matter at the local level, and are implemented—or violated—by local actors. How local law enforcement officers respond to efforts to prevent torture, then, is important for whether and how the principles of the Convention Against Torture spread.

Yet scholars and practitioners rarely seek the perspective of the local law enforcers who violate rights, as researchers who do pursue such inquiries note. In a volume on the local dynamics of state violence, editors Steffen Jensen and Andrew Jefferson rail against the tendency in human rights research and practice to see violent state officials as beyond the pale of understanding. Instead, they insist, we must investigate state officials' responses to rights reforms in light of the complex contexts in which they work.[13]

According to Jensen and Jefferson, in the design of most human rights training for police and military officers, "Violent practices are rendered illegitimate at the same time as they are ignored" as is "local logic that justifies violence or makes it seem rational."[14] Trainers seem to assume that state agents are simultaneously "empty vessels" ready to receive human rights knowledge and choice-bearing individuals who can act on this new knowledge. At the same time, police are understood as part of an undifferentiated state that can in a unified way protect rights. The authors argue that the failure to understand the ways in which state agents are situated in particular structures undermines the success of education and other efforts to spread human rights protections.[15]

Understanding Violence or Preventing It?

This does not mean, however, that there is always a straightforward complementarity between understanding police torture and preventing it. Indeed, although it can be tempting to see the different aims of this book as supporting one another, this is not always the case. For example, critics accuse the human rights movement of dividing the world into victims, saviors, and savages,[16] in the process painting perpetrators as monsters about whom there is little to understand. But activists may have good reasons to portray perpetrators in such stark terms. As James Dawes cautions in his careful study of Japanese war criminals, the refusal to understand violence can signify a well-founded refusal to accept it. Insisting that certain actions are beyond comprehension could demarcate crucial moral lines.[17]

And there may be more instrumental reasons that there is a conflict between intervening in violence and understanding it. Research on collective action frames suggests that public support is best garnered by simplifying issues with clear depictions of who is at fault and who offers a solution.[18] In other words, torture is complicated, but public pressure may be best mobilized by pretending that it is not.

In spite of these potential drawbacks, however, it is the contention of this book that recognition of perpetrators' personhood—which accompanies an understanding of the moral universe they inhabit—can and should coexist with a strong commitment to eradicate torture. Even though the goals are sometimes in tension, ultimately such understanding can support the human rights community's effort to prevent torture as well as enable greater reflection on how to treat those who violate its principles.

Such an effort, moreover, can be strengthened by careful consideration of how these goals support or undermine each other. In regard to the former, I discuss throughout the pages that follow how this research can inform human rights activism and education to prevent torture. To address the latter, in the conclusion I turn to the ethical dilemmas the research presents to activists, educators, and others who are engaged in the difficult effort to prevent police violence.

It is crucial to note that this book is not intended as a critique of human rights activists and educators. Rather, it is meant to inform their work as well as provide a resource for thinking through the dilemmas that haunt it. The human rights workers interviewed for this study were giving more of themselves than one might think possible. Belying the image of the elite and self-interested NGO staff that has garnered attention and debate recently, these advocates were working tirelessly, usually for little or no pay, out of a deep sense of commitment. Many were exhausted due to the emotional toll of trying so hard to stop brutality in the face of a largely unresponsive state. Rather than decrying the distance between what they are trying to do and what they are able to accomplish, this book puts into stark relief the difficulty and paradoxes human rights workers face. There can be no perfect way to advocate for equality, liberty, and protection from harm, and ultimately, sustaining the effort is more important than doing so perfectly.

Believing the Police

If it is easy to believe human rights advocates when they affirm ideals in spite of the circumstances that prevent their full realization, it may be harder to accept violators' claim that they are even trying to live by a moral code. One might ask, is there any reason to believe a police force that is known for its dishonesty? After all, among the police in India, deceitful practices such as framing false charges, fabricating evidence, and other forms of corruption are rampant.

Nonetheless, I take their statements seriously for several reasons. First, as I discussed previously, these officers do the opposite of what might be expected. They could have presented themselves as rights-respecting officers who do not torture. Instead, they answer my questions by passionately defending actions that they know are contrary to the human rights ethos, and as they sometimes guess, contrary to my own (their interviewer's) beliefs. They dedicate hours of their precious time off of work to explaining themselves to me. These are men[19] who wish to be understood. They do not exclude the violence they commit from their self-portrayal, but instead argue in favor of it in spite of their knowledge that this violence is contrary to what they "should" say according to the law and as students of human rights.

Second, I take these statements seriously because the officers had no motive to explain themselves to me in moral terms. They had not been accused of any misdeeds, nor did I have anything to offer them for good behavior. They chose to create a moral image of themselves without any identifiable fear of consequences or the possibility of reward.

A reader could argue that these officers may simply wish to impress me, regardless of whether there is a reward, and that they may care little about their moral image outside of its desired effect on me. If this was the case, however, it seems reasonable to assume that officers would say whatever might sound most impressive: if not as rights-respecting officers, then at least as police who use violence only in the most defensible ways, such as with the worst offenders when there is no other option.

Instead, officers tell complex stories, as the following will reveal, in which what is good is often elusive. Moreover, their stories are realistic. They speak in ideal terms about wishing to use violence against only the powerful and corrupt. But when I ask them for examples from their lives, they respond with believable accounts in which they act against people who do not fit their image of the villain. They then attempt to narrate these stories in relation to what they believe is right, which suggests an effort to understand their own actions morally. I suggest that how officers understand this moral dimension of their own violence is important to their ability to continue to engage in it, even if factors such as self-interest and external pressure are also significant motivations.

Furthermore, officers do not defend all police behavior. Although they defend torture and other types of violence as a legitimate part of police work, they resist admitting that corruption plays a role in it. When they do concede that police also use violence to extract bribes, they are quick to condemn such motives. This suggests that officers are not merely defending everything of which the police are accused, but only the practices that they believe are worthy of defense.

Nothing indicates that police actually live by this moral code; on the contrary, given the reports of corruption in the police force, it is unlikely that they do. But that they are selective in what they defend does indicate that police are genuinely articulating their beliefs about what they *should* do, which is the focus of this study.

Indeed, extensive reports by civil society organizations and the government itself as well as the interviews for this book suggest that in practice, torture and related violence are driven by motivations such as a desire to obtain a bribe, win a promotion, keep one's job, or please a supervisor, a politician, or the public. Physical and emotional states such as exhaustion, fear, and anger may also play a role. This book illuminates not these drivers of torture, which even police agree are wrong, but rather the reasons police believe it is good and right to use this violence.

The Officers

At the center of this study are thirty-three law enforcement officers who were participating in human rights education in India. They included civil police in North India as well as paramilitary and military officers in areas such as Kashmir that have been labeled "disturbed" by the federal government, where they have been given law enforcement powers and duties.[20] Hence, when I refer to "police" or "law enforcement officers" I include civil police, military, and paramilitary officers, using the definition of the United Nations in their Code of Conduct for Law Enforcement Officials.[21] Military and paramilitary officers ranged in rank, with many from the middle of the hierarchy. Civil police also included mid-ranking and very high-ranking Indian Police Service officers, as well as the lowest-ranking constables.[22]

The first officer I interviewed was an ambitious man enjoying an upward turn in his career. Although a member of the less prestigious State Police Services, he had been selected to serve temporarily in an administrative position with the central government in New Delhi. Given the rigid structure of the Indian police, it is not common for a relatively low-ranking officer to be given such opportunities, and he considered the post a promising sign that his work was being recognized. We met three times in the course of my year in Delhi, for several hours each time, first in a restaurant and later in his home.

He spoke often in our long conversations about his desire to advance professionally. He was especially excited about international work. Obtaining a security detail or joining a peacekeeping mission with the United Nations was first on his list of aims. This is why he was taking a human rights course, he explained, to increase his chances for such opportunities.

This, however, was not enough to compel him to change or even to hide his views on the human rights with which he disagrees. Like many other officers in this study, the majority of whom have aims similar to his own, he passionately defended torture and other forms of extrajudicial violence. He has succeeded in his aims, though, winning a security posting with the United Nations.

Although this officer may be unusual in his success, he is typical in his aspirations. All the officers interviewed for this book chose to enroll in a two-year distance-learning course that awards them a Master's Degree in Human Rights, hoping the degree will lead to professional advancement. Although most of the officers also wish to contribute meaningfully to society, their understanding of how to do so differs substantially from the human rights framework. The difference is most evident in their belief that torture and extrajudicial killing are integral to the maintenance of a just society, particularly given the weaknesses in the political and legal system that are pervasive in India.

Hence these officers are willing to engage with human rights education and have an incentive to do so, but they are not already persuaded of the validity of human rights norms. As police who are willing to listen to rights messages and learn rights principles, but who hold contrary beliefs, these officers offer an ideal case study of what happens in efforts to persuade local law enforcers to accept the messages of human rights activists and educators, the emissaries of the modern moral order.

But are these officers different from police who do not choose to enroll in a human rights course? One would expect police who elect to participate in such a course to be more receptive to its messages than those who do not. Instead, these officers express similar beliefs and similar forms of resistance to human rights as police who do not voluntarily take a human rights course. Educators who work with the general population of police confirm this, as does a lengthy report on the Indian police by Human Rights Watch.[23] Most obviously, these officers' support of torture indicates that they are not especially accepting of human rights concepts.

They may, however, be more ambitious than the average officer, demonstrated by their pursuit of education for the purpose of career advancement. The low-ranking officers may also be more financially comfortable than their peers because they must pay a fee to attend. Hence, if these officers are different from the average officer, they may offer the "best case scenario" for efforts to persuade police to accept human rights. This "best case" is rife with dilemmas, both for human rights educators and for theoretical perspectives on how human rights spread.

The Interviews

I conducted twelve months of fieldwork in North India for this book, beginning with two months in 2010 and followed by ten months from 2011 to 2012. This included sixty in-depth interviews with thirty-three officers. I met with twenty of the officers twice and in some cases three times. Each of our conversations lasted between one and six hours, with most ending after about two and a half hours. I began each interview with open-ended questions such as about the challenges they face and times when they felt satisfied or frustrated in their work. Usually, they identified human rights activists early in the interview as an example of a professional obstacle.

In the second interview with each officer, I approached human rights topics more directly. I gave them the NGO report discussed previously featuring a man named "Ajay" who has allegedly been tortured by police after reporting that his wife, "Namita," had gone missing. I asked each officer what he believes occurred, why the officers described in the report used torture, what the officers should have done, and why the NGO is criticizing the act. I also read them quotes from their human rights textbooks and asked for their understanding and views of the material. In addition, I asked them about recent cases of police violence that had appeared in the news as well as for their responses to the more general critiques human rights activists make of police.

These questions allowed me to examine the moral "horizons"[24] in which officers operate: their conceptions of justice, human nature, the nature of the society in which they work, the ideal police officer, and the ideal citizen. The second interviews allowed me to plumb their responses to specific material from the human rights course in which they are enrolled, as well as to human rights messages they receive from sources such as the media, NGOs, and the National Human Rights Commission.

Crucial to this process was how I presented myself to the officers. After contacting them through their human rights course, I explained that although the public usually hears about social issues from the perspective of NGOs and academics, I wished to learn from them because they deal with some of the most difficult social problems in their daily work. I was intentionally deferential and vague: deferential, so that they would not feel that I was accusing them of wrongdoing, and vague, in order to see whether and how they brought up and discussed terms such as *human rights* and subjects such as torture.

I interviewed officers in person in the North Indian states of Delhi, Punjab, Haryana, and Uttar Pradesh. Some of the officers were posted farther away in states such as Jammu and Kashmir and Assam. For these latter interviews, I either interviewed officers over the phone or met with them when they were temporarily in Delhi. I conducted all interviews myself, interviewing most in English and using a Hindi interpreter for six of the officers.

In addition, I interviewed thirty-five human rights activists and educators, police reform experts, and police leaders such as officials with the National

Human Rights Commission and Bureau of Police Research and Development in New Delhi. I also provided many of these interviewees with the NGO report of Ajay's alleged torture and asked them the same questions I posed to the police. Finally, I interviewed fifteen civil servants participating in the same human rights course as the police. These interviews provided a broader context in which to understand the statements of police. In total, I conducted 119 in-depth, semi-structured interviews with 83 people in India.

Finally, I will offer one note about language. I refer to human rights "activists," or "workers" interchangeably, as well as using similar terms without distinction. I do so in spite of the vast differences between people who advocate for human rights, such as variations between professionalized national elites and grassroots activists. Moreover, it is important to note that activism in India is not merely an extension of international discourses. The country has a long history of social justice organizing, rooted in a past that includes the fight against colonial power as well as resistance to the abuses committed under the emergency declared by Indira Gandhi. However, I refer to human rights workers using homogenizing terms because my focus here is on the police and their perceptions. Police speak about "human rights" as a monolithic idea, and it is their understanding that is the subject of inquiry here.

Local Methods, Global Politics

This focus on police perceptions of human rights does, however, include analysis of the meaning of their views for larger processes. Indeed, this research has required a dual approach, relying on anthropological methods to understand how particular people in particular places perceive the world, as well as international relations theory that considers the broader systems in which these ideas circulate. Hence I draw from in-depth conversations with individual law enforcement officers to reflect on a large-scale political process: the global spread of ideas.

Spreading Ideas: Education and Interdisciplinarity

The question of how and why ideas spread is at its essence a question about the nature of education. Although there are many ways of understanding education, I define it broadly, as purposeful efforts to spread concepts, beliefs, skills, and practices, including "intentional learning outside formal school settings."[25] Theorists of education such as John Dewey emphasize that education often occurs beyond the schoolhouse walls. In essence, Dewey writes, "education" is everything a society communicates in order to perpetuate itself.[26]

In keeping with Dewey's understanding of education and social transformation, one might add to this an understanding of education as also including that which a society communicates in its attempt to change itself. Thus education encompasses formal efforts such as human rights education, with its designated faculty and students, as well as other purposeful efforts to persuade others to learn, understand, and believe in new ways, such as human rights activism. In both cases, an explicit, strategic effort is made to spread information, values, attitudes, and behaviors to a target group, with the intention that this target group will become "learners" who are receptive to these messages and change in response to them. Understanding human rights work as an educational project calls attention to the processes by which the modern moral order spreads and to how the people who are asked to learn it then respond to what they learn.

An interdisciplinary approach is especially important for analyzing such educative processes. Human rights educators often belong to transnational networks[27] and, like activists, form part of the domestic movement that crucially accompanies international pressure.[28] These educators moreover draw from and also further the spread of the global scripts that are formulated through international political processes, infusing this international language into their curricula.[29] At the same time, human rights educators ultimately teach local people in particular settings, making sense of global ideas in local idioms. When the students are representatives of the state, the study of human rights education especially benefits from both anthropological and international relations theories. This is particularly so when the students are "ground level" state agents such as police and military officers who are responsible for the local implementation of global protections.

Moral Identity

Questions about education and the global spread of ideas presume that inner life matters, as efforts to change beliefs are premised on the assumption that people do not operate based on self-interest or external pressure alone. To illuminate how aspects of officers' inner lives inform their responses to human rights, I draw on Charles Taylor's concept of moral identity.[30] Taylor argues that one's conception of the good and of where one stands in relation to it are essential to a sense of self and the ability to function in the world. This does not mean that people always do what they believe is right. Rather, Taylor suggests that people cannot help but think of their actions in relation to some good, however far they believe themselves to be from it. This also says nothing about what counts as good; a person may be just as likely to see the good in the pursuit of self-interest, absolute freedom, or scientific rationality as in charity, duty, or piety. But Taylor argues that we cannot help but orient ourselves and our actions to what we see as good, even if we believe that we are failing to live up to it, or even choosing not to.

If such an orientation is crucial to actors' identities and choices, then understanding the actions of others entails gaining insight into their conception of the good and the beliefs that inform it. In order to understand the choices people make—about whether and when to use violence or any other weighty decision—we must understand how they define what is right and wrong, and their sense of self in relation to this definition. And to do so, we must understand the "terms in which people live their lives" rather than rely on explanations for behavior that the actors themselves would not recognize.[31] As I argue in what follows, such understanding is especially important for educators, who aim to enact change not by reforming structures or coercing compliance, but by communicating with individuals.

The Moral Imaginary of Violence

To illuminate the "terms" in which these police officers live, I depict not just how officers view a particular issue such as the use of torture, but also the larger moral framework in which their judgments make sense to them. I use Taylor's concepts of social and moral imaginaries, or the way people imagine what is true and good about their world. Taylor uses the term *social imaginary* to mean:

> something much broader and deeper than the intellectual schemes people may entertain when they think about social reality in a disengaged mode. I am thinking, rather, of the ways people imagine their social existence, how they fit together with others, how things go on between them and their fellows, the expectations that are normally met, and the deeper normative notions and images that underlie these expectations.[32]

The social imaginary includes moral beliefs and the perceptions that make these beliefs seem natural and good—the "normative notions that underlie expectations." At times, Taylor refers specifically to a "moral imaginary," though he sees this as part of the wider "social imaginary." Indeed, these two concepts are so tightly linked as to be part of each other. For example, as Taylor points out, contemporary moral notions of fairness are linked to a social ontology in which each person is viewed as inherently equal and autonomous. Hence a moral imaginary that normalizes a particular way of treating people is part of a larger social imaginary that includes the implicit beliefs (such as about human nature) that make sense of why people should be treated this way.

Taylor also uses the term *moral order* to denote particular conceptions of the good. The difference between a moral order and an imaginary is that a moral order includes an explicit, theoretical articulation of the good, whereas an imaginary describes the implicit beliefs that support it. Visions of moral order can over time migrate into the imaginary, and Taylor points to natural rights theories as an example of such migration from theory to imaginary. Thinkers such as John Locke articulated theoretical arguments for why people should be treated as equals. This vision of moral order is now part of the background assumptions people make about how they and others should be treated, even if each person cannot articulate the theoretical basis for this vision.[33]

Moral orders, as well as moral and social imaginaries, are not clearly distinct from each other; part of Taylor's point is that our beliefs about what is true are part of what makes possible our beliefs about what is good, and that also, conversely, our beliefs about what is good can influence how we see what is true. For the sake of clarity, however, I will use the term *social imaginary* to refer to all of the background beliefs people hold that are not explicitly moral and the more specific term *moral imaginary* to refer to the background beliefs that hold explicit moral content. I do so, however, with the understanding that the two are closely intertwined, and it is this interconnection that I explore in the chapters that follow.

Relationship of the Imaginary to Norms

Given these close connections between explicit and implicit beliefs, it is important for scholars who study whether, how, and why norms are taken up by different groups of people, and for educators and activists who persuade people to accept norms, to understand the background beliefs and perceptions that make some norms seem good and possible. Taylor advises:

> What an understanding of moral order adds to an awareness and acceptance of norms is an identification of features of the world or divine action or human life that make certain norms both right and (up to the point indicated) realizable. In other words, the image of order carries with it a definition not only of what is right, but of the context in which it makes sense to strive for and hope to realize the right (at least partially).[34]

I argue that such understanding is especially important for the attempt to create change through persuasion. Extrinsic explanations that focus on causes—rather than on actors' reasons—may be sufficient if the aim is only to coerce actors to behave or to rearrange structures in ways that promote compliance. But education programs strive to persuade officers to change their beliefs. Indeed, the human rights movement attempts not merely to alter laws and spread information, but to create a "culture of human rights" in which people not only adopt behaviors but also internalize values.[35]

Some scholars assert that such internalization is essential for the successful diffusion of human rights norms.[36] Furthermore, persuasion becomes particularly important in contexts where coercion fails. When the state does not hold police accountable for torture and laws bar civilians from prosecuting state actors, it may be especially important to influence officers' beliefs in addition to working toward legal change that would prompt greater accountability. To convince people to change their beliefs, though, it is essential to understand what they currently believe. Educators must understand more precisely the perceptions that support and challenge human rights principles if they are to fashion their messages in a way that connects to these perceptions. Moreover, perpetrators of violence may have important insights into the nature of this violence that are not evident to those who stand outside of it.

Arguments and Overview of the Book

This book aims to illuminate the moral universe inhabited by law enforcers who support or use torture, and the implications for how they respond to activism and education to protect human rights. In Chapter 1, I review research on human rights education and state violence in India and elsewhere. I argue in Chapter 2 that local law enforcement officers who violate human rights are neither "following orders" against their better judgment, nor simply ignoring them for personal gain. Instead, they hold moral beliefs that help them understand violence as right and good and enable them to deflect criticism. These beliefs are an important part of their moral identities, which contrary to previous scholarship, violent behavior does not require them to shed.

Chapter 3 demonstrates how law enforcers' ideals about when and why they should use violence break down in practice. How police understand and explain the breakdown of their ideals is instructive; their moral imaginary is further revealed by their judgments of when and why it is legitimate to compromise their principles. I show how officers' perceptions and the structures in which they work are intricately linked. Officers' perceptions of weaknesses in political, legal, and material conditions help them to justify using violence more often and against more people than even they believe they should. Although problems in the justice system are well known in India, this chapter examines how officers' perceptions of the best way to respond to these problems further weaken rights protections.

Chapter 4 reveals how police respond to messages in their human rights course. This reveals the microdynamics of resistance[37] among the ground-level state agents who are charged with upholding global norms once state leaders endorse them and shows the plasticity of moral vocabularies. Law enforcement officers neither simply reject nor ignore human rights messages. The moral authority of this modern order may make it difficult to maintain such a stance. Instead, they draw on rights language and logic to express their own conceptions of justice, using rights talk to justify violations such as torture. I show how state agents take on the language of the modern moral order while they disregard its protections, revealing the malleability of its theoretical vocabulary.

This is, however, not a matter of "local culture" resisting Western liberalism. It is the conception of security as a good upon which other goods are premised, a key facet of the modern moral order itself, which officers draw from to resist its tenets. In the following two chapters, I show that police resistance to human rights reflects not a conflict between global and local norms, nor a case of "good" Western norms confronting opposition from elsewhere. Rather, norms supporting human rights and those that undermine them circulate locally and globally, and local domestic actors situate their identities within some global and local discourses and use them to deflect others. Chapter 5 explains that officers largely accept educators' assertions that human rights are aligned with Indian religious, cultural, and national traditions, although some officers understand their traditions as making exceptions for necessary violence. They see their identity as law enforcers, however, as trumping their affiliation to such traditions. Moreover, just as police interpret, negotiate, and reframe the meaning of rights, they also do so in regard to their own cultural traditions, further revealing that norms do not simply emanate from the "Global North" or "Global West" and spread to the rest of the world. In Chapter 6, I discuss how officers draw from international norms and discourses around security to undermine the legitimacy of global rights norms, revealing that a primary obstacle to human rights is competing international normative discourse and action. In short, in the eyes of police, American torture in places like Guantanamo Bay legitimizes such violence in New Delhi.

In Chapter 7, I address the paradoxical ways that law enforcers respond to human rights activists. I argue that activism designed to coerce state agents to comply with rights, and education that aims to persuade them to comply, can undermine each other. In the final chapter, in addition to reviewing the main arguments of the book, I conclude by reflecting on the practical and ethical implications of these arguments for efforts to protect people from torture.

The book calls into question four assumptions about how human rights norms spread that are common among scholars as well as human rights activists. First, I question the often implicit assumption that failure to conform to the modern moral order can be explained by the absence of either ethical commitments or technical capacity.[38] Second, my research suggests that violators do not simply reject or ignore human rights messages, as researchers predict occurs when efforts such as human rights education are insufficient. Third, I argue against the suggestion that local cultural norms in the "Global South" are a primary impediment to human rights norms that originate in the West. Finally, the book undermines the assumption that human rights activism and education generally complement and reinforce each other.

The book shows instead the strength of officers' beliefs and how they interact with their environments. It reveals the ways in which police transform what they learn about human rights by using these ideas for contrary purposes. It also shows the diversity of ethical frameworks circulating on both the local and international levels. Lastly, the book reveals the paradoxical responses of state agents to human rights efforts and reflects on the political and ethical dilemmas that accompany efforts to prevent violence.

Chapter 1

Human Rights Education and State Violence

N'S EXASPERATION WAS EVIDENT. It appeared to be borne of working too hard for too long without seeing results—the suffering of caring so much about something for which there seemed to be little hope. As the program coordinator for the India office of a major NGO's police reform program, she conducts human rights trainings for police, as well as writes reports on police violations. "Sometimes the brutality is so bad," she lamented, "you feel like training is not making a difference."

Like so many of the human rights educators I interviewed, N has a dark view of the police. When I asked her why the police torture suspects, she replied, "One, they think they will get away with it. Two, they don't know how to interrogate people without torture." In other words, police behavior can be explained by immorality and incompetence. But when I asked her directly if the police think what they are doing is right, she said, "They think they are punishing rapists and criminals because the justice system is so bad the court will let them off. But that is none of their business."

In this interaction, she both acknowledges and rejects the moral self-conception of the police. The assumption that the first reason police use torture is simply "because they can" indicates a highly pessimistic view of their nature. And although she seems aware of their self-understanding, she quickly dismisses it as illegitimate. Like many dedicated human rights workers, she is consumed by the brutality about which she hears on an almost daily basis from victims as well as from police themselves. It is no wonder she states that police who use torture are "rotten people" and jokes that the only way to reform the police is to purge the current force and start fresh.

And it is not only the police about which she is pessimistic. "The trainings are very bad," she sighed, explaining that most human rights trainings for police inform them of international and domestic laws without explanation of their relationship or of how to implement them. She tries to improve upon this in the trainings she conducts by explaining the connection between global and national laws, and elaborating on what precisely police must do to uphold them.

As she continued to discuss the shortcomings of the trainings, however, it became clear that legalism without practical guidance was not the only problem. "I hate to mention human rights because you are shot down right away," she reflected. She explained, "There is so much hostility. They say, 'Human rights activists are pressuring us and they don't understand policing.'" Her view of police as violating rights simply because they can, and of trainers as ineffective due to officers' animosity, leaves her agonized about whether police human rights trainings serve any purpose.

She is far from alone in this view. The director of another human rights NGO in New Delhi is even more vehement. He once regularly conducted human rights trainings for state police colleges. He tells me that he no longer accepts the government's invitations to conduct such trainings, seeing the trainings, as well as the police, as hopeless. Like N, he insisted that the police use torture simply because there is nothing to stop them. As such, nothing short of punishment for police will change the situation. Human rights education is a "smokescreen" the government uses to "keep NGOs happy" and to fool the international human rights community, he asserted. Without real accountability that allows victims to sue police and that ensures police are punished, he said of human rights trainings, "it is all bunkum."

As these human rights activists and educators insist, removing the legal impunity police enjoy may indeed be the most important measure for reducing torture. Currently in India, it is necessary to obtain the permission of the government in order to press charges against an officer. Human rights workers emphasize that this inability to prosecute for torture is the primary impediment to stopping it. Yet the human rights regime has long been criticized for an overemphasis on legalism and an underemphasis on attitudinal change. Human rights education is seen by many researchers and practitioners as an important corrective, a means to go beyond the law to transform how people think.[1]

Moreover, educators' view of police as hopelessly resistant and responsive only to punishment may be stoking the resistance they encounter. By focusing so squarely on the need to punish the police, and by assuming that police operate according to only ignoble motivations, educators are limited in their capacity to understand the way officers perceive themselves and their actions.[2] This focus obscures a fuller picture of how police make judgments and the constraints, incentives, and ideals that matter to them. For educators who believe that human rights trainings may still be worthwhile in spite of their limitations, this understanding is crucial.

Human Rights Education (HRE)

International institutions, domestic NGOs, and many national governments embrace HRE as a means of spreading a "culture of human rights." According to some scholars, education represents the current direction of the movement as a whole: although human rights workers focused first on drafting treaties and later on establishing institutions, they now concentrate in large part on spreading their message through education.[3]

According to the United Nations, HRE "constitutes an essential contribution to the long-term prevention of human rights abuses and represents an important investment in the endeavor to achieve a just society in which all human rights of all persons are valued and respected."[4] The Office of the High Commissioner for Human Rights (OHCHR) accordingly funds local initiatives, creates education and training materials, and develops resources such as a Database on HRE. The OHCHR also coordinates the United Nations World Programme for Human Rights Education, which began in 2004 following the 1995 United Nations Decade for Human Rights Education.

Some methods have won consensus among scholars as "best practices" for HRE. Rights should be promoted not just in the content of lessons, but also in the means of instruction. In other words, in addition to providing students with knowledge of rights and with the skills and motivation to uphold them, educators should respect their students' rights and encourage the students to reflect for themselves on what they learn.[5] Some scholars especially emphasize the importance of using critical approaches in HRE and draw heavily on the Brazilian educational theorist and activist Paolo Freire's model of facilitating dialogue that eschews direct instruction and traditional student-teacher relationships.[6]

There are many different approaches to HRE, however, and not all fulfill these aims. HRE scholar Monisha Bajaj points out differences related to the social position of the learners and program administrators.[7] Elites such as governments and international organizations are more likely to emphasize "global citizenship" and international laws. HRE designed within and for marginalized communities, in contrast, usually aims to inspire learners to advocate for their own rights and provides them with the tools to claim those rights. Similarly, Felicia Tibbitts differentiates between a "values and awareness" model that is meant to socialize learners by imparting information and an "activism-transformation" model premised on changing what learners believe and what they are willing to do. She laments that the former approach typically fails to use participatory methods or encourage critical reflection. As a result, she predicts that at best, such approaches can prepare learners for more transformational methods and, at worst, be perceived by students as overly ideological and do little more than convey information.[8] This presumes that with better instruction, people across the world might come to accept human rights ideals, whereas with insufficient pedagogy, they are most likely to ignore or reject these messages. But how the ideals of human rights actually spread is not well understood.

The Spread of Human Rights through HRE

HRE is most often studied in two ways. Neoinstitutional sociologists often take it as evidence of the dissemination of contemporary liberalism, which they call "world culture."[9] Educational scholars typically study specific programs to evaluate their outcomes.[10] Although the former focus on the spread of HRE itself and on variables exogenous to its content, such as the legitimacy adopting HRE might bring to the government, education researchers typically focus on how well the content of HRE is learned.

This book instead asks what happens when state agents take up to this set of ideas, not to provide evidence that world culture has spread or that a specific program is effective, but to understand how the agents of the state respond to contemporary liberal principles and what happens to these principles when the agents interpret and use them.

Sociological studies have offered rich insights into how the increase in HRE reflects wider global trends. For example, Garnett Russell and David Suárez argue that "HRE gained traction at the global level because the broader social movement reflects widely held cultural scripts about progress, justice, and the individual," as well as because it spread concurrently with a worldwide expansion in schooling.[11]

These scholars view NGOs as a primary "carrier" of world culture.[12] But what precisely happens to this culture when educational NGOs attempt to explicitly teach it is not typically the subject of their analysis. Although research has revealed a great expansion of human rights topics in textbooks and curricula across the globe, the effect of this on human rights protection or even on beliefs about rights is uncertain.[13] Does HRE not only reflect but also expand world culture, producing modern citizens and state officials in its wake?

Educational researchers have shown that particular programs are effective at spreading human rights beliefs and even behaviors. For example, an extensive study by Monisha Bajaj revealed that an NGO program of great breadth and depth in India had a transformative effect on students and teachers alike.[14] In other cases, studies suggest that HRE increases knowledge or "awareness" and improves "attitudes," but with unclear implications for how people approach their lives and work.[15]

Moreover, not all research shows entirely positive effects. A study of an Amnesty International program at a high school in England revealed how the discourse of rights, on the one hand, was coopted by the disciplinary goals of the school administrators, and on the other hand, helped to destabilize that same administration when students and teachers engaged in protests against school leadership.[16] This suggests that who uses rights discourse, and why, matter for what the spread of this global script means, as scholars who emphasize the importance of domestic reasons and interpretations attest.[17]

HRE for the Police

If who uses rights discourse matters for the meanings that are attached to it, then its use by state agents raises particular questions. But scholars and practitioners rarely inquire as to what state agents mean when they speak in terms of rights. Instead, HRE for state officials is lauded by international organizations as increasing human rights protections and by scholars as signifying the diffusion of a global culture.[18] But the result of educating state agents in human rights and their subsequent use of this discourse is ambiguous. The lack of a clear and positive result should not be surprising, as HRE for actors such as police sets itself no small task: to transform through ideas and information what are often centuries of violence and inequality.

In their most ideal formulation, educators' aims are premised on a substantive conception of reason. They imply that if police understand certain principles, then they will know to transform their beliefs and behavior. This "knowing" is technical and ethical. If the police are given information about what is legal and illegal, and persuaded that torture is wrong, then they will stop using it. Less ideally, educators seem to be engaged in half-hearted due diligence: they suggest that if they educate police, then at least the police cannot say they did not know the law. Such educators concede that information and moral persuasion are unlikely to change police behavior, but reason that the lack of HRE guarantees that change will not occur. The human rights educators interviewed for this study mostly occupy an intermediate position, holding on to the hope that police will become convinced that rights claims are justified while retaining grave doubts about whether police will change their behavior accordingly.

The ambivalence among human rights educators interviewed for this book notwithstanding, international and domestic organizations around the world prioritize HRE for police and security officers. It is not surprising that human rights bodies would value state officials' compliance and knowledge: the state bears primary responsibility for upholding and protecting human rights, and police are "the first line of defense" for ensuring this occurs.[19] At the same time, the state is typically the body that rights are claimed against.[20] In fact, although this definition has been broadened in recent years to include nonstate actors such as corporations, typically it has been state culpability that defines an act as a rights violation.[21] As state agents on the "front lines" of rights enforcement, police officers especially occupy this dual position as the primary guarantors and the main violators of human rights.

And so, recognizing the crucial role of police in human rights protection as well as the frequency with which police violate human rights, the UN recommends human rights training for police as a primary means to improve conditions around the world.[22] The 2011 Declaration on Human Rights Education and Training emphasizes the training of law and security officers, as did the Second Phase of the World Programme for Human Rights Education.[23] UN bodies as diverse as the UN Development Programme, the Department of Political Affairs, and OHCHR, among others, provide trainings for police.[24] Many state governments around the world also train their police and militaries in human rights, as do nongovernmental organizations within countries.[25]

The majority of scholarship on HRE for the security forces consists of descriptions and evaluations of programs, as well as theoretical models of what such education should entail, rather than in-depth studies of police responses and experiences.[26] So while many educators are pessimistic about whether police care about their lessons, and international organizations continue to ensure the lessons are delivered, there is little research to guide expectations of what police make of what they learn.

The few rich empirical accounts that do exist suggest that more is at stake in officers' responses to human rights trainings than their recalcitrance. Researchers emphasize the complicated conditions in which police work, their belief that violence is a necessary way of responding to these conditions, and their animosity toward the human rights activists who tell them otherwise.[27] Moreover, they describe the contradictory expectations created for police by the many governments that wish to show their compliance with human rights standards, even as government officials continue to rely on the use of force.[28] These researchers argue that too few human rights scholars and practitioners attend to the complex contexts in which officers work, to the detriment of the trainings they study and implement.

A review of existing trainings around the world confirms that HRE for police is typically not based on an understanding of context. Researchers Danielle Celermajer and Kiran Grewal found that although police in a wide range of countries receive HRE, the curricula tend to be drawn from a small number of international organizations without prior research on the target population or their environment.[29] Moreover, most training is legalistic. Trainers understand the importance of relating legal education to practical guidance on how to implement laws, the researchers note. But it is unclear whether educators provide such crucial guidance. Finally, written materials and lectures are common formats for the delivery of HRE, though to a lesser extent, role-plays and interactive animations are also used. If evaluations are conducted, they typically take the form of questionnaires testing knowledge upon completion. In short, the trainings tend to be decontextualized and legalistic, frequently using passive instructional methods: not what most scholars of HRE would identify as "best practices."

The assumption that information will lead to change in beliefs and behaviors remains implicit in the work of human rights educators and scholars, in spite of the widespread recognition among both groups that this is not actually the case. Such an attitude can come in the way of putting research that has been gathered to good use. For example, one research team collected data on the beliefs expressed by police at a training conducted by one of the researchers in North Africa.[30] But rather than seek to understand and address these beliefs, the researchers noted that police "simply refuse to see the error in their arguments" and recommended that police practice would be improved by university provision of HRE wherein officers acquire better information (as well as by structural change within the police).[31] The beliefs are analyzed only as an error that can be corrected by better provision of HRE.

In contrast, a growing number of researchers argue that educators must understand the complex worlds inhabited by those they hope to influence. Celermajer and Grewal, for example, quote public health scholars on sexual assault interventions, who argue that unless an intervention is based on in-depth research on the intervention targets, "It is probably a waste of time to do, and it could even have unintended negative consequences."[32] They insist that the same is true for HRE.

The Aims of HRE for Police

Even if there is a lack of research on whether and how HRE for police can accomplish its goals, scholars have elaborated on what such education aims to accomplish. Labeling it the "accountability-professional development" approach, Felicia Tibbitts describes HRE for law enforcers and other professionals who protect human rights in their work as aimed primarily at providing skills. Tibbitts first developed this model in 2002, and then revised it for a forthcoming publication.[33] The differences between the earlier and later versions are indicative of the tensions of such training. For one, in the earlier version Tibbitts notes that professionals are motivated to protect human rights out of professional responsibility, and hence that this type of HRE does not focus on transforming their attitudes. In the more recent version, she indicates that motivating these professionals is an important component of such training. It is unclear, however, how such trainings can successfully motivate those professionals—in particular, state agents—who understand their interests and beliefs to be opposed to human rights.

Indeed, like many police reform researchers, Tibbitts notes in the more recent version that the effectiveness of this kind of HRE depends in part on its reinforcement by other mechanisms, such as reward and discipline structures within the professional organization and the state.[34] As the previously mentioned comments by human rights educators make clear, however, most educators have little control over organizational and state disciplinary apparatuses, and because they have no way to motivate their students, they often lose faith in HRE.

Second, Tibbitts reflects that "one of the learnings of the past decade is the importance of incorporating within any HRE—including that for professionals who might technically be viewed as perpetrators—a core focus on the learner as a human being."[35] This is a worthy goal, especially for police who feel, as later chapters reveal, that human rights professionals do not see them as fully human. This goal, however, can at times be in tension with advocacy for stronger disciplinary measures for police. Efforts to discipline police tend to emphasize officers' crimes rather than the difficult and quite human predicaments that inspire them. Such tensions in even a theoretical model of HRE for police are indicative of the difficulties of implementing this type of education in practice.

HRE in India

In spite of the challenges inherent in the implementation of HRE, the Indian government has in many ways embraced such education. It has promoted HRE since the 1980s, with increased attention to it emerging in the 1990s.[36] Federal institutions such as the National Human Rights Commission and the University Grants Commission sponsor HRE through the provision of funds and resources. It is also incorporated into school lessons and textbooks through the national teachers' associations.

At the same time, HRE has blossomed beyond this federal support in a wide variety of local programs, ranging from nonformal, grassroots community organizing to the types of postgraduate education on which this study focuses. Educators have vernacularized it to suit different outlooks, such as by stressing the importance of duties along with rights, as well as by advocating for the radical transformation of society.[37]

HRE for the Police in India

Police are one of several groups targeted by federal initiatives in India, along with, for example, judges, teachers, and university students. But police and other security officers are unique in that HRE is required for their employment. Human rights are included in officers' preservice training, and some have the opportunity to participate later in their careers in shorter workshops and debate competitions sponsored by the National Human Rights Commission (NHRC). Human rights professionals, NHRC officials, academics, or other police officers conduct these trainings.

The shortcomings of the required trainings for Indian police are reflected in the interviews with the disheartened educators that opened this chapter. They tend to be once weekly lecture courses or conducted through distance learning. Although the NHRC is attempting to create more interactive and practical formats, most focus on legal provisions and win little attention or support from the trainees.[38]

Extrajudicial Violence: The Problem and Its Context

The discouragement expressed by educators about the effect of their lessons reflects not just their observations of police in their trainings, but also their knowledge of the wider arena of criminal justice in India. Torture by police and security forces is pervasive to the point of being routine, according to reports by Indian and international NGOs and the US government.[39] According to human rights organizations, the Indian police frequently refuse to register or investigate cases against other police officers, so the majority of incidents of torture are not reported.[40]

The police are, however, required to report deaths in police custody to the NHRC. Between 2001 and 2010, the NHRC recorded 14,231 deaths in police custody.[41] As the Asian Centre for Human Rights points out, this means that at least 4.33 people die in police custody each day in India.

Torture in Kashmir, where India is combating an insurgency, has been the subject of particular controversy. International NGOs and media have reported the occurrence of widespread torture in Kashmir, including electrocution, beatings, and sexual humiliation. In an investigation by the International Committee of the Red Cross, of the 1,296 detainees they interviewed privately, 171 reported being beaten and 681 said they had been subjected to at least one of six forms of torture, such as electric shock and sexual assault.[42]

These problems are heightened by the provisions of emergency laws such as the Armed Forces Special Powers Act (AFSPA), which operate in areas the government has deemed "disturbed," such as Jammu and Kashmir and some states in the Northeast. This legislation provides legal backing for acts that are considered grievous violations of human rights under international law, as well as under the domestic law that governs the rest of India. For example, in addition to giving normal policing powers to security officers, the law also gives security forces the right to search without warrant, destroy shelters (including homes), and shoot to kill civilians whom they suspect of militant activities and for offenses such as gathering in groups of more than five persons.[43]

The NHRC has only partial jurisdiction over disturbed areas, leading at times to tension between the NHRC and state governments about what should fall under the commission's purview.[44] According to the 1993 Protection of Human Rights Act establishing the NHRC, the commission may only request a report from the central government on any alleged violations by security forces and make recommendations to the government in response. This is in contrast to its jurisdiction in the rest of India, where the NHRC is vested with the power of a civil court. It can conduct its own investigations, summon officers to appear before a judge at the commission, recommend or itself pursue legal action, and require action depending on the result of the investigation, which typically takes the form of monetary compensation for the victim.[45]

Difficulties abound in all of India regarding holding officers accountable for violations. In no part of India can civilians take legal action against public officials without prior consent of the government, which activists argue provides impunity for all police. But in disturbed regions, not even the NHRC can pursue legal action against security forces or conduct an investigation, heightening impunity considerably.

Emergency laws governing disturbed areas have garnered criticism from the international human rights communities.[46] Civil society organizations contend, however, that the problem is far from confined to conflict zones. Police violence is pervasive throughout the country.[47]

Defining Torture

The precise nature of this pervasive violence varies, and indeed, the issue of what constitutes torture may never be resolved. Those most concerned with preventing it tend to be most loathe to define it, because the more specific a definition, the more it narrows what is prohibited—and the more it implicitly permits. This is evident in the Bush administration's attempt to defend its own practices by asserting in an August 2002 memo that acts can be considered torture only if they cause suffering that is "equivalent in intensity to the pain accompanying serious physical injury, such as organ failure, impairment of bodily function, or even death," and if the acts are specifically intended to have these results.[48] Mental suffering must result in psychological harm that lasts "months or even years" and must result from a specific list of causes, such as threat of death, to be considered torture. The Bush administration used this narrow definition to justify techniques that are considered torture by the international community, such as waterboarding and forcing people to remain in stress positions.

Indian law has also sought a narrow definition of *torture*. The Prevention of Torture Bill, which has been passed by the lower house of the legislature and is pending in the upper house, limits the definition of *torture* to "grievous hurt" and "danger to life, limb, or health (mental or physical)" committed while "seeking to elicit information or a confession."[49] In contrast, the United Nations Convention Against Torture and Other Cruel, Inhuman, or Degrading Treatment or Punishment defines *torture* as:

> Any act by which severe pain or suffering, whether physical or mental, is intentionally inflicted on a person for such purposes as obtaining from him or a third person information or a confession, punishing him for an act he or a third person has committed or is suspected of having committed, or intimidating or coercing him or a third person, or for any reason based on discrimination of any kind, when such pain or suffering is inflicted by or at the instigation of or with the consent or acquiescence of a public official or other person acting in an official capacity. It does not include pain or suffering arising only from, inherent in or incidental to, lawful sanctions.

This definition broadens both the acts that might be considered torture and the motivations for torture.

The police officers in this study often use the words *torture* and *third degree*. They were occasionally more specific, such as one officer who mentioned putting suspects in stress positions: "For example, ask them to put their leg in one particular position until they tell us the truth." Usually, the officers are more vague, insisting, for example, that "physical torture" is necessary.

I did not ask officers to specify the details of what they mean by these words. They were wary of my interest in their behavior, and it was important that they not feel that I was investigating their actions. I did not want my interviews to resemble the questions an investigator for a human rights commission or NGO might use. Moreover, I aim to understand the beliefs that inform officers' views on violence, rather than the details of the acts they commit.

Speculations about the nature of police violence in India can be made, however, based on the reports of human rights organizations, such as those that list beatings, electric shock, sexual assault, stress positions, and exposure to cold as common among Indian police and security forces. Examples of torture can also be extrapolated from my interviews with human rights educators who work with the police in India, though these instances have not been verified. For example, the coordinator of police reform for a prominent NGO in New Delhi reflected:

> I was at a police training of sub-inspectors. A case came up in a casual way. An officer was caught torturing a man who was not answering their questions. He stripped him naked and put him on a block of ice. He poured kerosene into his

> rectum, put a candle in and lit it. Then he beat the man. This is a routine use of torture. And the response you get from police is that a seasoned officer would have known where to stop, but this man didn't know.

In addition, ethnographic research in North India reveals the types of torture that are common among police. The anthropologist Beatrice Jauregui writes of police in Uttar Pradesh:

> On any given day one would see police of all ranks—but especially the subordinate ranks of sub-inspectors and constables, who have the most regular contact with the general public—shove persons' bodies into walls or other objects; slap people across the face; leave them bloody, black and blue from beatings; pull hair and ears and other appendages; stretch and step on limbs; bang heads, and refuse to let persons in holding cells eat or have contact with outsiders for long periods (many of whom were illegally being detained without charge).[50]

Jauregui also writes of police abuse of suspects who are considered to be more serious criminals, including the use of "waterboarding . . . ; hanging from the ceiling by wrists or ankles; burning people with lit cigarettes or acid (or threatening to do so), and all manner of other creative cruelties."[51]

These reports offer examples of the violence that occurs regularly in India. The police in this study have not necessarily committed these acts. It is not possible to know precisely what these officers mean when they say the word *torture*. But this book focuses on how officers understand and justify the violence they do commit. Although human rights organizations do valuable work documenting the nature of acts, dramatically less is known about how officers make sense of what they do. Such an inquiry relies, however, in part on understanding the criminal justice system in India, which forms part of the broader context in which police operate.

Criminal Justice in India

The political system in India is seriously affected by corruption, and the administration of criminal justice is no exception.[52] Complaints that politicians use the police for self-interested political ends are common in India and have been the subject of decades of reform efforts.[53] The police as well as other public servants are accused of frequently accepting bribes, and even of demanding bribes as a condition to perform their duties.[54]

The perception of widespread corruption among public officials in general, and police in particular, is nearly ubiquitous in India; it is "common knowledge" that the police and other authorities are corrupt. In a 2013 Gallup poll, 75 percent of respondents believed that corruption is widespread in government.[55] Other polls show even higher numbers. According to survey results from the Lowy Institute for International Policy's India Poll 2013, 94 percent of respondents believe there is "a lot of corruption" in government.[56] This common perception is reflected in a political movement that swept the country during fieldwork for this book. Protests erupted across India under the banner of fighting corruption, winning international attention[57] and ultimately leading to the formation of a new political party, the Aam Aadmi (Common Man's) Party.[58] International attention to the issue has continued: for instance, *The New York Times* reported in 2015 that "India's Supreme Court ordered the country's Central Bureau of Investigation to examine a corruption scandal of astounding proportions, even by India's terrible standards."[59]

Beyond corruption, the criminal justice system is plagued by problems, many of which the state is working to mitigate, such as "inordinate delay in the lifespan of litigation between the institution of a case and its final outcome, often undermining the very purpose of administration of justice."[60] According to a Working Group's report, at the end of 2010 the number of cases pending in the subordinate courts exceeded 27 million, of which approximately 72 percent were criminal cases.[61]

The functioning of the police has been central to complaints about India's criminal justice system. Civil society groups contend that inadequate resources, poor training, and insufficient staffing stymie the effectiveness of the police. Reports point to police stations that lack proper equipment, as well as in some cases, basic necessities.[62] Governmental reviews and nongovernmental organizations find that police training is in need of improvement.[63] The police are also understaffed, with 3 million vacancies in the lowest rank of officers alone, according to a recent public statement by the Home Minister.[64] Some nongovernmental organizations also argue that the police force is poorly organized, with a significant number of officers fulfilling menial tasks.[65]

In addition to these problems in officers' working environments, nongovernmental organizations typically view police attitudes as central to the problems with criminal justice. They assert that the police incite communal violence and use torture selectively against minorities and the poor. Civil society groups assert that these problematic attitudes lead to high rates of extrajudicial killing, bribery, illegal and arbitrary arrests, falsification of evidence, and framing of false charges, as well as the pervasive use of torture.[66]

Reform Efforts

Flaws in the Indian police have garnered international attention due to the well-publicized rape and murder of a student in New Delhi on December 16, 2012.[67] Within India, however, problems in the police have long been well known and are the subject of frequent attention in the media and advocacy campaigns. Yet decades of reform efforts have failed to create significant changes. A series of reports by the National Police Commission (1979–1981) made recommendations, such as the creation of buffers between political power and police organizations, stricter legal accountability for police, and improved training programs. Policing in India is under control of the states, however, and for the most part, the states did not implement these recommendations.[68]

In 1996, two retired Indian Police Service officers petitioned the Supreme Court to mandate that states implement the National Police Commission recommendations. The case was decided in 2006, with the court concluding that states must comply. A small number of states have taken steps toward implementing some of the recommendations, but progress has been slow.[69]

Human rights advocates who work on police reform assert that the persistence of violations can be explained by a lack of will among political and police leaders: torture and other violations continue, reformers assert, because it serves leaders' interests. They contend that stricter legal accountability in which erring officers are punished, along with better training and resources, is needed to curb the problem. In short, advocates of reform frame the battle as that of moral norms against torture, embodied internationally in the Convention Against Torture (CAT), and against the political and individual ill will and insufficient resources that cause the problem.[70]

Historical and Structural Reasons for Torture

When police reform analysts look for causes beyond immediate circumstances and perpetrators, they often turn their attention to India's history. Colonialism is understood as a major contributing factor to problems in the police. As many scholars and police reform advocates note, India has inherited a police force that was created by the British to rule over a colony, not serve a democracy. Many facets of police organization, structure, and training, as well as the laws governing police conduct, such as the Indian Police Act of 1861 and the Indian Criminal Procedure Code, are remnants of colonial rule.[71] In addition, as in other postcolonial societies, the history of colonialism can undermine public trust in coercive state power and hence the legitimacy of police.[72]

This colonial legacy simultaneously empowers and disempowers the police.[73] On one hand, as human rights activists emphasize, laws protecting the police from legal prosecution without prior consent from the government make it difficult, and often impossible, to hold them accountable. This barrier partly reflects a colonial legacy in which the police are not intended to be accountable to the community, and on the contrary, are meant to serve the ruling power *against* the population. Police benefit from this relationship, many human rights activists assert, because it is in the interest of political leaders that police not be held accountable for human rights violations, so police have little to fear when they break the law.

Yet some analysts point out that police also suffer from laws and organizational structures that reflect the colonial legacy. One example of this is the clear division between an educated elite Indian Police Service, on one hand, and on the other, the lower-ranking State Police Service officers who constitute the majority of the police. This sharp division between ranks reflects a colonial policy of using the (native) lower stratum of the police to exert brute force against the population, with no intention of developing them professionally.[74]

These lower ranks are typically poorly educated and come from families of lower social and economic status. They are selected into the police from the state in which they serve. They have no possibility of promotions beyond this level, leaving them with little motivation to excel. Supervisors, on the other hand, are selected into the Indian Police Service (IPS) via a highly competitive national examination, trained in a national academy, and posted throughout the country. They tend to be well educated and often come from prestigious backgrounds. Although entry into the IPS requires a rigorous academic examination, selection requirements for the lower ranks are based in large part on physical strength. Many analysts argue that this selection procedure and structure undermine the capacity of the majority of police to function as investigators, responders in crises, and effective security in crowds, to name just a few limitations.[75]

In addition, lower-ranking officers typically work exhausting shifts, often on call for twenty-four hours each day, seven days each week. They often live away from their families in barracks and work in underresourced and difficult conditions. They are at times viewed by their supervisors with scorn, yet work within an authority structure in which they must strictly obey their superiors' orders.[76]

Just as lower-ranking officers are disempowered relative to the IPS officers who supervise them, higher-ranking officers are subservient to elected officials, who use the police to pursue personal and political agendas. The careers of IPS officers are typically subject to political discretion. For example, officers may be punished for failing to please a politician by being posted in an undesirable location, or rewarded by being given an attractive posting. Politicians take advantage of this power. They are widely known for using the police against their enemies and to help their friends. This often includes the exercise of extrajudicial violence, for example against groups making inconvenient political protests or against people whom they order the police to take into custody. Just as often, politicians order police to refrain from violence or any legal action at all against guilty parties with whom politicians are associated.[77]

Indeed, as scholars such as Jinee Lokaneeta and Upendra Baxi have emphasized, even if the colonial legacy laid the structural, attitudinal, and legal groundwork for such abuse of power, it is the current political authority that allows it to continue.[78] Baxi insists that "if the police retains its repressive colonial profile, it is due to the fact that the governing elites wish it so."[79] This aligns with what human rights activists and police themselves routinely insist: the problems may be rooted in colonialism, but are sustained because they serve current interests.

These factors frustrate the police officer's ability to uphold justice and decrease his or her legitimacy in the eyes of the public. A criminal with political ties may have more power than the police officer arresting him, as police in this study often lament. Indeed, such a situation would not be unusual: corruption pervades the political class in India, and politicians often maintain ties to criminals and illegal enterprises. As a police officer quoted in this study complains, if he tries to arrest a suspect, the person is likely to hand over his mobile phone so that the officer may speak to the politician on the other end, who then orders the police officer to "do the needful" and get the suspect released on bail.

In addition to the high levels of corruption and violence, researchers point to more subtle factors that contribute to the lack of legitimacy enjoyed by police. Officers contend not only with politicians, but also with sources of authority outside the state. These include cultural sources of legitimacy, such as family relationships and caste dynamics, as well as social and economic power. For example, the ethnographer Beatrice Jauregui recounts an episode in the North Indian state of Uttar Pradesh in which a constable attempts to intervene in a domestic dispute. He is beaten and chased off by the family, which refere to a mother's right over her youngest son and to the family's power in the local media to argue that the police officer has no authority over their affairs.[80]

Rather than indicating that the state lacks relevance, however, scholars suggest that these alternative sources of legitimacy offer civilians a way to compete for the status and advantage that state institutions can grant. Jauregui draws from earlier scholarship asserting that historically in India, civilians viewed the law as an arena in which to compete for power and prestige, rather than as a neutral adjudicator of rights.[81] For example, people might view a court case as an opportunity to increase local prestige rather than as an avenue for fair and neutral adjudication. She indicates that currently, citizens continue to compete for power not just *through* the state, but also as a means of capturing the state. The power that elected officials have over the police means that friends, associates, and even distant relations of politicians may be able to leverage power over law enforcement officers and use it to compete with formal state agents for authority.

Beyond India

As important as it is to understand this context, torture is hardly unique to any one country. Indeed, although the general publics of many countries may have once assumed that this violence is confined to the unenlightened past or the undemocratic other, recent history has shattered that perception. Nobody can ignore the reports of torture by American forces at places like Guantanamo Bay and Abu Ghraib.

Researchers are less surprised. In his comprehensive work on the subject, Darius Rejali has shown that modern torture techniques were pioneered by democracies interested in not leaving marks.[82] Sadly, subsequent research has found that rather than abolishing torture, democracies with stronger judicial systems are more likely to use stealthy techniques, whereas those with strong electoral politics but without institutions to protect minorities continue to engage in scarring torture.[83] Ambivalence in the law on such violence remains in democracies such as both the United States and India.[84]

The pages that follow will, however, best apply to police in countries with weaknesses in the legal system similar to those of India, above all: pervasive political corruption and judicial inefficiency. Other large, developing democracies, such as Brazil, exhibit similar patterns of police brutality as India.[85] Although the police are violent across the world, in such contexts it is pervasive, routine, and even expected (however regretfully and disdainfully) by the public.

The evidence from this book, as well as comparable research elsewhere, suggests that this reflects a volatile combination of officers' beliefs and the context of their work. Police in developing democracies characterized by weak legal systems are able to act on their beliefs to a greater extent than in countries with stronger mechanisms to discipline them. Moreover, obstacles to justice like corruption and inefficiency undermine the legitimacy of the rule of law in the eyes of the police as well as the general public, and provide police with yet another rationale to disregard it. And more than just undermining the legitimacy of law, corruption means that police are sometimes left with little choice than to use extrajudicial violence, as when a politician sees such violence as in their interest and demands that the police use it. Furthermore, police in such contexts work in environments that they perceive as chaotic and lawless, and this exacerbates their belief that it is right to use force.[86]

The responses of police to the human rights movement reflect this context as well. As I will discuss, police in contexts of significant insecurity, corruption, and legal inefficiency offer similar objections to human rights as the police I interviewed.[87] Moreover, research indicates that civilians faced with the same failures in the criminal justice systems in Bolivia and South Africa contest the rights framework in ways similar to the Indian police.[88] This suggests that the combination of certain beliefs about justice and the failure of formal criminal justice leads people across the world to contest the meaning of rights. The police, however, have particular power to act on such beliefs—especially in the contexts that most exacerbate these beliefs.

In short, contexts with pervasive corruption, inefficiencies in the legal system, and widespread public perceptions of insecurity provide police with the means and the motivation to use illegal violence. So while police around the world engage in torture and other brutal acts, police in such contexts do so for a particular set of reasons, do so pervasively, and as I discuss in the pages that follow, do so with the tacit support of many members of the criminal justice administration and even the general public.

Research on Torture and Other Illegal State Violence

Although there is broad consensus that extrajudicial violence continues to plague modern states, an intriguing divide characterizes research on the subject. Scholars of torture tend to view the perpetrators' environment as the main cause of violence. They typically treat perpetrators' beliefs as aberrations of normal human morality caused by pathological socialization, and view them as little more than rationalizations. Scholars of policing, whose focus includes torture but extends beyond it, are more likely to view officers' beliefs as genuine commitments, and many see "police culture" and the beliefs that partly constitute it as responsible for violence.

Studies of Torture

Most contemporary studies of torturers reflect Hannah Arendt's commentary on Adolf Eichmann: He disturbs not because he is unusual, but because he could be a neighbor or, more disconcertingly, you or me. His failure is that he does not think, and without the intervention of conscious contemplative effort, normal human beings can become monsters. Studies such as the Stanford Prison Experiment and Stanley Milgram's shock experiments support this chilling view of human nature.[89]

Recent qualitative research on torture draws on this perspective by insisting that we should not assume that there is something distinctive about perpetrators and that we should instead look to their environment and what within that environment socialized them into violence. Although such research notes beliefs that support the use of torture, scholars often view these beliefs as one more facet of a detrimental external environment: rewards for violence, the desire for approval from peers, brutal consequences for noncompliance, and legitimizing beliefs. These are often all conceived as part of a broader socializing context.[90]

A consensus exists between different qualitative studies on how external forces encourage violence. Brutalization of the brutalizers is a common theme. Police and military organizations humiliate and harm their recruits, who in turn are more able and more likely to humiliate and harm those in their custody.[91] These organizations also reward recruits for violence.[92] Early socialization to submit to authority helps produce men who will be violent on command; indeed, some British torturers cite their boarding school education as contributing to their later acts of violence.[93] And it is not only their superiors whom perpetrators aim to please. The approval of peers is a powerful motivator as well, as they strive to remain part of a fraternal order.[94]

Based on their research in Brazil, Huggins and colleagues identify three processes that transform people into "violence workers" who commit acts of torture and extrajudicial killing.[95] Political-historical processes such as the rise of a military regime can create both the structures and the rationale for violence. Governments create military and police trainings, for example, which socialize their recruits to believe that certain groups of people are threats to a valued way of life. These processes can also operate at the social-organizational level. Police organizations can encourage violence through formal rewards as well as through pressure from peers and supervisors, and legitimate this violence by normalizing and valorizing it.

Huggins and her colleagues assert that the transformation from "ordinary man" to violence worker is also a psychological process. But in their description, the inner world of the torturers reflects political-historical and social-organizational processes: Individuals internalize the expectations and ideology of the government and organization. They then disengage from genuine moral beliefs that they held before they were socialized into violence. In short, beliefs that support violence are understood as part of how people are socialized to "shed their moral identities" rather than as legitimately constituting them.[96]

A probing and nuanced reflection by James Dawes is suggestive of how moral disengagement may partially explain how people are able to commit violence. Dawes notes the ways in which Japanese war criminals he interviewed distanced themselves from violence they committed by using euphemisms for brutality. But Dawes also recounts that these men were raised from early childhood to valorize bravery and sacrifice for the nation.

Although Dawes does not make this case explicitly, this upbringing opens the possibility that these individuals may not have been disengaging from their moral identities when they committed violence; they may have been living up to them. It is true that a militant government socialized these beliefs. But most beliefs are products of socialization; indeed, human rights activism and education seek to socialize its addressees accordingly. And socialization itself cannot make a belief less legitimate or "genuine."

Regardless of whether police disengage from earlier moral identities, it is important to understand them as they are when they commit violence. Although perpetrators in most studies cite external pressures as reasons for engaging in torture, I will discuss in the chapters that follow how the police in this book make that claim only about certain types of torture.[97] They say that they are forced to engage in the kind of torture that they believe is wrong, such as when an innocent person is being framed for a crime. But when they describe the kind of torture they see as right, they present it as volitional even if not entirely free from the constraints of circumstances.

One reason for this difference may be that statements in other studies are often culled from perpetrators when they make confessions. These speech acts are especially unreliable, as they are typically performed for a public that has turned against these perpetrators, such as after a brutal regime has fallen, and hence blaming external circumstances is useful.[98] In the pages that follow, the police explain their current actions in confidential interviews and discuss current violence, which may be why they were more willing to claim responsibility and present their actions as aligned with their beliefs.

When assessing the protorture beliefs of populations that do not actually commit torture, however, researchers do not assume that they are disengaging from their more genuine moral selves. Survey researchers on the American public note the complexities inherent in support for torture.[99] Moreover, legal philosophers debate whether torture should be permissible, usually without being subject to the accusation that their philosophies are a rationalization. A recent case in Germany exemplifies this ambivalence. The administration sanctioned the use of physical force on a kidnapper in custody. Before the force was used, the man revealed the child's location, though too late to save the child. Legal theorists articulated mixed responses to this decision, including praise for the German government for "balancing" competing principles by finding officials guilty but not punishing them.[100] Officials at the National Human Rights Commission in New Delhi, who are responsible for punishing police who use torture, but who rarely punish them, mentioned this case in explaining their own mixed feelings about torture. It has been harder, however, for researchers to take seriously the beliefs of the people who actually commit this violence.

A robust literature on legal pluralism does explore how distinct legal systems, based on different normative orders, may operate within the same society. This research focuses on the tension between state and substate spheres, particularly in colonial and postcolonial societies. Although not all of these studies examine responses to efforts to spread a particular normative legal order, one rich study of such efforts is Richard Wilson's investigation of the Truth and Reconciliation Commission in post-Apartheid South Africa.

Wilson argues that the post-Apartheid South African government used rights discourse to centralize control. Racial cleavages deepened by years of violence threatened the unity of the new state, as did renegade local means of enforcing justice. Human rights discourse was a means of unifying the new nation through an ethics of forgiveness, according to Wilson. But people who understood justice as based on punishment rejected that discourse.

The Indian case is markedly different because the current human rights movement is not generally focused on forgiving past wrongs. Still, a similar moral imaginary pervades responses to human rights in India as in South

Africa: the idea that justice is upheld when people receive what they deserve rather than through protections that are equal and procedural.

Research on Policing

This conception of justice is prevalent among police across contexts, and a vast body of research has documented the police culture of which these beliefs are part.[101] At times police culture is described not as a moral orientation, but in terms of perceived flaws: police are depicted as insular, secretive, intolerant, and paranoid.[102] But such research also suggests a shared conception of justice. In his classic study of an American police department, William Westley interviewed police who argue that certain groups of people can be controlled only by violence and that it is right to use violence toward those people. Although the research conducted for this study is now more than half a century old and substantial police reforms have occurred since then, this view remains a central facet of police culture.[103] Indeed, the frequency with which policing scholars report on what they call "noble cause corruption"—which refers to the belief among police that it is right to bend the rules in order to ensure that "bad guys" are punished—indicates that this conception of justice is still common.[104]

For example, in their attempt to explain the 1991 beating of Rodney King, policing scholars Skolnick and Fyfe suggest that it is officers' sense of moral mission that leads them to sometimes use brutal force. "Police do not make their choices by a rational calculation of comparative economic values," they argue. Officers' "choices are made instead on moral grounds, developed within the subculture of a police department."[105] These moral grounds are strikingly similar to those of the police interviewed for this book, who believe they must control an "unruly and dangerous underclass."[106] The authors would not be surprised by the comparison; police culture is "everywhere similar," they argue, because police work is defined by the presence of danger and authority, which produce a distinctive outlook on the world.[107]

These authors acknowledge that police departments may still adopt different approaches, and more recent research seeks to diversify the concept of police culture.[108] Researchers insist that this culture is shaped by the wider social context, such as a recent history of violent conflict, elite agendas, and racial segregation.[109]

Moreover, other scholars emphasize the importance of police beliefs, but attribute these beliefs to individual personalities rather than to occupational culture. William Muir highlighted officers' moral orientations and beliefs about human nature and argued that the best police officers appreciate competing goods (in distinction from a simplistic pursuit of goals that trump all others) and perceive a shared human condition (as opposed to dividing the world into different types of people). He suggests that it is moral complexity, sympathy, and passion that restrain violence and discourage corruption.[110]

Policing scholars are divided on whether officers' beliefs "cause" them to be violent. Some researchers draw on evidence suggesting that police attitudes predict the use of force, while others insist that it is officers' immediate circumstances that determine what they do.[111] But most view these beliefs as authentic commitments rather than as an indication that officers have become alienated from their genuine moral beliefs.

Furthermore, the often remarked upon gap between what people say they believe and what people do does not necessarily undermine the importance of understanding the former. As one researcher has pointed out, officers' articulation of their beliefs, or even police culture overall, may serve the purpose of enabling police to justify to themselves and others their otherwise objectionable role as coercive agents.[112] Police may genuinely hold these beliefs but still feel discomfort about their role and actions. If so, these beliefs may not cause violence but may still facilitate it by helping officers to live with it.

I suggest one further reason that police officers' beliefs matter: They express what officers think they should be and do even if they do not live up to this idealized vision. Understanding this ideal reveals part of why efforts to introduce human rights reforms have met with so much resistance. Rarely, however, has the wealth of research on police beliefs been connected to the theory and practice of human rights diffusion, and it is to this connection that I now turn.[113]

Part 1

Officers' Ideals

Chapter 2

Police Beliefs and the Moral Imaginary of Violence

Police care about justice. That is why they have a temper.

—Mid-ranking police officer, Uttar Pradesh

"USING TORTURE doesn't mean the police are violating human rights. The police are also trying to deliver justice to someone," claimed a mid-ranking police officer in the North Indian state of Haryana. This officer will seem to some readers like one more example of what is wrong with the police. His statement suggests that he fits the profile of the low-ranking officer who lacks the capacity to understand human rights or the commitment to uphold them. But understanding the moral and social imaginary that informs his and many other officers' views can shine light on what he means. Such understanding will not make his statement less objectionable to those who are committed to the struggle against torture. Yet it will provide a partial explanation for why, despite decades of efforts to prevent it, so many police are able to engage in violence in spite of their desire to see themselves as decent people.

If there is anyone who belies the widespread notion that the less educated, lower ranks of police are incapable of careful thought, it is Y. He is a constable, the lowest-ranking police officer and, as the nation's home minister quipped, "India's most reviled public servant."[1] The government's own National Police Commission report referred to the constabulary as "poor specimens of humanity," warning that the dismal conditions of employment could never attract the right kind of people.[2] Many reformers assume that if only the lower-ranking police were better educated and more carefully selected, better able to reflect on their actions and more committed to justice—i.e., more similar to their elite supervisors—widespread violence would not stymie the professionalism of the police.[3]

Thirty-one years old at the time of our first interview, Y had recently married and taken his wife to his familial home just outside New Delhi. He had joined the Delhi Police (DP) after a period of time with the Central Industrial Police Force (CIPF), a paramilitary force chartered to provide security for government buildings. He left the CIPF because the members were required to live in barracks away from their families, whereas his post with the Delhi Police allows him to live at home. Still, policing in the lower ranks of the DP is known to be grueling, thankless work. That Y considers it an improvement upon the CIPF is suggestive of the even more difficult working conditions of the agency, rather than a promising statement about life in the Delhi constabulary.

Y wasted no time during our interview. By the second question of what would be an initial session lasting more than four hours, he was lamenting police corruption and praising some of the most outspoken and controversial critics of the government. Many of the officers I interviewed avoided any critical comments or sensitive subjects until the second, third, or fourth hour of conversation. Thoughtful and direct, Y expressed from the start his concern that because of corruption, he is unable to uphold justice. But what precisely does he mean by this contention? Has he imbibed the ideals of the human rights course in which he is a student? Does he wish he could uphold the rule of law and offer all people equal protection?

Y does share some views in common with the human rights activists who are his teachers and those across the country who view him and his peers as the source of so much injustice. He criticized the government for the violent crackdown on a peaceful protest led by Baba Ram Dev, a yoga guru who speaks out against government corruption. Y noted that "the government of India did what the Britishers used to do, giving orders during the night." This was no idle observation: he was one of the police officers to whom the orders were given, part of the force that "*lathi*-charged" (beat with batons) the sleeping men, women, and children gathered at the site of Ram Dev's "yoga camp," which was understood by the government as a protest. Y resented both the command itself and the fact that a police officer who refuses to follow such orders is transferred to places like Kashmir, the site of an armed insurgency, or isolated and eventually fired under false pretenses.

Public protests are not the only times Y feels pressure to use violence. He understands that his supervisors, elected officials, and judges expect him to torture suspects. He says right away that he is expected to force confessions from impoverished rickshaw drivers and to withhold help from people without resources.

But Y's complaint is not that politicians prevent him from protecting human rights. Corruption obstructs justice in his mind, not just because he is unable to protect innocent people but also because he is prevented from punishing the guilty. Political corruption means using violence against impoverished rickshaw drivers to force confessions; he detests this practice. But it also means *not* torturing the well-connected, powerful people he believes to be guilty—people he believes deserve and require violent treatment. It becomes clear that to Y, torture is not wrong. Rather, using it on the wrong people is wrong. In fact, to police, corruption and human rights are a problem for the same reason: both interfere with treating people the way they deserve.

Human Rights Activists' Beliefs about Violations

In personal interviews and written reports, human rights advocates attribute torture to two types of reasons. First, activists argue that police torture stems from the immoral and willful intention to harm. This includes motivations for torture such as the desire to punish a particular community, an enjoyment of power, and, particularly for civil police, the intention to extract bribes or please politicians.

Second, human rights advocates see police torture as stemming from amoral causes such as a lack of resources, facilities, and training; extremely poor working hours and conditions; and (for civil police) the poor organization of the police force. In this view, officers torture because they are too poorly equipped and trained, and too overworked, to do anything else. This suggests that improving the condition of the police and the adding resources, training, and equipment will reduce torture. These might be considered "amoral" motivations, because such acts are understood as unintentional lapses due to factors beyond the officers' control.

Law enforcement officers agree with these explanations yet view them as accounting for only certain kinds of torture. While the human rights community as well as Indian law asserts that all torture is wrong, law enforcers differentiate between torture that is justifiable and that which is not. So when human rights activists criticize police for using torture for immoral and amoral reasons, most officers agree with the criticism. But this agreement does not begin to account for all of the many reasons they believe police torture to be justified.

The Moral Imaginary of Violence: Officers' Conceptions of Justice

Law enforcement officers' conception of justice, and the background beliefs that support this conception, deeply conflict with human rights. Their conception of justice is grounded in principles of merit rather than equality. They generally believe that justice is upheld when people get what they deserve rather than when the rule of law offers equal protection. When they describe the ideal law enforcement officer, they describe someone who identifies evil persons and fights them, upholding justice by punishing wrongdoing. In their view, a hero understands that rules must sometimes be broken to protect the innocent and especially to punish the guilty.

This conception of justice is an important part of the moral imaginary from which officers draw to define their identity and purpose. For example, when explaining why he joined the police, a low-ranking officer from Uttar Pradesh asserted, "We do away with evil powers. We fight those with *ravana-pravathi* (demon nature)." Although most officers speak in terms of wrongdoing rather than evil, their understanding of justice is consistent with such a vocabulary.

Officers routinely draw from this "hero narrative" to justify and explain torture and other unsanctioned state violence. For example, a subinspector of police in Haryana who conducts human rights trainings in his department explains:

> Say a thief has committed a crime, say a robbery or a murder. If we ask him politely, he may not tell us. So we have to threaten him or use third-degree torture. But this is in the public interest. This is used for dangerous criminals. If we don't do this, justice will not be delivered.

Here, as in many cases, to explain torture the officer draws on a conception of justice that prioritizes not equal treatment, but rather just deserts—justice is served when people receive what they "deserve" because of their actions, as well as what is "required" to protect the innocent.

The Social Imaginary: Types of Human Beings and Categories of Exception

When I ask one high-ranking military officer who had previously been stationed in Kashmir how we should decide whether an act is a "human rights violation," he replied, "It depends on whom the violation has taken place against." Differentiating by the identity of the victim rather than by the act itself, is a key element in officers' conception of justice. This way of thinking is linked to and made possible by a broader social imaginary that is composed of a particular view of human nature and the nature of society.

Officers create and rely on different categories of people; members of each category have a moral worth peculiar to them and should be treated accordingly. These categories depend on distinctions between the guilty and the innocent, and between "hardened" criminals, "militants," and "terrorists," on the one hand, and "regular" criminals, on the other.

This way of categorizing people both constrains and supports officers' justification of torture. According to officers, ideally torture should be used with only certain "types" of people. Officers willingly defend torture without qualification when it is directed at what they describe as "hardcore" criminals. By defining someone in this way, the officer places the person into a category of exception. For moral as well as for instrumental reasons, the rules that protect "normal" human beings no longer apply. In this context, the explanation of an Indian Police Service officer from Punjab is typical: "If a police officer wants to extract information without using the third degree, he can do so, depending on the criminal. If he is a hardcore criminal, then you have to." Similarly, a high-ranking prison officer from Haryana asserted that torture is necessary to uphold justice, but only when dealing with "dreaded" rather than "regular" criminals. I asked how he identifies those who deserve torture, and he responded with a ready classification:

> The persons who are doing crime one after another, involved in serial killing, continually involved in robbery, gang rapes, ransom, kidnapping, et cetera, are dreaded criminals. The rest are normal, casual criminals or, you could say, casual law-breakers.

I then asked if it is ever necessary to use torture with casual law-breakers, and he replied, "No. Never."

This approach to torture, in which it is used only for certain types of people, breaks down in practice. As will be apparent in the next chapter, police officers admit this. But such distinctions nonetheless remain an important part of their understanding of right and wrong and of how torture becomes an acceptable, even morally necessary, action for these officers. This "hardened" criminal is the primary target of justice, in the officers' view. Anything that can be done to win in the battle against such criminals is justified.

The officers use the label of "militant" or "terrorist" in the same way, to identify and separate those who do not deserve the protections afforded to "normal" human beings. For example, one high-ranking Indian Police Service officer in New Delhi asserted, "I have been a senior officer for twenty-eight years. There was no situation where I had to be firing on someone. Except in encounters with terrorists." In this narration, a "terrorist" does not count as a "someone." Similarly, another officer argued that if police kill a "terrorist," then "it is not a human rights violation."

People categorized as "hardcore" criminals and "terrorists" should be tortured for several reasons, according to these officers. First, they argue that such people are fundamentally different from "normal" people. This difference provides a moral justification to torture them. Officers' comments suggest that they view people in this exceptional category as not human, or at least not in the same way that others are human, and hence not deserving of "human" rights.

Further, the officers use instrumental reasoning in their justification. The hardened criminal or terrorist's location outside the human community means that humane methods will have no effect, according to officers. They argue that this type of exceptional criminal has been "trained" to withstand torture; therefore, they "take more to break."

These different types of explanations are often combined, as in the statement of a high-ranking Indian Police Service officer. He insisted that these criminals are inherently different from other people, which makes it not only right to use violence, but also instrumentally necessary. He warned, "A criminal is a person without a soul, and the standard techniques for people with souls cannot be applicable."

Similarly, a mid-ranking police officer in Kashmir justified torture by explaining, "The *goonda* [professional criminal] element—such type of people—it doesn't matter whether he is from city or village—a person can be a big smuggler or small smuggler. These people are so tough they cannot understand the language of love, peace, and harmony." A low-ranking paramilitary officer previously stationed in Kashmir repeated this nearly ubiquitous rationale, saying, "If someone tells everything, then no officer is happy to use torture. But the hardcore-minded persons—they are called hardcore minded—they break in a difficult way, so police use methods to find results." The officer points directly to the system of classification here, noting that "they are called hardcore minded," signifying that he is drawing on an accepted system of division.

Beliefs about Utility

As some of the previous statements suggest, officers' conception of justice is also instrumental. Although these police believe that certain types of criminals "deserve" to be tortured, they insist that torture also serves the goal of "solving" cases and benefiting an abstract general public by keeping it secure. In this "ends over means" reasoning that officers so often employ, anything that serves the goal of punishing the guilty is legitimate. Indeed, officers sometimes defend torture by explaining that it is "only a method" for ensuring the conviction of criminals, as if its part in an ends-oriented process makes it legitimate.

The second way in which officers' conception of justice is instrumental, and in fact utilitarian, is their reliance on calculations of maximum benefit to explain their actions. This is particularly the case when there is no clear distinction between the guilty and the innocent, such as if a group is engaging in public protest. Officers often justify violence against protestors by drawing on the need for law and order, yet they also recognize that people have a right to protest. I asked a mid-ranking officer in Uttar Pradesh how a police officer should decide when to violate rights for the sake of law and order. He responded that it is a matter of "simple mathematics." He explained that if the "mass that is agitating" will "cause damage to a very large portion, to national property, then we must demand that they cannot break the law." He juxtaposed this with instances when the protestors "cause damage to very few persons." Acknowledging that the protestors indeed have a right to protest, he relates that this right is conditional upon how many people it will negatively affect.

The maxim that rights-holders should not violate the rights of others is part of the human rights framework itself. But not surprisingly, how police weigh the competing rights—how they perform the mathematics of utility—rarely favors the rights of those who question the state. Officers typically solve this "mathematical" problem by assuming that the interest of the majority and the interest of the government are the same. For example, the officer who referred to using "simple mathematics" to decide when to violate rights recounts a time when farmers were protesting and blocking the national highway. After fourteen days, the police were ordered to open the highway at any cost. As they did so, they fired into the crowd and killed a farmer.

The officer regretted that the farmer was killed and visited the house of the farmer's family to offer his condolences. But he believes that the killing was justified. This incident meets the conditions he laid out for just action because the blockage of the national highway affected many people and was not in the interest of the state. This highlights a central tension between utilitarianism and a rights-based conception of justice. In this particular use of utilitarian reasoning, the larger number of people whose lives are affected by a blocked highway trumps the right to life. According to many human rights advocates, in contrast, nothing short of the threat to another's life can negate this right.

Utilitarianism has been an important part of the liberal tradition. While the utilitarian theorist Jeremy Bentham was willing to sacrifice individual rights for the sake of the public good within certain limits, the liberal utilitarian thinker John Stuart Mill articulated reasons why protecting those rights promotes overall happiness and is hence consistent with utilitarianism. But human rights activists stress that rights hold an ethical status independent of such purposes. The aforementioned scenario exemplifies why activists sense a danger in secondary explanations for the value of rights: if they are treated as being contingent on utilitarian conditions, they cease to be inalienable.

Officers frequently use this type of utilitarian reasoning to justify torture. For example, a low-ranking paramilitary officer reasoned that torture should be used "when the gravity of the offense is very heavy for society and the nation." A high-ranking military officer explained, "As for an example of an inappropriate use of the third degree, any incident where the damage that will be caused [by the potential crime] is not as great as the damage you will do to this person."

This reliance on utilitarian reasoning often occurs in conjunction with the classification of different types of people, as in the assertion that "hardened" criminals should be tortured because they cause the most harm to society. As a result, officers argue, the suffering the suspect could inflict on others outweighs the suffering torture inflicts on the suspect. For example, a high-ranking prison officer from Haryana explained:

> In the case of professional criminals, dreaded criminals who are continually involved in serious cases of robbery, when a huge number of cases are pending against them and nobody dares to come and comment as witnesses, these dreaded criminals repeatedly are doing the crimes and always are acquitted by the courts in the absence of proper witnesses and evidence. In my view, then, there is no alternative but for the police to encounter them [stage an assassination] or do such type of severe physical torture to them. These dreaded criminals are like weeds in our society that harm the normal crop. It is a big hurdle in society. These must be eradicated like the weeds.

A mid-ranking military officer provided a similar argument for the need to torture "militants":

> If you spend time in Kashmir, you will realize these guys are the biggest problem in the world. So you have to resort to extreme measures. These people are fanatics. If you aren't tough with them, you will see thirty people dead. These people

> have to be dealt with a strong hand. You must show no mercy with them. A normal person like you and me may not understand that. But people in Kashmir—these people have no affection for Kashmir. Once you confirm that he is a militant, you find bullets on him, you should go all out. He is there to kill you or at least people in your country. But for normal people it is very wrong.

Hence this utilitarian rationale supports officers' belief that certain categories of people do not deserve human rights. Certain types of people, such as "hardened" criminals, pose the highest threat to society, so that "simple mathematics" proves that any harm caused to them will be outweighed by the harm they caused or could cause to society. But as will become clear in what follows, this reasoning also helps officers justify torture that expands beyond the "type" of person they claim deserves it most.

Beliefs about Intention

Intention is also a key feature of officers' conception of justice. Unlike merit and utility, this aspect is focused on the officer himself. When examining whether an officer has done the right thing by torturing, police typically emphasize whether he or she *intended* to act in accordance with their standards (i.e., by torturing the type of person who requires such treatment, when the benefit to society outweighs the cost). What matters is not whether the officer's evaluation is accurate, such as whether the suspect is actually guilty, but that the officer believes that the suspect is guilty. Police frequently assert that officers who torture or kill for the public good should not be punished, while they condemn torture that is done solely for personal gain.

This focus on intention is a central feature of many ethical systems, and is particularly important within Hindu theology. The *Bhagavad-Gita* famously declares that it is not the fruits of one's actions but the intention behind them that determines their merit, and advises that we let go of attachment to results and focus on the nature of our motivation.[4] The officers in the study identified as Hindu or Sikh; most said that their religious beliefs are important to them. Although I will later discuss how officers reconcile violence with their religious beliefs, it is beyond the scope of this study to examine whether their religious beliefs "cause" them to hold particular views. This issue becomes especially complex given the important role of intention in so many belief systems as well as in modern jurisprudence. But it remains that intention plays a primary role in how officers think about moral action and that the religious beliefs officers express support this.

This focus on intention as determining moral worth in some ways is in tension with the human rights framework and represents another belief with which rights activists must contend. If intention is the primary factor determining the moral worth of an action, there can be no universal application of law that bans any particular action.

Officers express this sentiment consistently throughout the interviews. When defending the well-publicized video-recorded abuse of a Bangladeshi man by an officer, another officer argued, "Human rights should rescue police if the policeman doesn't have any bad intention." And police do not limit this explanation to their defense of torture. A low-ranking police officer reflected that his father was a role model for him because he taught that "abuse is better than bad intention." In other words, it is better to abuse someone with a good intention than it is to do anything with a bad intention. The police officer I referred to previously reflected on the farmer's death by asserting, "If you do your job with full honesty 100 percent, then you must be satisfied with the results whether they are positive or negative."

Officers sometimes seem to assume that human rights activists share their reliance on intention as a determinant of moral worth. When I asked one Indian Police Service officer why human rights activists criticize the police for torturing, he presumed their criticism is directed toward officers who "torture just to torture." Officers often defend torture by exclaiming that "police have no personal interest in this"—as if that alone should quiet criticism. They argue that human rights organizations should "examine the intention of police" when deciding whether to prosecute for human rights violations rather than punish police for torture regardless of motivation or justification. In this way, they challenge a human rights framework in which certain acts are unconditionally wrong.

Negotiating the Law

Officers know that they endorse violations of Indian and international law when they say that certain types of people require and deserve torture. They sometimes address this uneasy relationship between law and their conception of justice. They point out that the law allows for some deprivations of rights already, such as the loss of liberty for those accused of crimes. They argue that, in this context, their use of torture does not violate the principle of law but simply adapts and extends it to exceptional people. Torture so understood is their own informal "emergency" crafted for individuals. At times, they argue that the law should simply change to accommodate the distinctions they make between those who do and do not deserve certain rights. For example, a mid-ranking officer from Rajasthan theorized:

> Offenders of heinous crimes and regular criminals who are in organized crime like repeated robberies, gangs, *goondas*—there also should be a certain code of conduct for this, like twenty shots to the lower back, then stop for a medical examination, then twenty more shots. The Indian law says that there is no place for the third degree in civilized society. But let me tell you, there is not civilized society in society. You need to recognize gradations in society. They say in civilized society you cannot use force. But where there are criminals you need to differentiate. Criminals need to be dealt with according to the crime.

This officer argues against one key premise of the rule of law by drawing on another key premise. He draws on a commonly acknowledged maxim that the punishment should be proportionate to the crime. By referencing this, he undermines the maxim that all people should be equal in the eyes of the law and enjoy equal protection of certain inalienable rights. He would like to reconcile the tension between the rule of law, on the one hand, and what he sees as the requirements of justice, on the other, by means of a legal system that recognizes the differences between categories of human.

More often, police discuss torture as a category unto itself that simply cannot be incorporated into the rule of law. In this view, torture is always an exception—no matter how frequently the exception is used. Officers who hold this view argue that they must be free to differentiate between those who should be protected by the law and those for whom exceptions must be made.

What is at stake for these officers is the understanding of torture as an exception for special cases rather than as an act that can and should be regulated and integrated into the daily work of law and order. Such normalization would undermine their justification of torture as outside of normal practice. This is exemplified in a dialogue with a high-ranking prison officer in Haryana:

> OFFICER: In our present law, torture is not allowed, even though it is a hard fact that it is necessary in cases of these dreaded professional criminals to maintain peace and proper law and order in society.
>
> RW: Why is torture illegal for dreaded criminals?
>
> OFFICER: In the eyes of the law everyone is equal. And in my view also, generally, it cannot be allowed because of the chance of misuse of this power. If it is generally legalized, then there is a big chance of misuse of such powers.

RW: What kind of misuse would happen?

OFFICER: If it would be legalized, then such types of incidents will happen . . . the officers will not use scientific interrogation. This is an easy way for the police personnel. I mean torture. Physical and mental torture is an easy way to get [confessions and information from] the criminals.

This officer suggests that torture and the discrimination on which it is based would become too prevalent if incorporated into the law. Once again, it is the restriction of torture—its status as an exception—that justifies it in the officers' explanations.

Torture and the System

As much as police feel they must reconcile a gap between their stance on torture and the law, this does not mean they perceive any tension with the legal system as it actually operates. On the contrary, officers assert that their superiors expect this violence of them. One high-ranking Indian Police Service officer explained, "Every day at *thanas* [police stations] there is some sort of illegality, but the acceptance is that you cannot cross [a certain] level. The level of acceptance is important. If you torture someone and you get information and crack the case, then it is win-win for everybody." That he sees torture as "win-win" for everybody suggests that he believes other actors in the criminal justice system, as well as the public, endorse this practice. Y, the Delhi constable introduced earlier, explained that "the judges understand" that the police need to use torture and asserted, "If a judge says, 'Ten days in police remand,' it is a hint to the police to torture him for ten days."

Moreover, officers often interpret the law as implicitly permitting torture, even though they know torture is illegal. A police officer who conducts human rights trainings for other police reflected, "The third degree is necessary. But 'third degree' is not the proper word. Indian law is flexible and so good [that] there is no law that specifies third degree." In other words, he interprets the lacuna in the law as implicit support for the practice.

In fact, officers' view of the relationship between torture and the law exceeds a perception that this violence is implicitly allowed, and for many officers, consists of a sense that their position within the legal system is at least partially defined by this violence. Y, for example, asserted:

Suppose a person is involved in a theft. Police present the man in court. The judge punishes him and he is sent to jail. That is judicial custody. The job of the police is over. In police remand—police custody—police try to use the

> minimum required use of force, but sometimes custodial deaths happen, say a heart attack. . . . This investigation, torture, all of this is part of the constitution. If the judges think police should not do this, then they should take it out. But how would police be able to do all this? If someone is in police remand, then it is legal. If NGOs have a problem, then they should please write to the prime minister and the president. What do police have to do with this? Police have no personal interest in doing all this. Just remove this particular chapter of police remand if you have a problem with this. Have the judge only allow police to take someone into custody but the police has nothing to do with this. If you don't want torture, then remove police remand. Police remand is legal. Police are instructed. Police did not write the constitution.

This officer views torture as inseparable from his role as a police officer to such an extent that police remand would need to be removed in order to eliminate this violence. While it at first seems that he misunderstands the constitution as allowing torture, further questioning reveals that it is the implicit rather than explicit support for torture that he intends to convey. When I asked, "What does the constitution say about torture?" he replied:

> The constitution and the [name of state] Police Rules don't use the word *torture*. But a little force is allowed. Like if you ask someone to stand in a position with their arms out, in half an hour they will confess. That is allowed.

Like the others, he experiences the criminal justice system as expecting police torture. Although they do not believe that torture is "legal," officers understand the law to implicitly allow it—and that the elected officials, judges, and police supervisors who represent the law expect it.

Human rights advocates would agree with these assertions about the flexibility of Indian law regarding torture. The Prevention of Torture Bill[5] ostensibly came into being in order to specify torture as a punishable offense and comply with the requirements for India to ratify (as opposed to only sign) the United Nations Convention Against Torture. However, the bill is widely criticized for making torture more permissible. The definition of *torture* it contains is far narrower than the definition used by the United Nations, limiting it to "grievous hurt" or danger to life, limb, and health. Human rights advocates note that severe physical and mental abuse could escape this definition. Also, the bill limits the time in which victims may report torture to six months after the incident. This period is prohibitive for many considering the frequency with which police refuse to register cases, especially against other police, and the length of time required for the Human Rights Commission to intervene. The bill further specifies that the victim must prove the intent of the officer.[6] These weaknesses in the law, which even in this compromised formulation has not been passed, suggests that there is broad support for the perception of the officers in this study: that when they torture suspects, they are not rogue actors but compliant ones.

Basis in Society

According to officers, it is not only other legal actors but also the public at large that expect the police to use torture. For example, when defending the officers' decision to torture the man suspected in his wife Namita's disappearance in the NGO report I gave the officers, a high-ranking paramilitary officer stressed both his own identity as an "investigator" and the public's expectation that he be a successful one. He first allowed that perhaps the husband was not guilty, but argues that he must torture him in order to find out. He asserted:

> But as an *investigator* [stresses this word and taps forcefully on his heart], I need to establish the cleanliness on the husband's part. I need first to give him a *clean chit* [clearance from wrongdoing] because the husband is the subject here. Only then will I proceed in another direction to arrive at a conclusion. But if there is persistent doubt on the husband, why should I look for other evidence? And if the husband is not cooperating, then what should I do? I need to grill him.

He then argued from the additional rationale of the public's expectation of police, stating:

> And I need to convince Miss Namita's family also because they have confidence in us that we will find their daughter. And the police is answerable to society also. They expect police to be effective, to be their guardian.

Police typically believe that the public's expectation that they torture to "find out the truth" is legitimate and part of their role as police. This officer also notes the scorn the public will have toward the police if they fail to succeed. He said:

> And if the culprit is not apprehended, what opinion will you have of police? They are helpless. You will come away with the opinion that police are helpless.

In this officer's eyes, the public will applaud him for a successful investigation in which torture has yielded evidence, and lose respect for him if the investigation fails.

Police leadership and human rights advocates attest to the accuracy of this perception that the public expects police to use torture. A high-ranking official in the Bureau of Police Research and Development notes that if, as a police officer, you beat a culprit, you will be a "hero" to the public. Human rights advocates who work on police reform also verify this. For instance, the director of the police reform program at a New Delhi–based NGO advises that one of their challenges is changing the public's attitude about what constitutes good police work. She asserted:

> Organizations like [ours] have a certain view of what policing should be, but the public often sees good policing as tough policing, which often means shortcuts. They want criminals eliminated the way the police do it, and they don't see the risks. People don't feel safe. They don't see that it could be gangs one day, or the Maoists one day, and them the next.

The consistency with which different types of actors endorse this perception suggests that the police are right in their assessment of the public's expectations. Unlike pressure from politicians to torture those who are innocent, or pressure from human rights activists to not torture at all, this public pressure often aligns with officers' conception of justice. Hence it may resonate more with police and reinforce their understanding of what they should do.

In fact, because of the perception that violence is a legitimate part of police work and that politicians and people of means can influence the police according to their will, officers may be suspected of corruption if they do *not* use force. For example, people may believe that an officer has accepted a bribe from a member of the general public or is acting under the control of a politician if he refrains from torturing a suspect. An officer who occupies a high rank at the National Human Rights Commission noted what can happen if an officer refuses to torture:

> Motives will be attributed. They will say, 'You are under the influence of the other person, of the accused person. You are hoodwinking us.' They will even allege that you have taken money from the other person to be soft on him and you will just produce him in court.

This statement suggests that if police follow the law, it could connote to the public that they are in fact corrupt. The legal action of "just" producing a suspect in court without torture implies corruption. This public belief signifies the broad salience enjoyed by the heroic justice narrative police use to explain why torture is legitimate. It indicates that police are not alone in assuming that torture has an important role to play in the administration of justice.

Indeed, many popular Indian films about the police embody this image of the heroic officer who breaks the law to uphold justice. In the 1973 hit film *Zanjeer* (*Shackles*), starring legendary Bollywood actor Amitabh Bachchan, a man becomes a police officer to avenge the murder of his parents, a murder he witnessed as a child. In the film, he relentlessly pursues villains and protects the innocent, even when this means going outside the law. In the words of a former director of the Central Bureau of Intelligence, who in my interview with him voiced support for torture, "Amitabh Bachchan becomes a hero because he disregards all the rules of the department." The film is wildly popular and still relevant to current sentiment; it was remade in 2013. Similarly, a popular Bollywood film from 2004, *56 So Far*, celebrates "the true story" of Senior Inspector Pradeep Sharma, known as an "encounter specialist" for the Mumbai Police Department. The title refers to the fifty-six people he has assassinated "so far." A more recent and by now typical film called *Department* features a band of vigilantes who help the police hunt down and kill members of the "underworld." The only crime of this vigilante group, the advertisement tells us, "is justice." These films celebrate the image of the police officer who sacrifices the law in order to punish criminals.

Some police refer to these films explicitly. The mid-ranking officer from Rajasthan instructed, "To learn about me, you should see a couple of movies," and then listed films that valorize a police officer who breaks all the rules for the sake of justice. He described *Zanjeer*, the Amitabh Bachchan film described previously, and *Cobra*, an American film starring Sylvester Stallone. In both movies, the rights of the accused are obstacles to the heroic police officer who knows that to fight wrong, one cannot always play by the rules. The officer explained that the films "tapped into his inner desire to resist wrong" and inspired him to become a police officer.

These films provide narratives in which violence is right, from which police can draw as they attempt to understand and explain themselves. These narratives likely reflect those that already exist within their work environment, and moreover, may make them more appealing. In this way, these films serve as resources for officers as they form and explain their moral identities.

Conflicting Imaginaries: Officers' Conceptions of Justice versus Human Rights

For the human rights movement to succeed, it must persuade people to accept a particular view of reality.[7] It must construct actors (as beings with an inalienable dignity) and actions (the equal protection of these beings) and explain why these actions are the right way to treat these actors. In other words, it must construct and spread a social and a moral imaginary.

But this imaginary confronts already existing imaginaries, and in the case of these law enforcement officers, it confronts imaginaries that conflict with human rights. First, there is a difference in the orientation to social change. Charles Taylor notes that social imaginaries can legitimize the status quo or offer prescriptions for how the prevailing order must be transformed. The modern imaginary of equal, autonomous, rights-bearing citizens began as a legitimation of the existing order. But as developed later by theorists such as John Locke, and increasingly so over time, this imaginary came to be a prescription for how society should change and why people are justified in trying to change it.[8]

Granted, as critics rightly point out, the human rights framework can be used to support the status quo. The "defense of human rights" can legitimize the opening of societies to market capitalism and excuse the aggressive actions of powerful states. Moreover, the human rights framework does not radically alter the structure of society, for example, by redistributing income.[9] But in spite of the fact that powerful states and corporations deploy rights talk, rights activists typically concern themselves with trying to change state behavior.[10] The police and military officers, in contrast, draw from a moral imaginary that explains why what they are already doing is right, and from a broader social imaginary that explains why their current vision of what is right is natural and rational.

There are other substantive differences between the moral imaginaries of human rights and of the police. The contemporary human rights movement has been shaped by myriad influences, from Christianity to Marxism, and no single source defines its moral order. But a particularly articulate expression of the moral order from which human rights has developed can be found in the philosophy of Immanuel Kant. Indeed, Kant's work is often identified as an important philosophical predecessor to human rights.[11]

The human rights movement follows Kant in two ways. The first is in the assertion that each person possesses inherent dignity and that, as such, people deserve a certain standard of treatment regardless of who they are or what they have done. The movement invokes this understanding of the person in codifying a list of rights that are inalienable, and in the many statements referring to the dignity that these rights protect.[12]

The affirmation of inherent dignity is a refutation of utilitarian, or more broadly, instrumental approaches to justice. For Kant, each person should be treated as an end in her- or himself. The dignity of a person cannot be violated as a means to an end, even if that end is "justice" or the protection of society. The human rights framework continues this tradition in its prioritization of individual rights over utilitarian calculations of the general good. And although the language of rights has been used to defend utilitarian goals, such as the sacrifice of economic rights for the sake of national development, many human rights advocates refute this use of rights rhetoric.[13] This explicitly non-utilitarian conception of justice means that there are some rights that people possess no matter what other social good may come from suspending them. The right to be free from torture is one such right.

Second, the human rights doctrine draws from Kant's imperative that moral laws be applied categorically rather than tailoring conceptions of morality to the specifics of a situation. This tradition is continued in the emphasis the movement places on the universality of human rights: state actors are meant to uphold basic rights equally in all circumstances.

There are several ways in which officers' beliefs are directly opposed to this moral order. Officers assume that there are different types of people who deserve different types of treatment. They base this assumption on a background understanding that is in direct contrast to the human rights movement's conception of a single human nature. In law enforcers' social imaginary, all people are *not* equal and to treat them equally would undermine justice, not enforce it.

Second, the maxim that people should not be treated as means to an end is contested in law enforcement officers' notion of justice. In the latter case, the end takes precedence over the means, as reflected both in the emphasis on fighting wrongdoing at all costs and in the more explicitly utilitarian formulations officers use. Justice is not procedural. It is an endgame in which, ideally, the right side wins. Officers emphasize that not only people but also rules are secondary to ends. Depending on the situation, justice may require that they be broken.

It may be unsurprising that law enforcement officers believe justice to be defined by punishing the guilty, protecting the innocent when possible, and creating categories that differentiate between the two. It may also be unsurprising that public officials rely on utilitarian considerations of the "public good." But little attention has been paid to how starkly this conception of justice differs from adherence to the rule of law and how much it differs from human rights doctrine. The rule of law and human rights principles both emphasize equality of individuals. Equality requires the neutral application of general rules for everyone regardless of who they are, what they have done, or how many people might benefit if the rights of some are violated.

In theory, there need not be a conflict between the neutral application of law and officers' desire to punish the guilty and thereby serve the public interest. Law prescribes punishments for those convicted of crimes, provided the process by which guilt and punishment are determined is neutral and fair. Yet officers prioritize punishing the guilty *above* neutral and fair procedures, and as such often believe that the guilty should be sacrificed if justice requires it. If neutral application of the law allows a criminal to escape punishment, then officers believe that justice requires illegal action.

In fact, it is sometimes the lack of neutrality that officers most praise. Police agree they should be "neutral" as to their personal interest in how they administer their powers, but believe they should be highly biased against anyone they consider a criminal. Their understanding of "criminal" is rarely based on conviction for a crime because most police work occurs before trial. Their understanding is based instead on officers' suspicion and their "knowledge" of the type of people who are involved in different types of crime. For example, officers often justify the torture of the man who reported his wife's disappearance by asserting that "someone in the family is always involved." Hence the premise that all are "equal before the law" is undermined.

A social imaginary in which people are grouped according to perceived differences in their character, and a moral imaginary that ascribes different levels of worth and treatment based on these differences, help to make sense of a dangerous perception that social theorists have long contended accounts for atrocities throughout history: the view that some people are human and others inhuman.[14] This view and the imaginaries that support it may allow people to view themselves as morally responsible within the community of people they consider to be fully human, while at the same time allowing people to commit atrocities against those who fall outside of this category. This seems to be what occurs with the police discussed here, who care about their moral identities yet defend the practice of torture.

Implications for Human Rights Protection

Insight into the imaginary or "background beliefs" of people who support torture and other forms of violence does more than serve as a reminder of the ethical particularity of contemporary liberalism. Ironically, such insight may also help to spread liberal norms, or at least clarify the obstacles to such efforts.

Social constructivist theorists in international relations argue that principled ideas—as well as how people determine their interests—are shaped by shared interpretations of the social world. In this way, perception is "socially constructed"; it is determined not by an objective reality such that behavior could be predicted by a survey of relative power and wealth but by how people interpret that reality. These intersubjective beliefs about reality are an important part of "what makes the world hang together."[15]

Perceptions of reality are subject to influence, constructivist scholars assert, and this malleability of public perception is key to how human rights ideals have spread around the globe. Those seeking to change norms, such as transnational activists, often do so by redefining how actors perceive a situation. Referred to as "framing," activists engage in "strategic social construction" wherein they intentionally change how a target audience understands the nature of a problem, who or what is to blame, and what should be done to solve it.[16]

Some rights are easier than others to frame in terms that will resonate with diverse publics. Constructivist scholars suggest that international norms governing the prevention of bodily harm spread most successfully because this is a value that is shared across societies.[17] Political philosophers also see the injunction to prevent suffering as a key development of the modern era and even suggest that "moral modernity" is based primarily in the belief that the state should protect citizens from bodily harm.[18] According to Judith Shklar and Richard Rorty, the modern liberal ethos is defined by the view that "cruelty is the worst thing we do."[19]

The centrality of this belief to the modern liberal order helps to explain why the Convention Against Torture (CAT) has won such widespread endorsement across countries even though it is a costly treaty for governments in the view of some social constructivists.[20] But this purportedly shared belief does not explain why countries that have expressed formal support for CAT have failed to ratify it and to implement it in practice.

India is an example of such a country. The government signed CAT in 1997. Ratification requires the passage of a domestic law to enforce the treaty. The lower house of the legislature passed the Prevention of Torture Bill in 2010, which many civil society actors anticipated would usher in ratification in spite of the law's flaws.[21] But the upper house of the legislature has not yet passed the bill. And although the government has presented itself in international forums as a supporter of CAT, the treaty has not yet been ratified.[22]

The government's aversion to ratification—in spite of consistent pressure from human rights organizations and other countries—suggests an unwillingness to change practices regarding torture.[23] Why do state actors continue to violate the convention, in spite of the government's desire to present itself as supportive of human rights norms regarding torture?[24] The answer might seem obvious: the state and its agents wish to use torture to advance their own interests without paying the price. These interests may range from a government's desire to quell protests against a profitable development project to a police officer's desire to receive a bribe for his trouble.

Yet recall that social constructivists emphasize the importance of beliefs and argue against purely realist understandings of human action. They argue that people are not motivated only by their self-interest, but also by their principles, and that their interests shape their beliefs.

But constructivists typically describe human rights violations as resulting from the *absence* of beliefs or other constraining factors. Scholars refer to a state's *lack* of desire to maintain a liberal identity; the *absence* of a network of principled transnational activists, an independent judiciary, the rule of law, and a free press; the state's perception that they will *not be held accountable*; or the *absence* of rewards and consequences tied to norm implementation such as aid money and trade agreements.[25]

Explaining human rights violations by the absence of beliefs and constraints suggests, first, that principled beliefs do not motivate human rights violations and, second, that the "default" position is for actors to violate human rights. Both of these assumptions suggest a realist understanding of human action in spite of constructivists' desire to expand realist assumptions. They imply that police are motivated only by self-interest, and when unconstrained by rights-friendly institutions and actors, will not act in accordance with any beliefs.

This neglect of the beliefs held by people who violate rights may partly relate to the focus of past scholarship. A rich theoretical literature explores the motivations of international actors such as diplomats, heads of state, and transnational activists. Like human rights advocates, elite state leaders may wish to support—or at least appear to support—modern liberal ideals, and this desire can motivate them to sign human rights treaties.[26] But international relations scholars pay less attention to the domestic state actors who are responsible for the direct implementation and physical violation of international norms. Such concerns are left to the researchers discussed previously, who focus on torture and policing but not on the global spread of norms.

But do the beliefs of individuals within the state matter to the global diffusion of norms? Some social constructivist scholars argue that state actors must "internalize" human rights to uphold them fully.[27] Many of these scholars assert that if actors' prior beliefs and values conflict with the new norm, they will be less likely to accept it.[28] Hence police officers' conflicting view of justice will likely make such persuasion more challenging.

But even if normative persuasion is not important to ensuring compliance, officers' conceptions of justice are problematic. Some theorists argue that what matters is not whether actors' beliefs truly align with norms but that they wish to *appear* to uphold norms. Actors can be shamed into compliance with norms even if they do not personally believe in them, so long as they believe that most other people do.[29] If this is the case, then what law enforcers "really" believe about torture is not important, whereas what standards they wish to appear to uphold and endorse do matter.

Officers' comments reveal that even the standards they believe they should uphold—or wish to appear to uphold—conflict deeply with human rights norms. Their ideal of justice is demonstrably opposed to equal protections from harm. In their daily life, they may use torture to obtain a bribe or please a supervisor, or they may not even use it at all. But they strive to at least appear to uphold the ideal of a heroic police officer who punishes wrongdoing, even when it means breaking the law or causing harm. This is the ideal with which they hope their actions will appear consistent.

Finally, social constructivist scholars do not suggest that the alignment of beliefs and new norms is all that is needed for human rights efforts to be effective. Recent research has outlined scope conditions within which human rights efforts are most likely to succeed.[30] The finding that poor rule of law and lack of economic development make rights treaties less enforceable makes sense in a larger structural perspective, but what might it mean close up? How do these factors inform local law enforcers' perceptions about whether they can and should uphold human rights protections? It is to these constraints that I now turn.

Chapter 3

Justice in Context

As a superintendent of police, the public wants us to beat up the criminal, which I personally feel is the wrong thing, because you can't treat everyone as guilty. But if you do that, then you are a hero, because the public knows if a case goes to court, it will take fifteen to twenty years. Nobody believes the accused will get actual justice, and the police internalize this.

—*High-ranking police official, Bureau of Police Research and Development*

I MET L IN THE BARRACKS of a paramilitary police organization tucked away in the outskirts of Delhi, too far from the capital for an auto-rickshaw to travel, so one of his subordinate officers picked me up in a jeep just outside the city.. We drove across the garbage-strewn Yamuna River and into an encampment of tents and makeshift buildings. I was given tea quickly, as I almost always am in these meetings, and I waited as L finished business, spoke to his wife on the phone, and for a while just sat, drinking his tea. Officers came in and out, sometimes giving him papers to sign, always saluting him with ritualistic precision, and then exiting by walking backward so as not to turn their backs on him. When he decided it was time for our interview, we left the tent and entered a temporary structure that was surprisingly plush on the inside. L sat at a broad desk across from me, and we began our interview.

L's battalion provides backup for the Delhi Police, as well as assists them in their regular law and order and security work. He was the highest-ranking officer present during both of our interviews, the first of which lasted four and a half hours, and the second of which concluded after nearly six hours. Hot lunches and snacks were brought to us at L's request so that we could continue to speak without interruption.

The interviews with L lasted so long in part because he loves to wax philosophical about justice. He is a student of law, he told me. He is concerned that people go hungry in modern democracies. He admires the Dalai Lama and knows a good deal about the Tibetan independence movement. He especially respects the Dalai Lama's commitment to nonviolence in spite of younger Tibetans' willingness to win freedom by other means. But he still believes that in certain circumstances, it is right for the police to torture people and to execute them without trial.

But it is not only the exceptional category of "hardened" criminals on whom he is willing to use violence, and it is not only because such people inherently deserve it that he justifies its use. Like most other officers, such categories and ideals break down once L begins telling stories about his work as it actually occurs. How, then, do police reconcile their ideals—different as they are from those of the human rights movement—with the reality of the much more extensive violence they commit?

Torture Expands: From Exceptional to Regular Criminals

Officers' circumstances—and importantly, officers' beliefs about the right way to respond to their circumstances—give further shape to their moral and social imaginaries. Indeed, beliefs do not exist in a vacuum, nor do the norms they support. There is a moral order that police endorse absolutely. But there are parts of their social imaginary—and the social reality that inspires it—that add caveats and conditions to the moral order. Perceptions of political, structural, and economic factors shape the extent to which police believe it is good to uphold their ideals. In this way, beliefs and circumstances together constitute the norms they believe are good and possible to live by.

L, like many other officers, believes that society is composed of good people and bad people, and that it is the job of the police to sort between them. Discipline in such matters is important to him, and he knows that it is the responsibility of the courts and not of the police to determine guilt.

But the circumstances in which he and other officers work make such ideal action impossible, he believes. Political corruption, inefficiency in the legal system, a lack of material resources for police, and legal protections for the accused all bias the system in favor of criminals and make it essential that police prioritize ensuring that criminals are punished. Because of the imperfect environment of their work, the police allege, this goal must trump all of their other duties, including upholding the rule of law. Moreover, they concede that they must use violence not only with the people who most "deserve" it—the "hardened" criminals—but with "regular" people as well. In such a situation, L and many others insist, police cannot uphold both the law and uphold justice. They must choose between them.

Here we see how wider social conditions, and perceptions of the right way to respond to them, shape the moral imaginary and the norms it supports. And we also see how the moral imaginary and norms in turn shape wider social conditions, as police sustain their violence in part by justifying it in moral terms.

Following, I turn to how police draw on political, legal, and material weaknesses in their working conditions to explain the use of torture on far more people than their ideal categories of exception allow. Due to these areas of weakness, police believe that they must use torture more broadly than they would in a better system. They believe, moreover, that this use of torture is a responsible way to deal with these weaknesses. Hence there opens an expansive category of torture that police do not see as intrinsically right, as with the torture of exceptional criminals, but which they also do not see as intrinsically wrong, as with the torture of known innocents for the officer's personal gain. It occupies a grey area of "right given the circumstances," and as will become clear, is flexible enough to encompass and legitimize so much of the violence in which police engage.

Political Interference

Police claim they must act outside the law and use torture on a broad spectrum of people due to pervasive political interference in their work. They frequently argue that criminals influence politicians, who in turn have power over their supervisors: a perception that is confirmed by both government and civil society reports.[1] This perception bolsters their conviction that they must use extralegal force on "exceptional" criminals, and also provides a reason to disregard the rule of law in regard to regular criminals. They assert that if they were to follow legal procedures and formally arrest a powerful criminal, it is likely that he would be released due to his political connections. For example, L argued:

> This is why there is extrajudicial killing, false encounter [staged assassinations] . . .Why are are the police agencies compelled to rely on false encounters? In the eyes of the police, he knows a person has committed a crime. With great difficulty, he arrested a person, a gun-toting person backed by politicians. If you arrest them, they pass on their mobile phone to you and the person on the phone says, 'He is my person, come on, do the needful, get him released on bail. Why are you taking this so seriously?' And the level of threat—'Hey, you want to lead a happy life?' He will be released, and after that he will not be silent, either. He will keep on teasing

> the police officer. And you will never feel secure. You will always worry about your children. If he is arrested and I know he is a habitual criminal, then my duty is to send him to prison. But if he is influential, the police will go on arresting and he will go on coming out. And there will be increasing pressure by society, 'You are not able to keep control of criminals.' So what will you do? This is how encounters [assassinations] take place.

Not all officers drew from perceptions of political corruption to defend extrajudicial killing and other violence. But even those who didn't explicitly mention corruption as a reason for violence do view it as constraining the ability of legal procedures to produce justice. For example, as was typical across interviews, Y, the constable in Delhi introduced earlier, complained that he is unable to act justly because of political interference. He provided an example that he described as commonplace: two groups of people were fighting with each other. The police wanted to arrest both parties, whom they saw as equally responsible. However, the majority of one party was released immediately because they called political connections, so only the members of the group without political connections were charged. Although he did not use this example to justify extrajudicial violence, later in the interview he argued that torture and bribery are justified because going through the legal system is no more likely to promote justice. This suggests that political interference in the legal system undermines officers' faith in the legitimacy of legal processes. In this way, officers' perceptions that the legal system is corrupt helps them to justify extralegal actions even in cases where police do not believe that such behavior is in itself right.

Judicial Inefficiency

A further way that officers explain why they must act outside the law to uphold justice is by pointing out flaws in the operation of the courts. They argue that if they were to arrest someone legally and allow him or her to stand trial, it is highly unlikely that the courts would produce justice, a perception that like political corruption is echoed in government and human rights reports.[2] They observe that trials often are delayed decades, so witnesses and evidence become increasingly tenuous and suspects are most often acquitted.

For example, L explained the legitimacy of extrajudicial killing in part by drawing on the anticipated failure of the court system. He asserted that the police agencies must sometimes assassinate suspects in faked encounters because otherwise, "Who will come and depose against [the accused]? Trials take years, and witnesses will have to wait and travel." Given this situation, police argue that if they leave justice to the courts, most crime would go unchecked and the lawlessness of society would increase.

At times, officers use this rationale to further justify the torture of criminals who are already in the category of "exception" and hence inherently deserving of torture. A high-ranking Indian Police Service officer in New Delhi uses this argument in favor of a now-overturned law known as TADA, the Terrorist and Disruptive Activities (Prevention) Act.[3] International and national NGOs vehemently criticized this act, because it eliminated protections for anyone who is accused of terrorism, including those thought "likely" to act against the government.[4] The presumption of innocence was reversed so that the burden was placed on the accused to prove that she or he is not guilty. Officers were not required to produce the suspect before a judge within twenty-four hours, as they previously had been and are currently. Confessions made to a police officer, previously and currently barred as evidence in court due to the high incidence of police torture, became admissible under the act. Along with these legal allowances, the act was criticized as being used against a broad spectrum of people outside the ambit of "terrorists," including rivals of the governing party. The officer referred to this act as a solution to the problem of communal and terrorist violence in India:

> The TADA act solved this problem. The trial of terrorists is too long, and witnesses don't show up. Also his masters try to get him released. During the trial, the criminal justice system will take years to convict, and due to lack of witnesses, there may be acquittals. I find that TADA, which has been repealed, was substantive.

This officer argued that democratic protections must be eliminated to compensate for an inefficient legal system. In his view, a law that allows for the easy conviction of criminals through reversal of the burden of proof and acceptance of confessions made to police (and hence presumably coerced through torture) mitigates the inefficiency of the court system.

Officers also sometimes use this reasoning to justify the torture of suspects who are not "exceptional." In this view, it is not that torture is necessarily right, but that the legal system is no better, due to fatal flaws in its functioning. For example, the constable Y described a case in which one man was owed money by another man, and explained the police rationale for using bribery and torture to retrieve it:

> If these people refuse to pay a bribe to the police, then he tortures. If they don't pay, they are tortured. But the legal way is also a kind of a torture. If police follow the legal way and deposit the money the man was owed with the court, he will have to fight for years to get his money back, and this is also a kind of torture, a mental torture. In these simple cases, people have to fight for sometimes twenty years. So this legal way is also a kind of torture. So both legal and illegal ways are a kind of torture. If the police start solving cases legally the way the NGOs want, the jail would be overflowing. People can be arrested for many things. And the courts will be overloaded.

Y argued not that this person deserves to be tortured, but that the legal system is so flawed that torture is no worse than turning him over to it. This is suggestive of how officers' perceptions of these flaws undermine the legitimacy of the rule of law and provide them with a means to justify major deviations from it.

Human rights advocates, experts on criminal justice in India, and the general public share this perception of the judicial system as stymied by delays due to a shortage of judges and other inefficiencies.[5] Human rights workers mention this problem with the court system in interviews, though they do not interpret it as a justification for using illegal violence. Police leadership understands this problem with the court system as a rationale for acting outside of it, even if they do not endorse this course of action. This is exemplified in the epigraph that opened this chapter. The acknowledgment by a high-ranking official that the police are seen as heroes for acting outside a flawed justice system suggests the pervasiveness of this belief.

This official's acknowledgement further suggests that inefficiencies in the legal system do more than provide police with a rationale for disregarding it. It suggests that these inefficiencies boost support for torture in a more substantial way as well, by indicating to the police and the public that police are the only source of punishment for culprits. Interviews with human rights advocates, police reform experts, and police leadership further support the assertion that police use torture as a form of punishment and that the police and the public see this as legitimate in part because judicial inefficiency means the courts will fail to do so.

It is worth noting that police do not say that they torture in order to provide punishment. Officers sometimes refer to the need to teach criminals a lesson and ensure that he is punished, but it is not clear that they are referring to the torture itself rather than to the legal punishment that torture could enable (in theory), such as through the recovery of evidence. In fact, officers at times specify that torture is *not* a form of punishment, noting that only the courts have this power. This suggests that police do not believe that "punishment" will succeed as a legitimate argument for torture in spite of other actors' insistence that this is a common motivation.

But police *are* willing to admit to and defend significant departures from legal procedure. Hence it is not the legality of the act that determines whether police believe they can argue for its legitimacy, but rather the reasons for the act. They know that torture is not legal, but defend it as legitimate when it aids the legal process, such as by equipping the prosecution with better evidence. Less frequently, they defend torture that disregards the legal process, such as Y's argument that the legal way is "no better" than torture. But they do not explicitly defend torture that coopts the legal process by embodying a form of punishment in itself. In short, police are not willing to argue openly that they can and should usurp a judge's power, while they are willing to argue openly that they can and should usurp a suspect's rights. This suggests that the hierarchy of the criminal justice system, in which judges are respected, carries more normative weight than the idea of equal and inalienable rights, even as they disregard the courts as too inefficient to produce justice.

Insufficient Resources

Law enforcement officers also draw from the poor material conditions in which they work to explain the torture of "regular" people. They argue that many police stations are not equipped to solve cases without torture. Police complain that they are understaffed, underresourced, and undertrained. They note that they lack tools to conduct scientific investigations. Officers also argue that these limitations put them at a further disadvantage compared to criminals. They assert that criminals are not only unburdened by any procedural norms governing their behavior, but also may have more resources than police. These poor conditions are verified by the reports of nongovernmental organizations.[6] For example, one police reform expert with the Commonwealth Human Rights Initiative noted that police sometimes do not have vehicles to travel to a crime scene, or enough petrol for the vehicles they do have. Unlike the human rights activists who note the same circumstances, however, police interpret these conditions as further justifying extralegal activities such as torture.

Explaining torture by referencing poor material conditions allows officers to express theoretical support for human rights while still endorsing extralegal behavior. This violence is construed as an unfortunate but necessary adaptation to the lack of better methods, contingent upon the straightforward addition of resources and skills. For example, one high-ranking officer stated:

> The system should be developed with respect to human rights. On the basis of technology. Technology can be a substitute for the third degree if police are equipped properly. Today, to get a lie detector test we have to go to the lab. Why can't there be a lie detector in a police station? DNA matching, finger-printing, narco-analysis[7] test should be in police stations. With competent officers. We have no technological support. We are left with nothing if we catch someone and we know he is lying.

It is likely true that some police torture would be eliminated with the addition of resources and skills, because those officers who desire to use other methods would have other options. Human rights and police reform organizations often point to lacunas in training and resources for police as a key reason for torture and other illegal behavior. Similarly, some scholars assert that torture has decreased in modern democracies due in part to the development of alternative means of collecting evidence.[8] However, other scholars emphasize the persistence of torture in modern democracies, casting doubt on technical developments as prime factors in torture.[9] Although analysis of a causal relationship between material conditions and incidence of torture is beyond the scope of this research, it is clear that poor material conditions, like political interference and flaws in the judicial system, help police to defend the use of torture while still endorsing human rights "in theory."

Officers sometimes argue that material conditions create the need for torture, while acknowledging that this is not a sufficient explanation. They typically express this view of torture as a stop-gap measure until conditions improve, but later note that there are certain criminals with whom nothing short of torture will work. For instance, a high-ranking paramilitary officer noted that sometimes, material conditions are not enough to explain the use of torture, even as he himself references material conditions to explain its prevalence. After he reads the NGO report describing the police torture of Ajay, he said:

> Normally, a police officer will do this thing [use force in an investigation] because I am of the opinion that both of these stations are rural. Rural police stations are not equipped with good police officers or good tools. For the purpose

> of investigation, you don't have any scientific measures. We have to depend on individual talent. How much a person is capable to interrogate, how intelligent he is, how much effort he puts in, individual interest, how much an officer is effective. The level of intelligence input he has—connections, public relations—these are the criteria the Indian police are judged by in the majority of police stations. There are few police stations or organizations that are equipped with scientific instruments. And even if some have scientific instruments, they prefer to rely on human methods only, do things the old-fashioned way.

He closed the statement with the observation that officers may "prefer" to rely on methods understood as "old-fashioned" as opposed, presumably, to "modern" methods that rely on scientific tools. This is in spite of his initial reaction, in which he explained torture as the result of poor resources. Material resources may be an important way that officers understand the justification for torture, therefore, but are likely only one piece of the multiple factors that contribute to it.

Legal Protections

Human rights activists agree with police that pervasive political corruption, judicial inefficiency, and lack of resources obstruct justice, though they have drastically different views from police on how law enforcement should respond to these problems.[10] Police, however, often view protections for the accused as being in the same category as these other problems: all represent barriers to justice and bias the system in favor of criminals, in their eyes. Without pausing, officers will include Indian evidence laws and other rules in a list of barriers to justice. In fact, these protections often comprise the main thrust of their argument for the torture of "regular" as opposed to "exceptional" criminals. Police argue that as a result of the law making confessions to a police officer inadmissible in court, there is heightened pressure to produce convincing evidence in order for courts to convict. To acquire evidence that withstands the restrictions that protect the accused, officers argue that they must use torture.

The irony that they "must" torture in order to work with laws designed to prevent torture is not lost on them. They believe that were they to refrain from torture, however, they would not be able to maintain law and order. They would also likely be failing in the eyes of the public, their supervisors, and the administration, who wish to see people convicted for crimes.

For example, L cited legal protections as part of the same explanation in which he listed political interference and judicial inefficiency as reasons that the police "must rely" on extrajudicial violence. He acknowledged that police should abide by the law and maintain positive relationships with the public. However, he explained that police must sometimes violate this trust in order to protect the "general interest." Moreover, he explained this general interest as needing protection due to the very laws that are meant to protect the public from abusive state power:

> A professional officer should have no personal interest. He should be transparent. He should win the good will of the people. People should trust him. That is why we are police. But sometimes we have to compromise. Sometimes we cannot take care of the value of some individual for the sake of the greater interest, the general interest. It is very difficult. We cannot always take care of human rights. . . . If you tell me you killed a person and hid the [weapon] in a bus, that is not enough to convict you. *[He points to the section of the Indian Criminal Procedure Code stating that confessions made to a police officer are not admissible in court.]* So what to do? You are confessing, and still I am helpless. We have to [prove] beyond a reasonable doubt, or he will go free after the trial. These are the legal obligations. What will happen to the police officer and the family of the deceased if the murderer escapes trial? In a court of law, you are reminded constantly that any statement you make can incriminate you. You are constantly warned that you are not supposed to make a statement like that, or you will be sent to jail. The accused is given so many safeguards. According to the Indian Evidence Act, no confession made to a police officer shall be used against the accused. The Indian judicial system has no trust in the police. Because we have the power to manipulate . . . Even if you take me to the place and show me the weapon, I need to prove that the process is transparent and take an independent witness.

The officer accepts the legitimacy of human rights arguments and the existence of flaws in police conduct. But he still argues that extralegal force is needed because he believes the system overcompensates for these problems by handicapping the police.

Officers often spoke about the courts' high standards for evidence as the primary reason for torture. For example, a mid-ranking police officer from Haryana stated:

> Police use torture when in a case they have to recover essential information, and they feel he won't do it easily [*sic*]. For example, in any murder case the police

> have many proofs [*sic*]. But the recovery of arms is important, because without the recovery of arms, the person won't be punished by the court, and he will be free.

Similarly, when I asked a high-ranking police officer to explain the biggest challenges he faces in his work, he immediately replied:

> The biggest challenge is human rights. This is the biggest obstacle. Our rules and regulations. The person goes free before our eyes. . . . As a policeman, suppose we get hold of a criminal. Because of human rights, we can just keep him up to a certain limit. Even if we keep him within proportion, because of media hype he goes free. . . . Because none of the persons will give evidence against him.

This officer sees "human rights" and rules governing police conduct as preventing police from properly upholding justice.

Government officials in leadership roles with the Bureau of Police Research and Development and the National Human Rights Commission share this belief. Many of these officials are committed to human rights, generally speaking, and to the right to a fair trial in abstraction. But they sympathize with the view that the legal system affords too many protections to the accused, leaving police with few options.

In essence, when explaining the flaws in the criminal justice system, officers tend to collapse problems stemming from political corruption and judicial inefficiency with legal protections for the accused. In the eyes of officers, these factors combine to create a criminal justice system that subverts justice by protecting criminals. They contend that the innocent and police themselves are powerless within this system and that they must act outside the system to do their job. This leads to the argument that due to the context in which they work, they must violate the rights of suspects in order to uphold justice—even suspects who would not require or deserve torture in a perfect system. In this understanding, justice (not to mention police success in the eyes of the public and the administration) depends upon the law's violation.

This is not to suggest that providing fewer legal protections to the accused would promote police compliance with human rights. Rather, this reveals that the ways in which actors interpret material and structural factors can inform their judgments on what is appropriate and right, complicating efforts to spread new norms.

Idealism and Materialism in Judgments on Violence

These officers' statements add empirical depth to a key claim of social constructivist scholars: that it is not only the facts of the social and material world, but also how actors interpret these facts that matter for the decisions they make about what is good and what is in their interest. It is well understood by human rights activists in India that politicians constrain the police by interfering to help friends and punish enemies. Police officers' comments reveal that how they interpret this constraint informs what they do with the agency they have. Similarly, the backlog of court cases and a lack of resources are well understood as obstacles to justice. Less attention has been given to how officers' interpretations of how to cope with these problems inform their choices, or at least their justifications. Moreover, laws governing confessions and evidence are intended to enhance procedural justice, but police officers' interpretations of them have unintended consequences.

As such, police officers' statements reflect a tightly bound interaction of ideational and material factors. They show how the effort to spread a particular moral vision and the norms that accompany it depend in part on the structures in which actors are embedded, and on their judgments about the right way to respond to this environment. Police hold philosophical beliefs about human nature, the nature of society, and the nature of justice, in which the use of torture is understood as right in certain circumstances and in regard to certain types of people. These beliefs inform how they judge the right way to respond to the pressures, constraints, and incentives of their circumstances.

The introduction of material factors into officers' explanations raises the question of whether the external situation is "real" and officers' beliefs merely epiphenomenal, an ex post facto rationalization. Perhaps the "reality" is that police are pressured and incentivized to use torture by structural and political problems in the justice system. Perhaps their beliefs simply rationalize their behavior, a superficial gloss on actions they would take regardless of what they believe. Although articulated most explicitly in Marxist theory that describes ideational factors as a "superstructure" that obscures the reality of power and economic relations, this perspective is broadly shared among researchers on violence. As discussed previously, much research on torture posits beliefs as rationalizations for actions that the perpetrator on some level knows is wrong.[11]

Officers' comments, as well as previous research, however, suggest that although beliefs are formed partly in response to environments, beliefs also have the capacity to shape an environment by making certain actions palatable. For example, ethnographic fieldwork in Thailand reveals the ways in which impoverished families explain the prostitution of their children, as well as the way the children understand their prostitution.[12] Ideals of filial piety matter within these communities; thus children understand themselves as fulfilling this duty by prostituting themselves. The anthropologist argues that although these are genuinely held ideals, the true "cause" of their prostitution is poverty. Solve that, and filial piety will not motivate prostitution. But at the same time, without a belief in the ethics of children's duty to their parents, it is possible that children and parents alike might have a harder time living with prostitution and hence engaging in it.

Likewise, one could conjecture that police elsewhere who hold similar ideals of justice as the police interviewed for this book, but who work in a system in which they are not expected to use torture, are in fact punished for using it, and have resources and training that enable different means of investigation, would be less likely to use torture. This points to the importance of the external circumstances. But it is also likely that beliefs matter as well: police who feel pressured to use torture, yet believe that all people are equal in possessing an inalienable dignity, may resist the temptation to use it even in circumstances that encourage it. The combination of external pressure, self-interest, and belief is likely what makes torture so common in some contexts. In other words, it is the perfect storm of material and ideational factors that produce the pervasiveness of torture.

Drawing on and extending Charles Taylor's argument that we form our beliefs in dialogue with others,[13] what these interviews suggest is that it is not only other people who function as interlocuters, but also the external environment. Police are "in conversation" with their environment when they form their ideals. Political corruption and judicial inefficiency figure into their explanations for what justice entails as much as their beliefs about human nature do. Officers' interpretations of their working environment help form their ideals and shape how they believe their ideals should be applied.

Torture Expands Further: Hurting the Innocent

OP is a mid-ranking officer working in one of a small number of "model police stations" being piloted in his district. This initiative is meant to facilitate better relations with the community through educational programs that bring officers into schools, among other measures. Most evident at my visit to the station was a chalk sign informing the public of the name of the complaint officer on duty and a list of free services offered to the public. Photographs on the wall showed how the station had been renovated, from a disorderly receiving room to one with chairs neatly arranged for people to sit in while they speak with the police.

OP wishes to do "what his soul says is right." He strives to live his vision of the professional police officer who uses scientific methods to solve crimes. In his estimation, his best moments on the job are those when he has been able to live up to this ideal. There was the time when he took fingerprints after a crime occurred in a bank. Even though his senior officers told him it was "just a formality," he stressed proudly, he "took it seriously and did a good job and satisfied the public." There was another case in which he was able to trace the calls made by drug smugglers, and through careful investigation, "arrested them in a very planned way." He criticizes colleagues who care little for forensic science, including supervisors who have told him that his efforts are a waste of time.

OP was outspoken from the beginning of our interview about the ways in which political pressure and corruption impede his ability to uphold justice. In response to my first question in our first interview regarding the challenges he faces in his work, he replied:

> We are stopped from doing what we really want to do by some selfish people. There are many difficulties police officers have to face. They want to do good work, but then they are pressurized [*sic*] by their senior officers, as the seniors are also pressurized [*sic*] by political leaders. . . . There is political interference in the police department. Senior officers interfere in the investigation process for their own selfish reasons.

Like Y, OP seems to be just the kind of officer for whom the human rights movement hopes, and a fitting employee of a "model police station": he is committed to professional policing and abhors corruption.

Then I asked him, "What are the things that allow police to do what they think is right, and what are the things that prevent police from doing what they think is right?" As with Y, he replied without hesitation, "We are pressurized [*sic*] because of human rights," and added, "We are hardly able to interrogate because of human rights." Outside interference, whether from human rights activists or corrupt politicians, is the kind of breakdown of ideals that OP sees as unjustified.

His ideals, however, also break down in ways he views as justifiable, as is made clear in the following exchange. He first differentiated between types of people who do and do not deserve torture. He then admitted that he also uses torture with people who fall outside this restricted category. Initially, he provided examples of those who seem to exist in a grey area between hardcore and regular criminals, such as criminals who deal in arms. However, by the time he provided a specific example, it was of torturing an impoverished man—a rickshaw puller—who had been accused of theft. Hence, although he began with a defense of torture for hardened criminals, he eventually defended torture of poor people who have been accused of stealing small amounts: a group with whom police express sympathy and yet are accused of torturing most often. Moreover, his reason for torture moved from the exceptionality of hardened criminals to the need to torture anyone who withholds information. Indeed, by the end of the exchange, he has justified not only the torture of petty criminals, but even those whom he acknowledges may be innocent. He does so even after initially placing such violence outside the boundaries of what he could ever do. I quote the dialogue at length to show how he transitions from idealized categories of exceptional guilt to the endorsement of violence for a far broader population:

> OP: It is necessary to physically torture the hardcore criminals, but human rights says not to do it. The law also protects criminals. The law does not allow physical torture. This makes our job very difficult. We are not able to make the criminal speak and confess his crime. . . . It has been told in human rights that we cannot undermine the self-respect of anyone, even if that person is a criminal. Man is not an animal. We cannot harm anybody. . . . I agree with it that people are born in an independent manner and have their self-respect, but those who are hardcore criminals, those who have murdered people, they should not get human rights protection.
>
> RW: Why?
>
> OP: The hardcore criminals themselves violate the human rights of other people. . . .
>
> RW: How about people like thieves and robbers?
>
> OP: They are not hardcore criminals. There can be many reasons for stealing. Reasons like poverty, if the mother is not well, needing money for studying. But the large-scale robbers with murder, they are hardcore. Those who are not hardcore criminals, they have our sympathy.

RW: Do you ever have to use torture on people who are not hardcore criminals?

OP: We have to do it many times, even though they are not hardcore criminals.

RW: Why?

OP: Many times, cases of stealing, theft, fighting, or arms—in such cases we have to go in detail and find the origin point. If someone is carrying illegal arms, we have to ask them who manufactured them and where they were purchased.

RW: Do you ever have to torture people you have sympathy with?

OP: It happens many times. We have to do it.

RW: How do you handle that?

OP: After something like this, we are sympathetic to them. It is possible he has some problems, so we have to pressurize [*sic*] our own minds to stop something bad from happening. So you have to think before you do anything.

RW: Could you give me an example of a time you have been in a situation like that?

OP: This happened in [location name]. There was a case of theft. We arrested a suspect. He was a rickshaw puller. He had stolen a box that had 2,500 rupees and gold in it. The rickshaw puller's father had died, and he took drugs. When we were physically torturing him, we had to control ourselves. It was difficult for us also, because he was not confessing his crime. His father had died. And he was taking drugs, but also he was not confessing his crime.

RW: How do you decide whether or not to torture someone?

OP: It depends on the criminal. If he accepts, then there is no reason for torture. But if he amends something he said or does not speak or does not tell the truth, then he must be tortured. . . .

RW: How do you know whether [the accused] really [committed the crime] or whether they [might] confess just because they want the torture to stop?

OP: It happens many times when we arrest a suspect, that during the extrajudicial confession, the suspect involves people who are not involved in the crime. And then those people also get arrested. . . .

RW: Does it ever happen that you torture someone because you think they are guilty, but they turn out to be innocent?

OP: I have not done anything like this. I have followed a free and fair path.

RW: Do police ever make mistakes and torture someone who is innocent?

OP: Yes, it happens. Police do make mistakes. Innocent people are sometimes beaten.

RW: Why does that happen?

OP: Many times police look in every direction. Many people come under suspicion. That is why innocent people are also questioned. Police are not God. Police are also not sure. So in such situations, we have to question the innocent.

This reveals the way officers use restrictive categories to create a normative space in which they can defend torture as an acceptable practice by limiting it to certain types of people. But they then extend these justifications to explain the torture of people who fall outside these categories. When OP transitions from defending torture for hardcore to regular criminals, he moves from an unqualified defense that is based on his ideal categories of justice to a defense that is instrumental and situational and can include anyone who obstructs police goals.

But OP does not see himself as violating his principles. When I asked him if he has ever tortured someone because he thought they were guilty, but they turned out to be innocent, he replied, "I have not done anything like this. I have followed a free and fair path." It is only "police," generally speaking who he admits torture innocent people by mistake: an error that he seems to see as understandable, if not something with which he is willing to associate himself. Moreover, it is only by mistake and not for nefarious purposes that he is willing to concede that police torture innocents. Revealingly, he is willing to admit to torture, but not to torturing the wrong people for the wrong reasons.

Doing a Good Job: Professional Identity and the Breakdown of Ideals

This expansion of whom officers justify torturing is connected, too, to their understanding of the role of police. Officers believe that it is their primary duty to "find out the truth" or, less idealistically, to "extract a confession" or strong evidence that will allow for conviction. This is, of course, connected to their understanding of justice as premised on the punishment of criminals; upholding the law, protecting rights, responding to the community, and other policing functions give way to this task. Police often make comments like that of the high-ranking paramilitary officer, who stated, "The main task of the police is to find out the truth and submit the truth to court," or that of another paramilitary officer, who asserted, "It is the duty of the police officer to verify the truth behind the information, to find out whether it is genuine or concocted." He continued to detail the priority of the police officer:

> Information is the foundation of a police investigation. The first information we receive is the foundation of the investigation. So the foundation of the investigation should be verified in order to make a good case. Then only will the police officer achieve his aim.

The necessity that police conduct a successful investigation at all costs is often invoked to justify torture, and was pervasive across nearly all interviews. For example, I asked a mid-ranking military officer what he thinks of the idea that "all people have a right to be free from torture." He replied, "Yes, it is a legal right. But it is also a duty of the police to extract confessions." Over and over, officers understand this duty as trumping the duty to uphold suspects' right to be free from torture. For example, when I gave a mid-ranking police officer from Uttar Pradesh the NGO report in which the police allegedly tortured a man who went to the police station to report the disappearance of his wife, the officer defended the torture and illegal detention of the man by arguing:

> If the lady has disappeared, they have to prove it. How will we get the proof? The human rights commission has claimed illegal detention. The point of view is that the police have not done their job properly. They have to get permission from the court. The work done by the police is not perfect. But in the last I would say the point is that the lady has [not been] found.

It is not that this officer believes it is inherently right to torture the man. After all, he is not a hardcore criminal. Rather, he believes that the officers' duty to get information trumps their duty to protect those from torture who do not deserve it. This is elaborated in the following, when I asked this officer why the police chose to torture Ajay in this case. He objects, "Police had not decided to torture Ajay. They wanted to recover the woman—that's why." When I asked whether torture was necessary, he said that it was not. When I then asked why the police tortured if it was not necessary, he replied:

> Shortcuts. The third degree gets results immediately. If we do our jobs perfectly, we have to go to court and get permission. The police have not done their job perfectly. But [this is] a very small part. We can't shelter Mr. Ajay. We have to find the lady. The human rights commission should also [try to] see where the lady has gone. Everything will be clear when the lady has been found.

In this explanation, the officer recognizes that the torture and detention of Ajay are illegal and unnecessary. But because the officers were doing their primary duty of trying to recover information (and hence acting for the public good), the treatment of Ajay is still legitimate.

At times, officers recognize and wrestle with the contradiction between their ideal categories that restrict torture to certain types of exceptional people and what they see as the demands of police work. This can be seen in the dialogue with OP. He asserted that those who are not hardcore, such as small-scale thieves, "have our sympathy" and may have stolen for understandable reasons reasons, such as to care for a sick mother or to afford an education. When I asked him whether he ever needs to torture such regular people, he conceded, "We have to do it many times, even though they are not hardcore criminals." He explained this not by reference to what these people deserve, as with hardcore criminals, but by the necessity of police work: finding the "origin point" of a crime or recovering arms.

Similarly, a high-ranking paramilitary officer responded to the NGO report by pointing out that the incident was a "personal" matter, rather than a case in which a hardened criminal or terrorist was threatening the general public. He stated that this suggests to him that the officers used torture for what he considers illegitimate reasons, such as political interference or bribery. In this way, he initially maintained the ideal categories in which it is only legitimate to torture exceptional people, and hence torture of unexceptional people "must" have been done for illegitimate reasons, such as to extract a bribe. As the interview continued, however, he conceded that the officers were doing what was necessary to solve the case and that because of this, the torture should be excused. This suggests that the torture of those who are not "hardened" criminals, which according to human rights organizations represents a large percentage of those tortured by police, occupies a grey area that police are not ready to defend as inherently right, yet believe is necessary in order to fulfill their role as police officers.

Human rights advocates sometimes try to dissuade police from torturing by arguing that their primary job is to uphold the law and that whether a criminal is ultimately punished is outside the scope of police work. Police, however, see a successful investigation and the punishment of criminals as primary, not secondary, to their duties. Hence, when human rights advocates tell police not to concern themselves with the result of an investigation, to police this may sound like advice to no longer care about doing or keeping their jobs.

Reconstituting the Exceptional

This understanding of the main goal of police work also informs how the category of "hardcore" criminal is constituted. The formation of this category is another way in which officers expand the types of people whom they justify torturing. In theory, the category of "hardcore" criminal is stable. It refers to a particular type of person whom it is inherently right to torture because of who they are and what they have done. However, how can police recognize a hardened criminal? Because most police torture precedes conviction, this must be known prior to official determination of guilt. And because one rationale for torturing hardcore criminals is that their hardened nature means that nothing short of torture will cause them to speak, police sometimes label people as hardcore when they do not do and say as police wish.

In the following passage, a low-ranking paramilitary police officer uses the term *hardcore* to refer to anyone who does not reveal what the officer wishes him to reveal. This quote was used previously to demonstrate the way officers justify torture by restricting it to certain types of people. It also serves as a strong example of how this conception of justice breaks down. The officer argued:

> If someone tells everything, then no officer is happy to use torture. But the hardcore-minded persons—they are called hardcore-minded—they break in a difficult way, so police use methods to find results. . . . Torture is not a way of giving punishment. It is a method of investigation. Only in situations where the person doesn't admit his offense. And the police think he is really guilty. And in making this inquiry, if he finds he is innocent, then it is within his discretion to release him.

The officer draws from the idea that hardcore criminals are different from regular people as a way to justify torture. His focus, however, is on the importance of obtaining information. The category of hardcore criminal is in this way construed in reverse: anyone who does not say what the police want him to say is "taking longer to break," and therefore must be hardcore. This expands the group of people to whom this label can apply significantly.

Making and Breaking Ethical Categories: The Imaginary and Its Failures

Officers' moral imaginary does not break down randomly, it makes possible certain kinds of breakdowns. By positing violence as sometimes right, these background beliefs make it possible for officers to see the much wider use of torture as an imperfect application of their ideals rather than as an outright violation of them. So although in theory, officers justify torture by restricting it to exceptional categories of people who "deserve" it, in practice, these categories expand and begin to disintegrate.

As evidenced in the previous chapters, police do not defend everything they do. Although officers justify violence against a wider array of people than they believe should ideally occur, they do not justify torture for the sake of personal gain. But officers know that their conceptions of justice break down in practice. Neither the views they profess nor the background beliefs such views imply match their actions. Yet these beliefs still play an important role in how they understand their actions. Law enforcers justify torture by restricting it to certain categories of people. Torture is right, they indicate, when it is used on the right people. This creates a premise in which torture is, in some circumstances, the right thing to do. When officers end up torturing people outside of this restricted category, they are then able to see this as less than ideal but permissible.

This is likely bolstered by the support for violence they perceive from other actors in the criminal justice system, such as judges and supervisors. Their perception of others' expectations of them and their own understanding of police work involve pervasive violence. This is understood as inevitable, which perhaps gives them further reason to view the use of torture on "*un*exceptional" suspects as a forgivable derivation from an ideal form of justice rather than as a clear failure of it.

Imaginaries then allow for some breakdowns more easily than others. In the moral imaginary in which people deserve different treatment, the category to which a person belongs can become loose. What remains is officers' belief that their aim should be to uphold this order of justice. Hence willfully harming people who are clearly innocent is not an acceptable breakdown, nor is acting for personal benefit. Officers deny responsibility for such actions, blaming the persecution of innocents on external pressure and condemning corruption. Attempting to enforce "justice" on people who can be construed as fitting loosely into the right category is acceptable, however imperfect they acknowledge this must be.

Implications for the Spread of Human Rights

The relevant point in the preceding pages is not whether officers live up to their own version of justice. What matters is that when human rights activists and educators try to convince police not to torture innocent people or demand bribes, the police readily agree. Police see these acts as wrong, too. But they place most of the violence in which they engage in another category. Troublingly, police are able to defend acts that contain some motivations they condemn, so long as they involve at least one justifiable motivation. If a police officer accepts a bribe to torture someone but also believes that the person is guilty, then they may see this as imperfect, but not reprehensible.

Moreover, officers' ability to reconcile their beliefs and behavior is not limited to the kind of violence they justify. They are also able to reconcile themselves to actions they see as wrong, such as failure to protect the poor. At times, they see themselves as powerless to do anything else, a perception that may be accurate. At other times, though, they interpret what they can do as in keeping with what they should do.

In addition, the foregoing comments suggest that officers are not merely projecting an idealized image of themselves in interviews. The stories they tell reveal the gap between what they believe they should do and what they do, which officers acknowledge. They speak in ideal terms of only torturing powerful criminals and protecting the poor. But their stories reflect frequent actions against the poor. Were they only trying to impress, they would likely omit these stories, or at least tell them only as episodes in which they had no choice. The interviews also suggest that police wish to reconcile their actions with their beliefs and that they are able to do so. This capacity may support their ability to engage in violence that violates their ideals, making it harder for human rights educators and activists to connect their messages with these ideals.

Of course, the differences in the moral orders of the human rights movement and of the police also pose an obstacle to activists' aims. Both human rights activists and police condemn torture that is motivated by the pressure of politicians and supervisors or by monetary gain. But the reasons they condemn it are radically different. Police believe that the wrong people are tortured in these instances, not that torture is wrong. Hence even officers' admission that they cannot uphold their conceptions of justice reveals the differences between their beliefs and the human rights ethos. And as this suggests, police are not alone in this view. The general public is often outraged at police violence. But media reports and interviews with reform experts suggest that their outrage often stems from a belief that the police use violence against the wrong people, not that they use it. The public complaint is frequently that the police abuse innocents and fail to act severely enough with criminals.[14]

This presents a challenge for human rights activists and educators. Advocating for the rights of "imperfect" victims is challenging in any setting.[15] Scholars have written about the difficulties activists face in convincing the American public that even those convicted of crimes should retain rights.[16] Torture victims who are later found to have been wrongly accused make easier rallying points than criminals whom the public fear. As such, activists often point to the torture of innocent people to garner public support and decry the corruption that often leads to such torture.

As activists know, focusing on innocent victims does not convey the importance of rights that are universal and unconditional. Activism always involves a trade-off between connecting to previous beliefs and changing beliefs, though, and this is no exception.[17] But officers' distinctions between legitimate and illegitimate forms of torture may present a further obstacle to their acceptance of rights principles and norms. Police agree that torture for corrupt reasons is wrong, and they also agree that innocent people should not be tortured. But they tend to believe that the people *they* are torturing are guilty. At most, they will concede that innocent people may on occasion be tortured by accident, but that such collateral damage is necessary in order to identify the correct suspect. So when activists condemn the torture of innocent people, police may agree, believing that such criticism in general does not apply to them. And trumping all of these competing messages about justice, officers believe that violence is a necessary part of investigation and is expected of them. In their view, because the main duty of police is to extract information, anything that accomplishes that end is justified, even if the suspect does not inherently deserve or require such violence.

Ideas and Environments

Much research on human rights activism focuses on how activists change the minds of government officials and the public, such as the many investigations of how activists "frame" norms.[18] This focus makes sense given social constructivists' contention that it is not simply material reality, but interpretations of it that matter for judgments. But the foregoing demonstrates how interpretations arise in response to material conditions, a point constructivists also make, but that is not as often the focus of such research. In this case, human rights workers might be successful in changing officers' perceptions of how they should respond to political interference, judicial inefficiency, and insufficient resources. But police may more readily accept human rights norms if activists address the structural problems that give rise to such perceptions.

Substantial scholarship has examined how civilians' perception of the legitimacy of the law influences their willingness to follow it.[19] Studies have also shown that members of organizations are more likely to follow rules when they believe the procedures of enforcement are legitimate and when the rules correspond with their moral values.[20] Some research has showed the relevance of police and military officers' judgments on the legitimacy of law for their adherence to it: a study by Tyler and colleagues revealed the importance of American soldiers' and police officers' perception perception that rules and policies are legitimate and moral for their willingness to defer to them.[21] Clearly, the perception of the law's legitimacy is important for whether people feel compelled to follow it, even including the law's enforcers, and there are many components of an environment that can undermine this legitimacy.

Human rights reformers who see bad attitudes or insufficient knowledge and resources as the only relevant obstacles to reform neglect both the complexities of this context and officers' perceived need to cope with it.[22] Indeed, researchers have revealed that police officers do not make judgments in isolation, nor do they do so as part of an undifferentiated state. They frequently negotiate the perils of insecure and contradictory circumstances, and this negotiation greatly informs their judgments about violence.[23]

A unique comparative study of police in the United Kingdom, Germany, Australia, Venezuela, and Brazil indicates the importance of both officers' perceptions and their circumstances. Although the judgments of police in all countries were remarkably consistent, those in Venezuela and Brazil were more likely to anticipate using deadly force. The authors attribute this to the reality of insecure conditions in those countries, as well as to officers' assumptions about danger.[24] Such qualitative studies do much to explain why there is a relationship between context and action; the environment informs not just what police can do, but also their beliefs about what is desirable, necessary, and right.

This book builds on such scholarship by revealing how material reality inspires a particular imaginary, as officers respond to a context that they perceive as pervasively corrupt and inefficient. Law enforcers see this corruption and other flaws in the legal system as reasons to disregard the law. Like the perception of threat in Brazil and Venezuela, this disregard for the law is generalized, as it extends beyond their response to specific instances of corruption and other problems and characterizes officers' view of the legal system overall.

Moreover, this points to the significance of state actors' perceptions of other sectors within the system in which they work. Political interference and judicial inefficiency undermine officers' faith in the legal system and contribute to their view that only by acting outside it can justice be upheld. Moreover, these same flaws in the political and judicial systems decrease the likelihood that police will be held accountable when they act on these views.

This bolsters constructivists' claims about the important role of subjective interpretation,[25] but also supports the conclusions of research that shows the limits of advocacy in contexts lacking institutional and political support for human rights standards.[26] Like beliefs, structural problems do not "cause" police to use torture. But these problems may inspire and legitimize violence among police who hold moral beliefs in support of violence and whose interests are also on the side of using it. Spreading a moral order depends not only on changing beliefs, then, but also on addressing the relationship of beliefs to the structures that inspire them.

Police know, however, that their interpretations of how to respond to problems in the justice system are not the only ones possible, and in fact that their "solutions" are sharply criticized. All police are exposed to human rights messages to some degree through their initial training, NHRC programs, and media, as well as NGO campaigns. But the choice of the officers to enroll in a human rights course means that they, in particular, must respond not only to the demands of judges and the public, but also to the claims of human rights activists and educators. In the next chapter, I address how they do so.

Part 2

Human Rights

Chapter 4

Police Respond to Human Rights Education

How can you say that someone who is not observing the human rights of others has human rights?

—*Indian Police Service officer, Madhya Pradesh*

R IS A POLICE OFFICER STATIONED IN KASHMIR, a contested region of India that borders Pakistan. He works in a context of armed insurgency, State of Emergency laws, and according to international and national civil society groups, frequent violations of human rights by the Indian security forces. Although a low-ranking officer, his name suggests that he is of a high caste. He is also well educated, which is unusual for an officer of his rank. He once considered pursuing a career as a lawyer on the High Court. Lately, he has gained recognition as an orator and writer, delivering lectures and drafting correspondence on behalf of his supervisor. R has also become a human rights educator, assigned to lecture other police. He gives them lessons on the rights of children and women, for example, and on how to conduct investigations without violating suspects' rights. Recently, he won an award for human rights protection.

I spoke to R six times during my year in India, because after our first interview, he liked to call me to discuss human rights over the phone. At times he would slip into his role as a lecturer, explaining to me the history of the ICRC or the Geneva Conventions. But often he wanted something more; he wanted to get to the bottom of this concept called "human rights" and its relationship to justice. One evening he called to tell me a story. He had been at a party with other police officers, where, he said, they were "talking about human rights." When I pressed him for details, he explained that they had been discussing a famous case. Years ago, when R was a child, the son of a powerful politician was arrested for murder. The politician bribed the police, who destroyed the evidence, and his son was freed. "But you know," R tells me, "there is a court of God, of the Almighty. You can influence man, but not the Almighty."

Years later, the politician's son murdered again. This time, he killed the son of another politician. Again the killer's father tried to bribe the police to let him go. Initially, he was successful. But the people of the town gathered and protested. "The matter came before the media," R explained, so "the case was taken away from the corrupt police officers and given to honest police officers."

As we seemed to be nearing the climax of the story, justice appeared to be imminent. But there was a twist, and R wanted to know what I thought of it. In spite of the suspect's powerful political connections, the "honest police officers" tortured him. "He was abused, he was beaten, and dirty language was used by the honest police officers," R stated. "So the question is," he continued, "if the police are using this kind of method, is this a violation of human rights?"

Here we see a particular moral and social imaginary—and the reality that surrounds it—confront the universal schema of human rights. R seems to pose a question: if "honest" police refuse the bribes of politicians and use violence against the people who "deserve" it, how can an international language of justice not side with these brave officers?

R knows the answer. He knows that no matter the intent of these officers, torture is still a violation of human rights. But informed by a moral and social imaginary in which justice depends upon differentiation rather than equality, and a context in which the struggle is understood as against the leniency inspired by corruption, this does not feel right to him.

Negotiating the Moral Order

This chapter explores how officers respond to the messages they receive from human rights educators and activists, including the lessons in their master's degree course as well as National Human Rights Commission activities and media campaigns launched by NGOs. What happens when concepts that spring from one understanding of moral order are interpreted and used by people whose background understanding of what is true and good is very different?

The conflict between the moral imaginary of the police and that of the human rights movement does not mean that officers reject human rights. But nor do they endorse rights superficially while continuing to violate them, as might be expected. Instead, they actively engage rights concepts and negotiate their meaning, using the language and logic of rights to contest the very principles on which rights are premised.

This reveals the plasticity of moral vocabularies. Although language remains the same, concepts change depending on the background understanding and goals of the speaker. Here, "human rights" take on new meanings not as part of an unconscious process of diffusion, but when people with conflicting beliefs and interests actively reinterpret them.

These officers have reasons to align themselves with the human rights framework that scholars would predict. Social constructivists could point to the desire of many of the officers to obtain postings with the United Nations and infer that they enrolled in the human rights course to acquire the image and credentials associated with a modern, liberal identity. A realist perspective might emphasize the more immediate, tangible rewards, such as promotions that may be forthcoming with a postgraduate degree. Critical postcolonial scholars might direct our attention to historical and structural power relations. The resulting inequality means that the ideals promulgated by Western states are privileged as markers of modernity. Human rights becomes a discourse that constitutes the modern moral actor. In the terms of Gayatri Spivak, human rights are that which "we cannot not want."[1] Although the explanations among scholars differ, simply dispensing with the discourse and concepts of rights is a difficult proposition for state agents of contemporary democracies. But they could be expected to simply pay lip service to rights, to "talk the talk" and continue to violate them.

Instead, officers engage. They maintain the discourse of rights protectors while still defending the use of torture. They provide their own interpretations of rights by articulating what they believe rights should entail. They also negotiate rights by explicitly arguing against more standard interpretations. These processes are linked, as they draw from their interpretations to explain and defend their negotiations.

Interpretation: The Social Contract

Officers often interpret rights as conditional rather than inalienable, and invoke a version of social contract theory to do so. Classical liberal theorists viewed rights as based in a contract between the state and citizens: each person upholds the laws of the state and respects the rights of others, so that she or he may be protected from the intrusions of others and of the state itself. In this view, it is rational to restrict one's own natural freedom if the state ensures that in exchange, other citizens follow the same code.[2]

The course in which officers are enrolled discusses classical liberal philosophers such as John Locke and explains social contract theory. It is not clear whether officers are consciously drawing on this framework or whether their logic simply reflects it. But officers echo this conception of society when they argue that only those who abide by the rules of the state deserve its protection.

However, liberal theorists would object to officers' use of their theory. For early liberal thinkers, it is the state's respect of citizens' rights that lends it legitimacy.[3] Instead, more reminiscent of Thomas Hobbes, officers reverse this and view all rights as conditional upon citizens upholding their end of the social contract. To officers, people who fail to respect the law lose all rights.

If this interpretation of liberalism aligns poorly with the views of its classical theorists and contemporary adherents, it matches officers' conception of justice well. A view of rights as conditional upon the respect of others' rights is consistent with their belief that what each person deserves is dependent on his or her actions. Rather than reject human rights in favor of their conception of justice, then, officers express their conception of justice through those aspects of the rights framework that are most consistent with it. They then use these complementary aspects of the rights framework to undermine rights principles that conflict with their views.

The words of a mid-ranking army officer serving in Kashmir exemplify this. Human rights advocates accuse the security forces in Kashmir of frequently arresting and torturing political activists. When I asked whether he is concerned about arresting innocent people or using too much force, he replied, "There are concerns about human rights values, but it is give and take," and added, "Only if you abide by the law will you have it." This officer does not explicitly reject human rights laws. Instead, he articulated his disregard for the law as a principle of the law itself.

To some extent, the contemporary human rights movement also abides by this maxim. Human rights workers as well as domestic legal institutions agree that convicted criminals should lose some rights. Officers draw on this shared premise, but extend it in two ways. First, they suggest that those who violate mutual security should lose all, rather than only some, rights. Officers reject the human rights regime's insistence that some basic rights must be inalienable in favor of the tenet that those who violate rights must be controlled. Second, officers extend *who* should lose rights to those who have not been given a fair trial. These modifications undermine key tenets of liberalism. But officers nonetheless use rights language to legitimize themselves as representatives of a modern democratic state.

Officers also invoke social contract theory when they make a related argument. They point out that liberty is dependent on security. They argue that if they do not violate the rights of those whom they believe violate others' rights, security will be compromised. If security is compromised, the innocent will lose their liberty. They assert that liberty thus requires them to violate the rights of some people. In this way, officers reframe "human rights" and "liberty" so that they are both synonymous with "security," and defined by it. For example, a high-ranking prison officer in Haryana asserted:

> In all situations, we have tried to our last to maintain human rights. But in some situations, we use the minimum required force. Because to maintain law and order is primary. If the authority fails to maintain law and order, then there will be great violations of human rights by antisocial elements, by miscreants, by terrorists. So it is necessary to maintain law and order in the nation and in the world. To maintain law and order, sometimes the human rights of some people will be affected.

Rather than seeing universal protection as possible, he believes the rights of different people are in tension with one another. As such, he justifies violating the rights of some people with the need to protect others. Similarly, when I asked a mid-ranking military officer how he interprets the meaning of "human rights," he asserted:

> When I say human rights, from whatever I have studied—I am in my first year at [the human rights course] only . . . or from my experience, is people must get basic needs. That includes security. In J and K [Jammu and Kashmir], security of normal people is jeopardized. Who should you blame, militants or the armed forces? This is the difference of opinion. We are trying to bring peace while terrorists are the ones violating human rights.

Here the officer does more than justify violence in Kashmir through the need for security. He makes a rights-based argument for violence: security is a basic right, so the armed forces are protecting basic rights by violating the rights of those who threaten security. This draws from, but reverses, the widespread criticisms of violence in Kashmir made by the international and domestic human rights regime, which typically posits the armed forces as violating the rights of Kashmiris.

Similarly, a high-ranking prison official who justified torture earlier in the interview interprets liberty as defined by security. I read him a quote by Woodrow Wilson from the human rights textbook used by his course: "The history of liberty is the history of resistance. It is the history of the limitations of government power." When he asked for clarification on the quote, I asked him, "To be free, is it necessary to limit government? How should we balance security and freedom?" He responded by asserting:

> Freedom is our birthright. Liberty is part of freedom, and security comes after liberty. To maintain freedom and liberty, security is necessary.

This officer first endorsed the priority of liberty. He then moved to base liberty in security. This allows him to support human rights while still justifying violations of key rights. The officer goes so far as to say that liberty comes before security, but that, paradoxically, it can only exist with security.

Negotiation: Narrowing Who Deserves Rights

In addition to expressing their interpretations of human rights, officers negotiate them by explicitly arguing against more standard interpretations. They draw on the aforementioned interpretation of human rights as based in a social contract, in order to negotiate who deserves rights. Starting from the premise that the state must limit the rights of those who violate the rights of others, they argue that certain categories of people should be excluded. This includes "hardened" criminals or "terrorists," or in some cases, anyone they suspect committed any crime. One low-ranking paramilitary police officer summarized this viewpoint in an assertion that is typical among law enforcers. He asserted, "Human rights should be for the people who are really innocent."

This negotiation creates the normative and rational premise for officers to support human rights but still rely on categories of people (e.g., hardened criminals) who stand outside the community of such deserving humans. Interviews abound with examples of this negotiation, in which officers endorse the concept of human rights but narrow to which kind of person they should belong. A high-ranking Indian Police Service officer exclaimed, "How can you say someone who is not observing the human rights of others has human rights?" He then concluded that in cases in which officers are accused of violating the rights of civilians, judges should generally favor the officers. He asserted, "So in flagrant violations yes, but in borderline cases it should be interpreted in the favor of security officers. I deeply feel that way." Another police officer argued, "Human rights should come to the rescue of the innocent person. Criminals are taking advantage of human rights." Similarly, a mid-ranking police officer reasoned, "Human rights is necessary but there should be . . . criminals should not be able to take advantage. Nowadays criminals are very smart." A low-ranking paramilitary officer asserted:

> Society is constituted by the people. Everyone has a responsibility to behave as he wants to be treated. One man is respecting human rights and another is not. If someone is trying to commit a wrong, then it is not possible. Treat them as they require. Tit for Tat. If someone doesn't understand in the simple way, then they must be taught.

In this way, officers frame rights as contingent on rule following rather than as inalienable. They adapt this to their conception of justice, in which criminal suspects do not deserve the same treatment as others. And hence they can support human rights as well as endorse practices that violate them.

Officers use their reasoning to negate arguments to the contrary. For instance, I asked the previously mentioned paramilitary officer whether he thinks that "people who are suspected of wrongdoing should have any rights." He replied:

> Now that I am enrolled in [the human rights course], I know they should have the right to life. But I consider that their life is not more important than the hundreds of people they kill. . . . People who commit crime knowingly, they are out of society. He [who] loves to kill, it is not possible to put them in normal civilization.

Some officers explicitly argue that the human rights system should change to accommodate these divisions. One high-ranking Indian Police Service officer advised that human rights should apply "when the criminals are not terrorists, when the criminals are not serious." Like other officers, he then makes the case for differentially applied rights, asserting:

> Criminals have to be classified. When the criminals are very serious, then the police may resort to extrajudicial killings, violence, but this is rare. [In] 99 percent of cases, police must adhere to the law, keeping human rights and civil liberties. If we act in this way, and there is some profiling and classifying and making extrajudicial killings permissible and keeping human rights for others, then the system can work.

By narrowing who deserves human rights, this officer is able to identify himself as a supporter of human rights while still defending extrajudicial killings.

Officers often respond directly to the course material by affirming the aspects of it that align with their narrowed conception of who deserves rights. As I did with other officers in the second interview, I asked a low-ranking police officer for his opinion on quotes from the human rights textbook, this time regarding an assertion made by Thomas Jefferson that "The God who gave us life gave us liberty at the same time." He replied:

> This is right. Human beings can think. They have conscience. Wherever they go, they will respect each other and cooperate with each other. Such people have the right to live freely.

This officer seemed to entirely endorse the textbook's view until the qualifier at the end, where he added that "such people" deserve to live freely. Here, he uses the human rights course material to make a subtle argument for his conception of justice, which he had earlier articulated, in which it is right to detain and torture suspects. Only such people who abide by certain standards have rights, in his view.

Negotiation: Rights in Conflict

Officers similarly negotiate the human rights framework by drawing on the argument that rights can be granted only up until the point at which they infringe upon the rights of someone else. This is closely related to the previously discussed negotiation in which officers narrow the definition of who deserves rights. The difference is that narrowing who should be granted rights is primarily an argument about what is inherently just: officers suggest that regardless of the result, some people do not *deserve* rights. In contrast, in this negotiation related to rights in conflict, officers make a primarily instrumental argument about what they must do for the sake of a larger goal.

For example, a mid-ranking police officer asserted, "The people who do not respect the rights of civilized society need a strict hand." Similarly, a low-ranking paramilitary officer argued, "Human rights are unless and until other people get problems from your rights," and "Your rights are only until your rights harm the rights of others." Rather than focus on whether the person in question inherently deserves to have his rights taken away, in this negotiation officers focus on the pragmatic need to limit rights for the sake of a larger aim.

This argument in itself would not be objectionable to human rights activists. The difference, again, is in how officers extend which rights should be taken away and when. The aforementioned officer includes freedom from illegal arrest and torture as human rights that should be suspended when other people "get problems" from your rights. He also extends the human rights regime's understanding of what constitutes someone "getting problems from your rights." For this officer, mere suspicion that someone has or may in the future violate rights, rather than a guilty verdict in a court of law, is sufficient.

Officers often position the rights of suspects against the rights of the general population of innocent people, though sometimes more specifically against the rights of the victim. For example, one high-ranking Indian Police Service officer reflected:

> If you do not use some force, the larger section of society will suffer. *Lathi-charge* is legal. [*lathi* refers to a police stick used in crowd control]It is a minimum use of force. If that is not done, there will be more deaths by inaction. It is in the best interest of society.

This same officer explained:

> Ultimately, miscreants cannot be allowed to do the stone pelting. Otherwise, there would have been a stampede. People would have been killed. Then we can handle them a little harshly. You can say a little violation of human rights.

Similar to other negotiations, the premise of this statement alone need not necessarily suggest a deviation from the rule of law or from the human rights framework. It is true that the police have a responsibility to control crowd violence. It is again the extent of the police response and the nature of it that may contradict the rule of law and human rights. Carefully containing crowd violence is significantly different from intentionally treating protestors "harshly," and even "a little violation of human rights."

Another mid-ranking police officer argued that human rights and police duties are inherently in tension. I asked, "Is it possible to maintain everyone's human rights, and also maintain law and order, or are they ever in tension?" He responded:

> There is tension. Human rights and police duty, maintaining law and order. They look as if they [complement] each other. But then this is not the case. If on one hand, police protect the human rights of some people, they also violate the human rights of others. For example, if the public jams the road for some small demand like water or electricity supply. If the police do not interfere, then the human rights of other people are violated. For example, if someone is in critical

> condition and is unable to reach the hospital [because of the jam]. So police have to see whose right is being violated more.

Officers also often position their own rights against the rights of citizens. When I asked one military officer why human rights activists criticize the armed forces, he replied:

> Sometimes human rights violations take place. That's why NGOs criticize. There are chances for human rights violations to take place because security forces also have their rights. And sometimes when their rights are violated, then they violate others' rights.

As I discuss further in Chapter 7, officers' sense that their own rights are disregarded informs their stance that they cannot and should not respect the rights of those who threaten them.

In sum, law enforcement officers draw from aspects of liberal social contract theory and human rights that are coherent with their conceptions of justice, and then use these to reframe human rights norms in ways that justify their actions. In other words, they use the language of liberalism to justify violations of it.

Imaginaries in Translation: Responding to Rights

Why do these officers not simply endorse rights in speech and then proceed to ignore them? Why spend hours wrestling over these issues with an interviewer, using rights concepts to endorse practices they know violate rights? And moreover, why do so with an interviewer who has contacted them through the human rights course, when their self-interest seems to rest squarely on the side of paying lip service to rights, playing the part to reap whatever potential benefits might come from a foreigner who may have connections to international NGOs?

One reason is that these officers care about their moral identities, and they care about what is true. They want me to understand the situations in which they work, and they want to make this dominant language of rights into something that can express what they believe. In Charles Taylor's words, human rights are not "the terms" in which they live, but officers are trying to make them more so.[4] In the process, they subvert the very meaning of rights. Their terms remain relatively intact.

Taylor writes that "the underlying idea of society as existing for the (mutual) benefit of individuals and the defense of their rights . . . [has come] to be the dominant view, pushing older theories of society and newer rivals to the margins of political life and discourse."[5] Officers' statements suggest two things about Taylor's claim. First, alternative theories of society and the moral order connected to those theories persist. A moral order based on difference and merit continues to challenge the order of mutual rights and equality.

Second, however, this does not mean that Taylor and the many others who speak of the dominance of human rights ideas are mistaken.[6] The rights-based moral order is so dominant that even some adherents to alternative moralities articulate their claims in terms of rights. This suggests that background beliefs do not necessarily dictate whether someone takes on the language and concepts of an ethical or political framework. Such beliefs shape the very meaning of the framework, the way a person interprets it, and the way a person uses it. Police draw from an imaginary in which there are different types of people who deserve and require different treatment. When they interpret and use the concept of human rights, it is in light of this imaginary. Rights are understood as based on what someone deserves, even as another way of distinguishing between people: there are those who respect and therefore deserve human rights, and those who on both counts do not. Hence Taylor writes of the social imaginary as the context in which norms make sense or do not, and appear worth striving to realize or not.[7]

Police are aware that their interpretation of rights differs from that of most human rights educators and activists, and many are genuinely perplexed by the standard meaning of rights. This is in part because the moral order of rights is an abstract theory to them, which they comprehend but have not internalized. They understand that in theory, all people are equal. But, they ask, "How can you say that someone who violates the rights of others has human rights?" In a social imaginary in which people are inherently different, and a moral order in which those differences mean that different treatment is required and right, the premise of universality seems wrong, even if its theoretical basis has been taught and learned.

Implications for the Spread of Human Rights

Informed by different moral and social imaginaries and situated in different contexts, people interpret human rights according to their own conceptions of what is good and necessary. These interpretations exemplify the "multivocal" nature of rights discourse that enables it to accommodate a wide variety of beliefs and interests.[8] On one hand, this adaptability makes it less hegemonic:

people with different worldviews can use it from within their own traditions. Activists in diverse parts of the world use rights language to acquire the international support they need, while continuing to speak other ethical and political languages with their constituents.[9] This raises concern that rights talk may crowd out these other languages, rendering local activists with no choice but to organize around rights.[10] But it does mean that however imperfect the fit may be, diverse local activists can use rights language to support their aims.

On the other hand, such malleability means that rights discourse can be "captured" by powerful actors and used to support their interests. This can include corporate and government emphasis on the "right to development," interpreted in ways that diminish individual rights and hurt the poor, as Upendra Baxi indicates in *The Future of Human Rights*. This can also include the use of human rights laws to undermine the freedom of women, as Pratiksha Baxi et al. show in regard to police and *panchayats* [local governing councils] in India.[11] The police in this study similarly interpret human rights according to their own beliefs and aims, leading to judgments with which most human rights advocates would deeply disagree.

As a result, international norms change as they travel, as they are negotiated and adapted by the people who use them. To explore the implications of this for human rights protection, the next section turns first to international relations theory on the global spread of human rights, and subsequently to anthropological research on how those rights are translated into local "vernaculars" of meaning.

The Global Diffusion of Human Rights Norms

Social constructivist theorists argue that state agents adopt human rights norms in part because they wish to identify as representatives of a liberal state.[12] Government officials may do so only tactically at first, endorsing human rights without intending to protect them. But following what scholars refer to as a norm "spiral," states eventually become rhetorically trapped by their commitments and shamed into narrowing the gap between their public proclamations and their actions.[13]

The ways in which the officers in this book negotiate human rights reveal what may be one obstacle to this process. These officers have good reasons to project a human rights–friendly identity. They have enrolled voluntarily in a course that will grant them a master's degree in human rights. They hope to advance professionally by representing themselves as qualified in this area, a goal that should provide them with incentives to at least articulate human-rights beliefs, even if they do not always follow them. They should also then be vulnerable to shaming when they fail to protect rights.

But these officers do not even pretend to endorse human rights activists' views in order to take on a liberal identity. Instead, they reframe rights so that they align with their already existing beliefs and practices. They argue that they are better representatives of human rights than the activists who criticize them. Hence they can take on a rights-friendly identity without undermining—even in speech—their support for torture. There is no gap between their speech and actions that could be exploited by activists' shaming efforts because they modify human rights discourse to support violence.

Theorists might point out that their arguments about identity and norm diffusion are applicable to state leaders on the international stage, and not to domestic actors such as law enforcement officers. If so, this suggests a problematic gap between the interests of international actors who endorse norms and the domestic actors who implement them. This gap may help explain why pervasive violations of rights continue long after a state has endorsed their protection.

This, however, is unlikely to provide a full explanation. Scholars and state leaders alike have long identified the principal-agent problem as a challenge for governance. Indeed, both human rights researchers and elected officials point to the difficulty of controlling what local police do as a problem for human rights compliance. But police officers' statements and human rights reports on India strongly suggest that they are not rogue actors, but rather are expected to engage in torture and other illegal actions by supervisors and politicians.[14]

If there is a principal-agent problem, then, the disobedient agents occupy a level far higher than the police. In interviews, investigators with the National Human Rights Commission, who are responsible for holding law enforcement officers accountable, also express concerns about sacrificing security for the sake of rights, and they articulate doubts about whether it is always possible or good to maintain the rights of suspected criminals, including their right to be free from torture. Even the public statements of high-ranking officials that are intended for an international audience suggest ambivalence about torture. In a 2012 interview with *The Wall Street Journal*, India's Minister for Home Affairs stated:

> I cannot say that a police station located in a remote part of Chhattisgarh or Jharkhand, where they apprehend a chap who is alleged to have committed burglary or murder, I certainly won't say that they use forensic evidence to decide

> whether he's guilty or not. They probably use some rough and ready measures like the olden days, but things are changing.[15]

Such comments imply a tacit acceptance of torture at the highest levels of government. As such, shaming methods seem to fall short in regard not only to local police, but also to superiors and more visible elected officials as well.

This all suggests that even if state actors wish to present themselves as maintaining a particular kind of liberal identity on the international stage, it does not follow that domestic state actors prioritize presenting themselves this way, even among high-level officials speaking to an international audience. Although scholars disagree on whether state officials must genuinely believe in a norm in order to be shamed by it, at the very least they must wish to appear to uphold a norm in order for shaming to work.[16] These officers are not successfully shamed by accusations of human rights violations, because the standard against which they judge themselves, and against which they believe people who have power over them will judge them, is radically different.

Moreover, they are able to draw on the legitimizing language of political modernity to make their claims. The police in this study do not explain torture by reference to caste or religious affiliation. Instead, they frame their assertions in terms of their identity as protectors of the liberal security state. This allows them to bolster their legitimacy even as they undermine principles of liberalism.

This ability to adapt international norms to support existing beliefs and practices is not limited to educational efforts, nor to only low-level state officials. In a groundbreaking study, Amitav Acharya showed how policymakers within an intergovernmental organization, the Association of Southeast Asian Nations (ASEAN), "localize" international norms.[17] Whether or not ASEAN changed its goals and procedures to reflect international norms depended upon policymakers' success in making those norms congruent with regional interests and values.

Such translations occur within Western countries as well, though as with the police in this book, this can take the form of local actors coopting a reform, rather than the creative localization of policymakers. A study of police responses to the Human Rights Act in England and Wales found that "instead of shaping police work to make it more responsive to human rights, bureaucratic processes are used by officers to legitimize and justify their existing practices."[18] The police welcomed the documentation required by the Human Rights Act, but saw it as a way to protect themselves should their actions be later questioned. They actively engaged with the reform, but used it to strengthen extant norms.

Such uses of global norms and accompanying reform efforts highlight the importance of connecting international relations theory on how global norms diffuse to anthropological research on how domestic actors use these norms once they have spread. It suggests that local uses of global norms can deflect or transform the mechanisms that in other circumstances might promote compliance, and it points to the importance of understanding what happens to these norms when they are translated into the "vernacular."

Vernacularization

A rich body of ethnographic research examines how international human rights norms are translated into local idioms of meaning, a process referred to by Sally Merry and those who build on her work as "vernacularization."[19] This process exists on a continuum between instances of a near "replication" of the international norm and times when a "hybrid" is formed as local values infuse and alter its meaning.

The concept of vernacularization is modeled on how languages change as they spread, but this process is also similar to religious syncretism. Christianity took many forms as it moved across the globe. Missionaries connect Christian values to local rituals, and local converts combine elements from Christianity and preexisting religious traditions, leading to new forms of worship. Such mixtures have generated controversy as church leadership attempts to maintain a pure and universal form of the religion.[20]

The same can be said of human rights, which activists and educators adapt to local beliefs. Human rights workers in India draw on images of female goddesses to promote women's rights, for example, a process that may produce a new conceptualization of female power that mirrors neither source exactly.[21] Scholars refer to such symbolic adoption of local images and signs as "indigenization" when they involve shifts in meaning.[22]

Although activists who mediate between transnational networks and local communities intentionally vernacularize rights in order to make them salient locally, rights norms may also be subverted and used for contrary purposes.[23] This occurs when "the name and transnational referent are retained but the content of the ideas and the structure of the organization is dramatically changed."[24] Some scholars refer to this as a "decoupling" of policy and practice, wherein the international norm is adopted with little meaning for what people do or believe.[25] Indeed, legal anthropologists argue that like any law, human rights laws can be a vehicle either to contest or to reinforce power structures, depending on who is using them and for what purpose.[26]

This subversion has often been described as occurring in three ways, which I categorize as cynical, unintentional, and insufficient. I use the term *cynical subversion* to refer to scholars' descriptions of actors who use rights language with no intention of fulfilling its aims, and instead pay lip service for the sake of rewards or to avoid punishments. Social constructivist scholars in international relations largely focus on such cynicism, or "tactical concessions" on the part of state leaders, and see this as a stage in their socialization to rights norms. Other scholars have also described the cynical adoption of rights language without any intention of fulfilling its standards among lower-level security personnel.[27]

I use the term *unintentional subversion* to refer to scholars' descriptions of local actors who may believe they are implementing a human right or other global norm, but who interpret it differently than international funders. For example, teachers in Tanzania who were trained to implement "learner-centered pedagogy" do so in ways that meet their own standards of good educational practice and are not necessarily altering the policy on purpose.[28]

Lastly, subversion due to *insufficient* adoption refers to scholars' judgment that a rights norm has been accepted only partially. Merry discusses women who speak of their human rights under *Sharia*, for example, which extend to special circumstances such as the right to leave the house for medical attention, but do not encompass the full range of rights under international law.[29] I also include researchers' arguments that local actors use rights language in vague and uncertain ways in the category of insufficient translation. For instance, in his account of the Truth and Reconciliation Commission in South Africa, Richard Wilson argues that human rights norms failed to encompass local actors' conceptions of justice and their desire to see the perpetrators punished.[30] In spite of this lack of resonance, South Africans sometimes use human rights language superficially, asserting that their human rights have been violated as a way of saying that something is unjust, rather than because they know and believe in the validity of specific rights.

My research suggests another way in which rights discourse is subverted in the process of vernacularization: through intentional contestation that is earnest rather than cynical. The police officers in this study do not merely use rights discourse superficially, paying lip service to rights while continuing to violate them. They also go further than infusing rights discourse with local meaning. They engage actively with rights discourse, reasoning with it and questioning it, and ultimately using it to contest rights principles.

Vernacularization in Context

Why the officers vernacularize rights in this particular way may seem to be a question that does not merit asking. They are state agents, hence using rights to argue for the importance of security bolsters their authority and serves their interests. But although this may offer part of the explanation, it does not provide all of it. For one, it does not explain why officers feel such a need to bolster their authority; assuming that police simply have an insatiable desire for power is not sufficient.

This, and the limited number of studies that exist on the topic, reveal the importance of officers' contexts, not just for how they make judgments about violence, as discussed in Chapter 5, but also for what they do with human rights messages. In South Africa, for example, a police officer may present her- or himself as supportive of human rights in order to escape the particularistic and ill-respected reputation of policing, as well as to identify instead with the middle-class professionalism signified by the rule of law. Nonetheless, public perceptions that the police are only responsive to private relationships mean that human rights become one more advantage that can be acquired through cultivating a relationship with the right officer.[31]

The decisive role of context is also revealed in an insightful study of how prison wardens in New Delhi respond to human rights messages.[32] These wardens work in conditions in which they are expected to use violence and see no alternative to doing so. The author sees wardens' manipulation of human rights language as a demonstration of their volition, drawing on Richard Wilson's conception of agency as expressed by actors' capacity to deal with and respond to their circumstances.[33] He argues that it is prison wardens' need to survive a complex environment, rather than the more typically blamed local culture, bad attitude, sadism, or simple lack of resources that inspires their resistance.

The importance of context is further supported by evidence that state officials in comparable contexts vernacularize rights similarly. The prison wardens in New Delhi, a city in which many interviews for this book occurred, express remarkably similar interpretations and negotiations of human rights to the police I interviewed. The prison wardens draw from the same social imaginary, in that they view security and order as under threat due to the rights accorded to suspects, and in that they see state officials as themselves suffering from a lack of rights to basic welfare. And just like the officers in this book, the prison wardens interpret rights as privileges rather than as universal guarantees. In this way, they negotiate who deserves them, arguing that the prisoners do not.

It is not only state officials, with their obvious interest in interpreting rights in terms of security, who take on this usage. In conditions of widespread insecurity, civilians also negotiate rights in this way, pointing again to the importance of context for how rights are vernacularized. For example, in his book *Outlawed*, Daniel Goldstein describes how impoverished people living in insecure conditions in Bolivia invoke their "right to security" to justify lynching local criminals.[34] Like the police in this book, their perception that the criminal justice system fails to deliver justice informs their view that extrajudicial violence is necessary. And so, also like the police in this study, they use the very language and logic of rights to contest its principles.

Idealist views that prioritize beliefs and meaning-making, and materialist analyses that emphasize the role of structures and circumstances, are both indispensable for understanding how police interpret and use human rights language. Indeed, it is both a social imaginary and the social reality on which it is based, as well as a moral, imaginary that move police to negotiate human rights. Moreover, these are hardly separate: the moral imaginary is both constrained by the social imaginary and as enhanced by it. As discussed in chapter 2, police draw on a moral imaginary in which they view violence as good in certain circumstances and for certain people. As chapter 3 shows, police believe they are unable to uphold ideals regarding when and against whom violence should be used. They believe that due to these contextual constraints, it is good to use violence more widely than they otherwise would. As such, the moral imaginary informs officers' judgments of what is not just a way to cope with circumstances, but of what is a good way to cope.

This combination of ideational and material factors is acknowledged, if not highlighted, in several studies, even among scholars who see the context of police work as so powerful that they judge any effort to spread a universal normative order as bound to fail. In her study of police reform in Nigeria, for example, Alice Hills argues that while the police and political elites welcome instrumental technical knowledge, they implement normative reforms—such as those regarding human rights—only superficially.[36] Hills focuses on the self-interest of police and elites given their circumstances, but notes the possibility that "transmission sometimes depends on a moral response to a specific situation," and reflects, "This raises the as yet unanswered question of what norms ground the moral response, and what the limiting factors might be".[36] The Indian police officers interviewed for this book elaborate on the nature of those norms, and their statements reveal how their beliefs combine with their perceptions of their circumstances to ground their judgments. Both beliefs and structures, officers' inner and outer lives in interaction, inform their responses to human rights and make torture commonplace.

Teaching and Learning Human Rights

Is there any hope for human rights education?

If officers' inner lives matter for their judgments on violence, then education has the potential to make a difference. Unlike the structures within which police work, their beliefs represent a realm that communicative approaches might influence. Indeed, although police use liberal language to contest rights principles, this does not imply that they mechanically adapt international norms to their own views, using them in a purely strategic way to their advantage. They are willing to reflect on the gap between their beliefs and human rights principles, and show interest in doing so. Police at times question both their own assertions and those of human rights advocates, expressing doubt and curiosity about how and to what extent they should protect human rights. Officers' negotiation of human rights is their means of reconciling questions, rather than an indication of an absence of reflection.

In addition, although in this case human rights education fails to transform these officers' outlook, this does not mean it has no effect. Officers speak at times of human rights messages affecting them unexpectedly, almost in spite of themselves. For example, a low-ranking paramilitary officer used a clever metaphor to explain the way human rights may exert subtle influence, even when an officer has not been convinced to "believe in" them. He explained:

> If you know a place has danger—for example, let's say that someone tells you a tree is haunted by a ghost and you shouldn't go at night. And let's say you don't believe in ghosts. But when you pass the tree in the night it clicks in your heart—a ghost. This is human rights knowledge. It will click in your soul the moment you are about to commit a mistake. That may overcome your mistake.

The officer does not imply that he has been converted to a belief in human rights. And he does not even suggest that if the "ghost" of human rights arises at a key moment, it will change his behavior. He says, instead, that it "may." At the least, it may give officers a reason to consider whether their action is in fact a mistake. This pause is likely fleeting, and probably could be nothing more substantial in the circumstances in which violence typically occurs. But it is at least possible that every once in a while, this pause will transform what follows.

Torture is an especially hard case for human rights education, though, given that such violence is entrenched both in officers' beliefs about what is right and in the environments in which they work. In the concluding chapter, I address how educators might tackle this challenge. But it is also worth briefly examining how police respond to human rights messages that do not present such an obstacle.

Beyond Torture: Responses to the Human Rights Course and Conditions for Accepting New Norms

I now turn briefly to how officers respond to other messages they receive from their human rights course. I do this for two reasons. First, there is a danger of seeming to suggest that the course has no effect by omitting any mention of it beyond the especially difficult subject of torture. Second, and more importantly, contextualizing officers' responses with how they respond to other types of human rights reveals what makes torture and related violence such a challenging subject on which to change officers' views.

Officers' comments suggest that they read, understand, and remember at least some of the course material. For example, a mid-ranking officer from Rajasthan discussed knowledge he had acquired about the history of rights, such as about the *Magna Carta*. When I ask him about the value of such information, he replied:

> In order to have faith in anything, you need to understand its roots. You need to know, who was this man who fought for human rights, what were the obstacles it overcame, how has it developed.

Officers often make comments of this sort, wherein they repeat information from the course and assert that it was worthwhile to learn. Some also speak positively of conversations they have with faculty of the human rights institute, for whom they express genuine respect: a view of human rights educators that is unusual for officers.

This does not mean that officers agree with the material, but rather that they read it and are engaged with it. For example, officers would sometimes say that now that they are participating in the course, they know that people should technically be granted particular rights, and then proceed to give the arguments recounted previously to negate this claim.

But this resistance does not hold true for all human rights. Officers often express their support for rights that complement their interests and beliefs, such as social and economic rights. They particularly express enthusiasm for the rights of children, the elderly, and the poor: people who fit more easily than criminal suspects into the category of the "innocent."[37]

This suggests that officers may accept human rights when they see them as aligned with their beliefs and interests as police. Officers often speak of wishing to help children, and frequently voice their support for aid to the poor. Some become involved in voluntary organizations such as to help poor children become educated. Some officers also report that the course has made them more sensitive to the plight of people who may not have seemed vulnerable or innocent to them before. For example, compare the way one low-ranking police officer spoke of his response to course material on refugee rights and to material on torture. I asked him if he has learned anything from the human rights course, and he responded:

> OFFICER: Yes. For example, there are many refugees from Bangladesh now in India. They are mostly involved with rickshaws and petty crime. Sometimes the police slap them and arrest them. Now after learning about refugees, I make other officers aware of the problems faced by refugees. I try to help them sort out their problems.
>
> RW: Could you give me some examples of how?
>
> OFFICER: Like I tell them about night shelters, and about getting a refugee card. They are provided with a refugee card with which they can get subsidized food. They can get education. They can work in small industries. I tell them about the rights of refugees. . . . Human rights training taught me about why they become refugees and what problems they face, so it made me feel that we should not be so strict with them. Also the rights of criminals.
>
> RW: What did you learn from the human rights program about the rights of criminals that you did not know before?
>
> OFFICER: That we cannot force confession.
>
> RW: Has this changed your behavior at all, or has it not been able to due to the pressures you are under?
>
> OFFICER: It changes my behavior by about 20 percent.

The rest of this officer's interview is suggestive of what he may mean by this 20 percent, as he is one of many officers who express the belief that some criminals require torture. In contrast, he seems to embrace without reservation ways that he can help refugees, perhaps because this is a way that he can fulfill a desire to act ethically, as well as attain and project a desirable identity, without compromising his interests and beliefs. Hence the extent to which a norm matches actors' interests and beliefs is likely important for the extent to which they accept it.

Furthermore, the officer now has clear, easily transferrable information about how to help refugees, such as informing them about cards that entitle them to education and food aid. In contrast, officers often do not believe that they have the skills or the agency to conduct investigations without torture. Hence the spread of a normative framework may also depend upon the ease with which actors can implement it. The seeming success of educators' efforts to cultivate this officer's sympathy for refugees may be related, then, to both the ease with which he can act on this sympathy and the alignment with how he understands his interests and his beliefs.

Moreover, interviews suggest that the human rights course and the human rights framework overall provide officers with a further incentive to align themselves with rights-friendly practices. Although officers may already have a desire to contribute meaningfully to social causes, the human rights movement could increase the likelihood that they will act on their inclinations by offering opportunities that make it in officers' interest to "do good." For one, most officers joined the course in hopes that it would lead to professional opportunities, though quite a few also expressed what seems to be a genuine desire to contribute to society. Second, officers sometimes spoke of volunteering with human rights organizations in which higher-ranking officers are involved, which offers them the opportunity for networking.

Such professional incentives are a key goal of the director of the human rights education institution, who argues that it is vital to make it in the interest of actors in all professions to engage in human rights work and to tie professional success to human rights involvement. Officers' comments suggest both the benefits and the limits of this approach. They do seem eager to become involved in causes that complement their beliefs and interests. This is constrained, however, by whether officers believe the organization and human rights are supportive of the police or undermine them.

At the same time, officers' readiness to endorse the rights of vulnerable groups does not mean that they will always abide by these principles. Officers may genuinely support the rights of children they consider innocent, for example, while still behaving violently toward children whom they believe have committed crimes. But the foregoing does suggest that officers' responses to human rights education is informed by the extent to which they believe the particular rights they learn match their beliefs, interests, and capacity.

The Trouble with Learning Concepts

As this case suggests, teaching concepts does not necessarily spread those concepts, even when learners successfully learn them: it spreads the language used to describe them. Drawing on Wittgenstein's theory of language, the philosopher of education Megan Laverty highlights the ways in which the meaning of any concept is always in flux and subject to revision, which occurs through reflection and interaction with others. As such, we "learn our concepts as we use them."[38] Given this observation, the education of police and military officers can be understood as occurring only initially through their encounters with texts and instructors. It is when they use the concepts they learn in conversation that the substantial learning of the concept occurs.

A learner-centered pedagogy might exert some influence on how students use concepts by guiding them in the practice of such use.This course, in contrast, is an example of the "Global Citizenship" model[39] and the similar "Values and Awareness—socialization" model,[40] in that the educators provide students with information rather than offer skills training or inspire a transformation of attitudes. Such approaches tend not to engage students in active learning exercises or encourage critique—features of the most effective HRE, according to scholars.[41]

This didactic approach focused on the transmission of information is typical of human rights training for state agents in India and elsewhere, and as such is important to understand. Such programs represent what can be referred to as a "loose diffusion" of human rights messages. This is how global norms often spread: police learn about these ideas in a piecemeal fashion from many different sources, including but not limited to formal training, which exposes them without intensively socializing them.

The director of this particular HRE institute views his method as a means to reach the largest number of students, particularly those police and military officers who would be unlikely and even unable to commit any more time to a human rights course.In spite of the limits of distance-learning, moreover, he hopes that his program will both enable and inspire professionals to protect human rights in their work. And opportunities for more active learning are there for students who seek them, as the faculty and director are available to students to speak in person, on the phone, and online.Some students do report having meaningful conversations with faculty that changed their views, and faculty told me that they enjoy active student engagement in such conversations. But these additional interactions are not required, and not all students engage in them.

As such, this common approach to training state officials does not meet the requirements that scholars and practitioners of human rights education insist upon. As discussed previously, these experts argue that HRE should use participatory methods.[42] Some go further to suggest that ideally, HRE should utilize the kind of critical pedagogy described by the Brazilian educational theorist and activist Paolo Freire.[43] It is possible that by meeting standards such as the use of active learning methods, police might come to use these concepts in ways more closely aligned to what educators desire.

But ultimately, no educational program can control what students do with the ideas they learn. This is both a strength and a weakness of education: it is a weakness from the perspective of fidelity to the message the educators hope to communicate, but a strength from the perspective of human freedom.

Of course, not all education is equally respectful of human freedom. The nationalism taught by an authoritarian state, or even more subtle messages that are supported by both formal schooling and other socializing institutions, leave less scope for freedom than a distance-learning human rights course that is teaching against the grain of officers' presuppositions. And not all freedom is worth celebrating. It is desirable from a human rights perspective for a student to question the meaning of rights and to seek to understand the concept on her own terms, but not if her conclusion is that brutality should be condoned.

Moreover, the contention that concepts are learned through their use does not imply that there is no essential meaning of any concept and that officers' interpretations are adequate. The human rights framework is premised on the priority of individual rights, even though concepts of responsibility and duty are also part of the framework. Educators who emphasize responsibilities and duties over rights are, in the words of other researchers, "miseducating" about rights as defined within contemporary liberalism.[44] This is not to say that the educator is teaching something unethical, only that she is not teaching the concept of "human rights" with fidelity.

As such, concepts can be understood as in flux and open to interpretation and renegotiation. But there are certain bounds beyond which the idea would be better described by drawing on a different, and even competing, concept. In the case of police and military officers in India, they retain the language of human rights, but interpret them in ways that bear more fidelity to competing ethical frameworks.

The importance of using ideas in order to learn them, and the potential flexibility of any concept, suggest that there may be restrictions on the extent to which deep normative change can occur through the transmission of ideas, in settings in which learners hold beliefs and interests in opposition to them. The learners in this case end up learning human rights concepts as they use them, but when they do so, they stretch these ideas almost beyond recognition. It may be better, then, to attempt to connect human rights messages to what police already believe than to change their beliefs. This, too, is a difficult and problematic proposition, though, to which I return in the concluding chapter.

Conflicts within Concepts

There are further difficulties inherent in teaching human rights to state agents. Whether analyzing activism or education, scholars often discuss the spread of norms without reference to their content. But the transformation that occurs through teaching human rights concepts may be exacerbated by tensions within the history of the concepts themselves. The objections of the Indian police are not a reflection only of their particular context or idiosyncratic beliefs. Rather, they articulate an objection that predates the human rights movement. They articulate a much older criticism: that belief in the existence of "natural rights" is bad for society because it encourages dissent, and this dissent undermines the real good for man, which is security. Thomas Hobbes thought as much, in contrast to John Locke's affirmation of natural justice and his expectation that governments conform to it.[45] This critique has haunted liberalism and led one scholar to describe Hobbes as "Locke's own evil angel with whom he wrestled throughout [a] lifetime."[46]

It seems that liberalism must continue to wrestle with the ghost of Hobbes. Rather than uphold rights that transcend the state, these police invoke a Hobbesian version of social contract theory to refute the validity of such rights.

In this creation myth of society, people enter into a social contract because it offers better protection than the state of nature. In this natural state, everyone is vulnerable to the intrusion of everybody else. The state offers protection from this "war of all against all," as Hobbes called it, but requires obedience in return. Hobbes argued that the rule of even an imperfect sovereign is preferable to the state of nature, and hence emphasized the importance of maintaining the state above individual rights. Arguing over rights, or even over conceptions of the higher good, only destabilizes and hence undermines the true good of security. Therefore, not a transcendent natural law, but state-made, imminent law should guide behavior.[47] In contrast, early liberal theorists, such as John Locke and Jean-Jacques Rousseau, emphasized that obedience is owed only when the state protects certain natural rights, viewing a sovereign who violates natural rights as no better than the state of nature.[48]

Echoing Hobbes, law enforcement officers note that liberty is based in the security of a state that protects citizens from each other and that citizens must uphold their end of this agreement by respecting others' rights. Otherwise, they lose their rights to state protection. This introduces a conditional clause on rights in the premise that state protection is dependent upon a person's respect of the law and of the rights of others. Also like Hobbes, officers see human nature as tending toward self-interest and violence that results in chaos, which they believe requires the control offered by a strong state and which justifies the exercise of state power. They argue that without the presence of the state to restrain those who threaten the rights of others, society would devolve into worse conflict in which nobody would enjoy rights protections.

The liberal tradition from which the contemporary human rights movement emerged has shifted dramatically away from Hobbes's assertion of the near-absolute authority of the sovereign to enforce its law for this purpose. It evolved from the arguments of thinkers such as Locke, Rousseau, and later theorists of democracy who assert that the state has a right to assert its law only so long as it actually protects the natural rights of its citizens.

But police still have recourse to a language of rights that is based in state sovereignty rather than in natural claims that transcend its power. They may learn this in their human rights course, which covers the different social contract theories, or they may reason their way to it. Either way, it provides them with a discourse that carries some legitimacy in its use of a secular, rational defense of security.

Indeed, it is noteworthy that these police use the discourse of the state rather than an alternative normative framework to resist human rights standards. They do not draw on the idea of "Indian culture" or religion to argue that human rights should not apply to them. That officers did not need to reach beyond the language of social contract theory to defend torture suggests the plurality of conceptions of justice that may be articulated using the same theoretical language. Contemporary human rights activists and police officers speak the language of rights and view the state as the protector of these rights, yet with very different views on how conflicts between the state and its citizens should be resolved. Such malleability presents an obstacle for the spread of human rights, as actors draw from the logic of a normative framework, and from aspects of it with which they agree, to negotiate those elements with which they disagree.

This examination of how state actors in a particular context interpret rights provides empirical support to theoretical assertions of the tension between the asserted universality of human rights and the requirement that such rights be upheld in specific political contexts.[49] It provides insight into how rights move from their universal articulation to their particular enforcement. The interviews demonstrate how state agents can exacerbate the inevitable tension between universal and national legal frameworks by interpreting rights in decidedly non-universalistic terms. But as the foregoing suggests, the obstacle to universality is not "local culture" as traditionally understood. As I explain in the chapter that follows, local culture is too complex to unilaterally resist or support human rights, as are officers' understanding and use of it.

Chapter 5

Complications of the Local: Violence, Religion, and Culture

Cross-border terrorism cannot be solved with Gandhian methods. A criminal is a person without a soul, and the standard techniques for people with souls cannot be applicable.

—*Indian Police Service officer, Delhi*

I SPENT ALL DAY AND EVENING with A for our first interview. He lives in the state of Uttar Pradesh, and the train schedule from Delhi that day meant that he would need to be my host for many hours. A servant who lives with him cooked our meals, and our conversation ranged over the course of the day. Forty-eight at the time of our interview, he had been a police officer for thirty years. Although a member of the State Police Force rather than the elite supervisory ranks of the Indian Police Service, he had recently been given specialized training in a research division. He was relieved to no longer be working out in the field, where, he lamented, his desire to serve the public was compromised by political interference. In the evening he drove me to a local temple, where he asked for a blessing on his work and on mine.

As it is to many of the officers I interviewed, religion is important to A. The Hindu swastika was painted prominently over the hood of his police car. A tape in his car radio played religious music, and he was eager to explain to me that the song was dedicated to the worship of the Lord Shiva.

Many assertions have been made about the relationship of the rights framework to Indian religious and cultural traditions. Some scholars suggest that in spite of their diversity, ethical traditions in India tend to focus more on relationships of collective care, reciprocity, and duty than on equal individual rights, and give more attention to specific contexts than to universal moral rules.[1] Some scholars draw on this premise to suggest that the human rights framework privileges a Western conception of the good.[2] Others emphasize the convergence between Indian traditions and the rights framework, pointing for example to the value placed on all forms of life, compassion, tolerance, and the obligations of the ruler to the ruled in Indian religions.[3]

Human rights practitioners tend to embrace both views. They often identify religious and cultural beliefs as constraining acceptance of human rights by positioning the latter as emblematic of progress against the bulwarks of "tradition." But they also see religion and culture as important sources of support for human rights, and religious and cultural leaders as crucial partners in human rights efforts. Local beliefs are often referenced within United Nations documents and discussions as reasons a community may resist social change.[4] But they also often assert the universality of human rights values, sourcing them to every religion and culture.[5]

Indeed, connecting to local religious beliefs is a common way that activists frame and vernacularize human rights.[6] Many international organizations prioritize partnering with local religious authorities, and some even define their mission in this way.[7] Practitioners and scholars alike typically suggest that human rights educators will be most successful if they can connect their messages to those aspects of local traditions that best support human rights.

The educational NGO on which this study focuses takes seriously this admonition. Lessons emphasize the ways that human rights embody the same values as Hindu, Buddhist, Christian, and Muslim beliefs. The textbooks also discuss the ways in which national icons, such as Mahatma Gandhi and Swami Vivekananda, promoted values that are similar to those of human rights, and how historical struggles, such as for independence, realized those values.

By revealing the continuity between the modern liberal moral order and the moral orders that preceded it in India, educators hope that human rights will be accepted more readily. This reflects an attempt to separate the moral order from the moral imaginary that supports it. Educators connect the explicit beliefs of the human rights movement, such as the dignity of all individuals and the protection they deserve, to similar beliefs within Indian religions, such as the value of every life, in spite of the differences in the background beliefs within which these explicit beliefs make sense.

What is perhaps surprising about this effort is that in one sense, it is successful. Police often agree with their educators that human rights are based in the same values as their religious and cultural traditions. This is not sufficient, however, for them to endorse the right to be free from torture and other forms of extrajudicial violence. This is not because they see their religious and cultural traditions as opposed to human rights, but because of a conflict with another moral order, which is also secular and modern. Officers grapple with the gap between what they see as worthwhile principles of human rights and their traditions, on one hand, and their belief that it is right to violate them in order to uphold state security and justice, on the other.

There are several ways in which officers respond to this tension. They at times interpret the meaning of both human rights and what they see as traditional values, so that both could support the violence they believe policing requires. This shows how police are active interpreters not only of human rights, but also of their religions and cultures, providing their own reading of these traditions. At other times, they reject not only human rights but also what they consider traditional values in favor of the violence they believe police work requires.

Officers Accept Human Rights as Traditional Values

Officers often speak of human rights as consistent with their religious beliefs, as well as with what they understand as their traditional culture more broadly. "Tradition" can of course have many meanings. Scholars have elaborated on the values that they assert are central to different Indian traditions.[8] The officers sometimes refer to the values with which they were raised by telling specific stories about their upbringing. At other times, they reference a more generalized "Indian culture" and describe what they see as its characteristics.I foreground these times when officers themselves articulate the meaning of what they consider to be their traditions.

Religion and Human Rights

The police who articulate religious commitments typically view human rights as a more recent version of religious values. A mid-ranking officer from Uttar Pradesh responded to my question about where he had learned about human rights by explaining, "I am religious from birth." I asked another mid-ranking officer from Haryana for his interpretation of "the meaning of human rights." He responded, "Human rights means the justice by God which has been given shape by various governments and committees." When I asked if there is a difference between what human rights and religion teaches, he replied, "There is no difference. Just as the sun is the source of all life, religion is the source of all rights."

Even when officers define *human rights* in terms that are associated with secular individualism, they sometimes go on to explain themselves using religious language. For example, another mid-ranking officer from Haryana explained that "self-determination" is the most important human rights value, because "these decisions are related to a man's soul." Hence this officer endorses the secular and individualistic value of self-determination, but explains it through the religious concept of the soul.

Tradition and Human Rights

Officers often speak of human rights as a manifestation of the values with which they were raised. They sometimes explain that they joined the human rights course because of these values. For example, a high-ranking military officer in Delhi described human rights as carrying on the values of his mother. When I asked him why he had enrolled in the human rights course, he answered that his mother had taught him to treat people with compassion, and explained:

> The value system we imbibe from parents, teachers. . . . To respect elders, to be compassionate, put yourself in others' shoes. . . . They are human rights. . . . I feel that every person in the world deserves some basic rights. One is you pay him. But if you speak to him nicely and he feels 'I am being treated as a human being also, not like a machine.' . . . Like we have some casual laborers, poor families. . . . These people, their work is harder than mine. It is only by the grace of God, by my education, that I can sit here and dictate. But people who are sweeping the floor, bringing *chai*, if you ask them about their family, not out of duty but from the heart, they are at peace and you also are at peace. So human rights brings a lot of peace I have found.

This officer uses "rights" language to talk about the compassion with which his mother taught him to treat people. Rather than seeing a contradiction, as some scholars do, between the individualism of rights discourse and the relational values that some say are important to Indian society, this officer sees them as accomplishing the same thing. Recognizing each person's individual humanity and acting with compassion are the same, and both bring inner peace.

This does not entail a conversion of the entire imaginary; officers have not come to think in terms of rights-bearing autonomous individuals who are inherently deserving of neutral and equal treatment. But the course does not stress such a conversion. Rather, as is typical, the course emphasized the resulting attitudes and actions that are common to Indian religious beliefs and human rights, rather than the background beliefs that inspire them.

So when I asked a mid-ranking officer in Uttar Pradesh for examples of times he had protected human rights, he did not narrate stories in which he upheld an individual's *right*. Rather, he spoke about times in which he acted with kindness in response to people in need:

> We saw a couple with children. There was an accident. Nobody was there to help them. We helped them. This is how human rights starts. People were avoiding talking to the police . . . and nobody was willing to help them.

I asked him how this was an example of human rights, and he replied:

> It is about the right to life. Every human being should try to help others. This is where human rights starts.

This suggests that officers can interpret human rights in terms of values that are "relational," such as helping others, as well as in terms of values that could be in tension with these beliefs, such as individual liberty. Furthermore, a relational interpretation does not necessarily cause police to act differently than if they had thought in terms of rights. For example, the officer from Uttar Pradesh thought it was important for him to help others, even though he did not suggest that people have an inherent "right" to such help.

Other officers refer to rights and traditional values, such as duty, interchangeably. A retired officer in Delhi argued that society requires "moral education" that would teach:

> *Sanskar*, meaning good qualities. . . . Parents have to teach their kids. When families are healthy, society will be healthy. Honesty, courtesy, hard work. Respect for others. Others' rights.

In this passage, the officer attaches rights language to a discussion that is primarily about values that could be considered traditional, such as respect. This use of rights language to express "good qualities" suggests that the human rights course has been successful in making the connection between traditional values and human rights, or perhaps, that officers already saw this affinity.

That officers see human rights as embodying their idea of general goodness but still sometimes reject the legitimacy of rights suggests something more complex than a straightforward opposition to rights as such. It suggests that officers contest the rights framework regarding *who* deserves rights (or good treatment), and why. This points to a difficulty in reframing human rights in terms of other ethical traditions with which they may resonate. Officers associate values, like charity with human rights, and support rights along these lines. However, these values are distinct from the concept that each person has an indisputable right to the goods that charity might divulge. As such, officers may endorse human rights without being convinced that all people deserve them unconditionally.

Still, this is not a conflict between the background beliefs of contemporary liberalism and a homogenous imaginary of "Indian religious beliefs" as such. Notwithstanding the diversity within the many different Hindu, Buddhist, and other religious traditions, each tradition bears much that is in fact more compatible with the rights framework than both the imaginary and the explicit views of police. A Buddhist might understand the good as unconditional compassion for all creatures, for example, and in fact be more likely to endorse inalienable protections on this basis than a secular liberal who believes that people deserve rights proportional to their compliance with the law.

Indeed, it is precisely this secular, state-centric deviation from the rights framework that poses the main ideational obstacle to officers' acceptance of human rights, not their religious beliefs. The power of this secular imaginary and moral order to undermine both human rights and religiously derived values is evident in officers' responses. But officers' acceptance of rights language nonetheless suggests again how actors may find in a normative framework that which resonates with them or infuse concepts with meanings that are coherent with their values. *Human rights* becomes *goodness*, however each person defines it.

Negotiation: Officers Reconcile Violence with Human Rights and Tradition

Although no officer articulated an opposition between human rights and their religious beliefs, they did identify tension between the values supported by human rights and religion, on one hand, and by policing, on the other. For example, a high-ranking prison official from Haryana admitted that when he first heard about human rights he rejected them as antithetical to his work, even though, he noted, the same values are taught in his religion. He reflected on when he first was required to attend human rights trainings:

> As a law and order agency, it was my thinking that I couldn't understand the values of human rights. Technically, I could understand the values of human rights. The values of human rights are already available in our literature, in our

stories. . . . Human rights are in our tradition in every story, in the *Mahabharata*, in primary school books, in Gandhiji.[9]

This officer compared what he sees as part of his religious tradition to what matters to him as part of "a law and order agency." The tension is between the values that he asserts both human rights and religion promote, and what he believes is required of a law and order agency.

Officers attempt to reconcile the tension between the values they see as supported by human rights and tradition, and the violence they associate with effective policing. They sometimes negotiate with human rights and what they see as religious or cultural values in almost identical ways, using terms from human rights and Indian traditions interchangeably. One way officers negotiate is by endorsing human rights and what they see as traditional ideals "as far as possible," meaning until these values conflict with police goals, national interest, or security. An army officer who served in Kashmir described how soldiers should behave in the following way:

> They should be compassionate and thoughtful. If a government policy is there, if force is required, to be legal and compassionate as far as possible. Being in government it may be required. But as far as possible be compassionate and protect the inalienable rights of the people.

He used the language of both a traditional value—compassion—and inalienable rights to express the same sentiment regarding expectations of police behavior. While the irony that "inalienable" rights should be respected only "as far as possible" is obvious, the idea that one should be compassionate only when the state's interests are conducive to it would also likely be considered problematic in ethical traditions that prioritize compassion. Yet he endorsed both rights and compassion, without undermining his commitment to the use of force when the state requires it. Interestingly, both Indian and international human rights law are based on the principle that force should be used only when necessary. Officers' disagreement with human rights law, then, is related to their beliefs about when and how much force is "necessary."

At other times, officers negotiate in similar ways with rights and with traditional values at different points in the interview. A mid-ranking officer in Delhi highlighted the importance of his religious beliefs and the value of being "humane." Yet throughout the dialogue, he continually justified torture. He reconciled these traditional values with violence by suggesting that torture should be conducted in a way that is "humane" and that a religious person would be more likely to torture in a humane way. Later in the interview, he engaged in a very similar negotiation, only with human rights rather than with religion and "humane" behavior. In answer to my question about whether torture should be used in investigations, he replied:

> OFFICER: Yes, if I am the person investigating I will use torture.
>
> RW: Why?
>
> OFFICER: Because we have no alternative means. There may be a conspiracy against the entire nation. Then he must be tortured. But again, humane torture.
>
> RW: How can we ensure that torture is only used when it is necessary?
>
> OFFICER: The person who is in the investigation. A lot will depend on his mind, his training, his religion, his upbringing. Maybe I will use only 50 percent of force but a younger person will use more. . . . I have compassion. I have a different mindset. The degree of torture will depend on the mindset.
>
> RW: How does religion make a difference?
>
> OFFICER: What I learn from my parents and from society I will never forget throughout my life. Before I could pronounce *mother* and *father* I was taught to pronounce *Lord Krishna*. In school, the first class is prayer class. First, we swept the school floors and then we had prayer. What I learned will always be in my mind. When I have to kill someone, I will think one hundred times before I kill.

This officer reconciles his religious beliefs with his support for torture. He does so by insisting that if someone has cultivated a religious quality of mind, the way in which he uses violence will be moral. He will be more likely both to use only the amount of force necessary to do a job.

At another point in the interview, he negotiates with the human rights framework in an almost identical way. He stated:

> OFFICER: It is the duty of all of us to protect human rights. But at the same time, you must support him who is doing the investigation. If you ask him just for the sake of human rights, he cannot do the investigation, and the law and order situation will go out of hand. There must be an equilibrium.
>
> RW: How can we find this equilibrium?
>
> OFFICER: It is purely training of the investigators. On one hand the rights of this person, the international conventions on human rights. At the same time,

> various techniques that he can improvise . . . I always think that training makes a big difference. There must be deterrence in law against police or whoever is doing the investigation. They also must be afraid of the law.

He maintains that human rights should be protected, but that torture is sometimes necessary, so we must find "equilibrium." The way to find equilibrium, he suggests, is to train officers well and instill fear of the law. This mirrors his previous suggestion that the way to balance religious ideals of nonviolence and the need to torture is to ensure that the torturers have been raised with a religious sensibility. Torturers who are have been raised with religion will torture in a more humane way, just as torturers who have been trained and are operating under the law will better protect human rights. Religion and the law moderate the torturer by instilling certain limits and qualities in his mind, not by barring any actions completely. This reveals that the officer negotiates religious values and human rights in highly similar ways. In addition, this officer's comments again pose an opposition between values the officer recognizes as positive and what he believes is necessary for police work. These values should be upheld, in his estimation, but not to the extent that they compromise police goals.

Officers often negotiate by framing torture as something that can be done morally or immorally, rather than as an inherent wrong. A high-ranking police officer from Punjab stated:

> It is wrong to torture if someone is inflicting pain in an irresponsible manner for small information . . . but if it is beneficial, then it is positive. It is beneficial for everyone at the *thana* [police station]. Responsibility is very important. For human rights, dignity is very important. Maintain the dignity and be responsible.

I then asked him how one can maintain dignity during torture. He wrestled with this question, admitting the conflict between them. Ultimately, he negotiated a compromise: torture should not go beyond a certain point, and human rights values should be maintained, but not if they undermine security. He reflected:

> Torturing and maintaining dignity are contradictory. But . . . you should not do it in front of someone. You should not cause lasting damage.

Similarly, I asked a low-ranking police officer in Haryana for his opinion on a quote from the human rights textbook, which was Thomas Jefferson's assertion that "the God who gave us life also gave us liberty at the same time."

He agreed, adding, "The God who has given birth to humans has also given all the liberties to him." He continued, "Death is also in the hands of God. So something that has been made by God, nobody else has the right to finish it." He then negotiated between his endorsement of a seemingly transcendent belief with the needs and norms of a state. When I asked him, "What if someone commits a crime?" he replied, "It should be seen in the context of a particular country. The kind of laws framed there. And if it doesn't harm the self-dignity of a person, then he should be punished."

Here the officer faces a contradiction. On one hand, he endorsed universal ideals drawn from religion and human rights concepts, in which taking life is in conflict with God, and all people deserve to be treated with dignity. On the other hand, he asserted the importance of national law and punishment. He resolved this by deciding that how much dignity a person deserves depends upon the extent of the problem the person poses for the state or society. When I asked whether criminals deserve dignity, he responded, "Every living being deserves dignity, in my opinion." I asked whether dignity is deserved even by hardcore criminals, whom he had previously asserted need to be tortured, and he stated, "Even a hardcore criminal deserves dignity." He then qualified this universalism, first with national law and then with a justification of police violence, adding, "First of all, he should be interrogated psychologically, and if he is actually very dangerous for society, he should be punished according to law." When I asked him what he would do "when you want to maintain someone's dignity, but you think they have information and you have to torture them?" he replied:

> In these cases, the police should take care that his dignity is not affected. He should be interrogated on the basis of the crime he has committed. . . . If it is a small theft, then he should not be interrogated the way someone who has raped or murdered is tortured.

First, this officer endorsed a religious and a rights-based ideal that protects all people. He agreed that all people "deserve dignity" and that nobody but God should take a life. He then asserted that how criminals should be treated depends on state laws. This seems like a further contradiction, asserting first a universal ideal of dignity, and then arguing for context and particular laws. But as he continued, he reconciled this contradiction by implying that although all people deserve dignity, how much dignity they deserve depends on their actions. Protecting the dignity of an innocent person may mean not torturing him, but protecting the dignity of a petty thief may mean torturing him less than you would someone suspected of murder.

The officer moves from a universal conception of human dignity to the admonition that the extent of torture should depend on the crime. Human rights and religious values become matters of degree. Police do not contest their value, but rather to whom and in what circumstances such protection should apply. The point here is not that this officer lives by his theory, but rather what it suggests about how individuals engage with normative frameworks that undermine their practices, and some of their beliefs, in cases where they are motivated to engage with those frameworks. It suggests that they incorporate the language and concepts of the new framework into their already existing conception of right and necessary action.

No Need to Negotiate: Officers Understand Traditional Values and Human Rights as Already Containing Compromise

Although values of compassion and nonviolence present a conflict for officers who endorse torture, these officers sometimes draw from their religious traditions to explain the legitimacy of violence. A mid-ranking police officer in Kashmir explained that he "learned about human values from the religious books." When I asked him to explain, he stated:

> In our *Ramayana* . . . our Lord Rama was a great believer in human rights. When he killed Ravana, he gave so many chances first, said 'you return my wife, my Sita.' Only when Ravana did not do that did Ramji attack and kill Ravana. So these human rights concepts are not new. They are ancient.

This officer understands religious values and human rights not only in the elimination of violence, but also in the care one takes to avoid it when possible.

A mid-ranking police officer from Uttar Pradesh was unusual: he was the only officer in the study who consistently condemned torture. He enthusiastically expressed his admiration for Gandhi and asserted, "Nonviolence is the most important religion." When I asked how it is possible for a police officer to do his job without violence, he replied, "Those who do not have nonviolence in them, they cannot stop violence." Like the other officers, however, he sees religious and human rights ideals as possible to maintain only as far as the goals of officers and of the state are not compromised. He argued, "Religion does give us permission to use violent methods when the situation is bad and a lot of wrong things are happening," and provided an example:

> OFFICER: From the Ramayana, when there was a fight between Ram and Ravana. Hanuman was asked to find Sita. He went to Lanka, and he wanted to see the city and started to eat fruits from the garden. The guards saw him and caught him, so they tried to punish him by burning his tail. So he changed his body into a small form, and then he burned the whole city by jumping around.
>
> RW: How is that an example of how violence is okay?
>
> OFFICER: It was apparent that in Lanka there were more bad people, and Hanuman gave them an answer by burning their city. There was a fight between Ram and Ravana, and the right side won.

These interviews reveal how officers can draw from religious ideals to support both human rights and violence. They are also suggestive of the complexity of any tradition. Just as the human rights framework contains conflicting tenets, so, too, do religious traditions. Officers' comments show how state actors draw from different aspects of these traditions as they reconcile them with violence. Traditions of nonviolence, propagated in the modern era by figures like Gandhi, as well as ancient religious stories in which violence is sometimes just, are both salient to officers and available to them when they explain their actions.

Negotiation Concluded: The Trumps of Justice, Security, and the Nature of Policing

Officers are not always able to resolve tensions between human rights and what they see as traditional values, on the one hand, and violence, on the other. At times, they acknowledge their stance as a rejection not only of human rights, but also of Indian cultural or religious values. For example, a high-ranking officer in Delhi related:

> The basic Indian culture adheres to the Gandhian way, where violence has no role. . . . The majority of the population believes in this nonviolence. But younger people are believing that the Gandhian way of life is not successful and that a little state violence is required. Cross-border terrorism cannot be solved with Gandhian methods. A criminal is a person without a soul, and the standard techniques for people with souls cannot be applicable.

This officer made distinctions between those who do and do not deserve the benefits of values celebrated by national icons. He elaborated:

> There are two categories of criminals. [The first is] indoctrinated criminals who want to spread communal violence. Gandhian methods won't work on them. But for others, Gandhian methods of reform can work.

He did not only negotiate in this way in regard to Indian traditions: he made an almost identical statement at another point in the interview, this time positioning the violence he endorsed against human rights and democratic culture:

> Democratic culture says that arbitrary killing is not permissible because no life should be taken without the opportunity to defend himself. So extrajudicial killings are not possible. Only capital punishment after trial. State violence is not possible. But dreaded criminals are so strong [that] they need to be killed on the spot.

He argued that "human rights activists" try to protect criminals from torture and extrajudicial killing because they view everything from "a human rights perspective," rather than in terms of the "potential loss to society" if criminals are left unchecked. This police officer does not equate human rights with "the West" and his values with "Indian" society. Rather, he sees human rights and some Indian values as endorsing the same nonviolence, but rejects them both for certain types of people. Similarly, a member of the armed forces admires Gandhian nonviolence but dismisses it as impractical for national interests. He stated:

> I admire Gandhiji because of his way of presenting in a nonviolent way. He had a great way of dealing with things. That's why we achieved independence.

When I asked about the relevance of Gandhi for the armed forces, he replied:

> We don't work on that policy. Arms and ammunition are there to protect. Violence as such should not come out in a bad way. But we have to protect our country.

Even though these officers acknowledge nonviolence as the philosophy of the "father of the nation," as Gandhi is considered, they still reject it, just as they reject human rights. What is significant is not merely that the officer admires, but ultimately rejects nonviolence. Rather, the important point is that when officers justify violence, it is not only a Western notion of "human rights" they are rejecting, but also values that they see as part of Indian traditions.

Cross-Pressures

Charles Taylor discusses the ubiquity of "cross-pressures."[10] He means that almost all people now experience the pull of both religious and secular worldviews. Few people in the contemporary world, he argues, are exposed to only one way of understanding their lives. The hallmark of our era is the "fragilization" of each moral order. Even for deeply religious people, the awareness that many others live according to other frameworks is unavoidable. A past in which a particular conception of the world was the only one possible is now inaccessible to us.

Taylor depicts variations not only between religious and secular traditions, but within secular worldviews as well, particularly on the question of violence. Secular traditions include warrior ethics that valorize violence, for example, as well as humanistic stances in which self-interest and mutual benefit align in peaceful coexistence. Likewise, the same religious traditions have inspired righteous violence, as much as they have respect for all life.

The officers in this study understand the secular "right to life," but know that violence is supported by an (also secular) culture of policing. They see nonviolence as affirmed by their religious traditions in the values of compassion and care, but also understand their religions as sometimes supporting violence. In such a cross-pressured world, ultimately people emphasize one set of values over another, but it can be difficult to predict which values those will be. Police recognize competing goods and feel they must negotiate and reconcile them, but when they do, they do so in favor of what they believe is required of their profession.

These competing ethics do not represent anything as straightforward as a clash of cultures. In some ways, officers' statements align with assertions about Indian ethical traditions. Police frequently attest that it is not possible to follow rules unconditionally, because so much depends upon what is required by the situation. And they also sometimes explain their actions by referencing their relationships with others, such as the importance of responding to the parents of the missing woman in the NGO report discussed in the introduction. This is, in a sense, consistent with depictions of Indian ethics as based in context and relationship, as what matters to officers is what the situation requires, and responding to people who inhabit certain social roles.

What may be more significant than *that* officers emphasize context and relationship, however, is *which* aspects of context and relationship they see as important and why. Although they believe they should adjust their behavior to the requirements of the situation and respond to significant people, police explain the importance of doing so by reference to abstract notions of justice and order. When they speak about relationships, they prioritize fulfilling their duty to those they see as innocent or to their supervisors. They draw from abstract categories of guilt and innocence, like "hardcore" criminals and regular criminals, and from goals, such as "maintaining order," to articulate the reasons for which they act. This suggests that a clear dichotomy between a "Western" justice-based orientation and an "Indian" tradition focused on context and relationship does not exist among these police officers.

Moreover, as discussed in previous chapters, police across the world share these officers' beliefs about justice. Law enforcers from Western and non-Western countries alike often believe that they should be able to bend the rules—and the law—for the sake of justice and security.[11] Taken in this light, these officers' beliefs reflect the aims, ideology, and pressures of policing across contexts, rather than an Indian as opposed to Western viewpoint.

Any dichotomy between Indian and Western conceptions of justice is also complicated by the long history of Indian movements for social justice. Indian theorists have pointed out that although Western political philosophers were the first to articulate the liberal tradition of universal rights, in practice, Western governments typically failed to extend rights universally. The legal scholar Upendra Baxi notes that the independence movements of former colonies, as well as the struggles for equality of oppressed groups within the West, were key in actualizing the freedoms Western liberal theorists merely described.[12] Baxi and others have noted that the Indian independence struggle spoke many ethical languages and was by no means confined to that of rights. But it did seek the recognition of rights that the British celebrated at home and failed to grant others abroad.[13]

Richard Shweder and his colleagues suggest that different societies articulate and endorse different values, but competing values are often still recognized within each society.[14] Another way to think about this is that people in all societies likely experience similar tensions, for example, between attending to relationships and respecting moral rules that are neutral in regard to relationships. And even this is fraught—for most individuals, particularly in the current world that is cross-pollinated by so many conceptions of the good, conflicting ideas about how one should act are likely to abound. The history of colonialism, the spread of media and other modes of communication, and numerous other forms of globalization make this especially likely. Culture may be defined not by whether people recognize and experience the pull of competing values, but by how they believe they should resolve them.

Implications for Human Rights Protection

That officers resolve these cross-pressures by favoring their identities as police above their religious and other cultural affiliations is problematic for a human rights movement that has long emphasized making connections to local culture. Indeed, scholars suggest that reformers conduct a "cultural audit" to identify the local beliefs that best support their agenda.[15] Researchers frequently assert that new norms spread more easily when there is a "cultural match," and that activists and educators can make norms seem like a better match by framing or vernacularizing them to accord with local culture.[16] But it is clear that any culture contains competing values from which individuals may draw as they respond to such efforts. In the case of the Indian police, at least, a "culture of policing" trumps more traditional ways of understanding local culture.

This is not to suggest that human rights scholars, activists, and educators should not connect rights to a community's religious or other cultural beliefs. It is possible that the police in this study would not have so enthusiastically adopted the rights-friendly views they do endorse, such as in regard to children, had educators not connected rights to their religion. Moreover, one police officer interviewed for this book, who was highly unusual in his consistent and passionate condemnation of torture, is also deeply religious, and asserts that his stance on torture is due to his religiosity. The following dialogue with him demonstrates the depth of his religious commitment and its influence on his views:

> RW: Is torture ever right?
>
> OFFICER: No, never.
>
> RW: Why?
>
> OFFICER: The human being is a good and beautiful creature made by God. Humans can think, so we can come to the conclusion that if a person commits a crime, then there are other ways to solve it. Nowhere in the constitution of India or anywhere in the world has this been mentioned [that torture is acceptable].
>
> RW: Why do you think differently about this than other police officers?

OFFICER: The reason perhaps I am more sympathetic is [that] since childhood, I have been reading Hindu religious books. Humanity has been discussed in great detail in these books. Somewhere that influenced me to study the human rights course.

My Hindi translator informed me that although this man is a low-ranking officer, he speaks eloquently on religious topics and has been especially well educated in them. So it is possible that framing human rights in terms of religious values may be effective for some officers who are already deeply committed to a rights-affirming understanding of their religions. Moreover, connecting rights to religious and other beliefs may be more successful in a course that meets the pedagogical standards human rights educators argue are important, such as learner-centered methods.

What these interviews suggest, however, is one way that people respond to efforts to connect a new moral order to an older one: by drawing on competing beliefs that deflect both the older and newer order, or by interpreting the new beliefs in ways that do not compete with the beliefs they prioritize. Given the complexity of any local context revealed by this response, educators might best reach beyond conceptions of geographically bound locality to draw more specifically on the mores of the particular group in question.

In this case, knowledge of the culture of policing with which these officers identify would inform educators' approach at least as much as understanding officers' religious beliefs. Understanding this culture, as well as its local particularities, may be more pressing for human rights workers than a broader conceptualization of a country's cultural heritage.

This is rife with obstacles, however, as this policing culture is the most resistant to rights norms, and framing these norms in officers' terms has the most potential to distort them—as is clear from officers' own formulations. Furthermore, the human rights movement, and the religious ideals to which it most readily connects, are not only in competition with other local beliefs. Police also readily draw support for violence from international sources, which have diffused in India at least as widely as human rights. The next chapter explores how officers reference international norms and actions to bolster the legitimacy of torture and other forms of extrajudicial violence.

Chapter 6

Complications of the Global: Competing International Norms

NGOs think in one way. Their point of view is purely in favor of civilians. But officers think about security. NGOs think terrorists can be scared, but innocent people should not die. But security forces say anyhow that the culprits should not escape. All action has been for the good of society.

—*Low-ranking paramilitary police officer, Kashmir/Delhi*

SPEAKING TO T, one is more surprised that he has spent his life as a policeman than that he possesses a degree in politics. His conversation is peppered with references to Plato, Aristotle, Marx, and Locke, as well as Indian thinkers such as Gandhi and Vivikenanda. He is a high-ranking member of the Indian Police Service, which he entered after having completed a degree in political science and scoring well on the competitive national exam. He hopes to return to academia after retirement and has ambitions to write a book on his theory of policing.

In our first and third interviews, he was articulate but conflicted. He lamented the corruption and disorganization that plague the police. These limitations, coupled with the challenges of policing a complex society, make extrajudicial methods seem sometimes necessary, he conceded. Ultimately, though, T told me that he is a "great believer in democracy" and insisted that it should be possible to police without resorting to torture.

His second interview was radically different from our first and last conversations. The conflict seemed to have evaporated since we first met. He insisted over many hours that only after sustained physical torture can terrorists and hardcore criminals "break." He saw an irredeemable conflict between democracy and policing, and viewed human rights as an unwelcome constraint that has caused terrorists and other criminals to increase in number. Human rights monitoring makes it more difficult for the police to torture and kill criminals, he told me, and this undermines security.

It is unclear what caused this temporary change of heart. Shortly before this conversation, a bomb exploded in a district of Delhi that is within his jurisdiction, killing several people. It is possible that this radicalized his position. But whatever the reason, what is clear is that when he changed his mind, a ready-made discourse of security was available to him to justify his position. Torture and illegal executions are not a problem of Indian police, he is able to say, but are a response to the inherent requirements of any modern state. To prove his point, he, like other officers, has a quick point of reference: Just look at what the United States has done. For these officers, Guantanamo Bay, Abu Ghraib, and Bagram justify the torture that occurs in New Delhi.

Rejecting Rights in Favor of Security

When there is a conflict between rights and security, and they cannot interpret the former in terms of the latter, police are explicit about which must trump. Moreover, rather than draw on what might be thought of as local beliefs to oppose international human rights, they often base their arguments in a competing principle of contemporary liberalism: the protection of the state. Furthermore, officers defend their stance by referencing the actions of countries such as the United States. Hence, when they contest human rights, they have recourse to a competing international order composed of the discourse and practices undertaken for the sake of security by powerful Western governments.

The Trump of Security

While the term *public good* could denote the protection of individual rights, officers use it to refer to national security, and to them, rights that undermine security are untenable. Human rights activists typically agree that security is important, but see security and human rights protection as beneficial to each other. They assert that it is not necessary to violate rights in order to uphold security, and that rights protection creates a more secure society. But in the eyes of law enforcement officers, security and human rights are inevitably in conflict.

Officers frequently articulate this belief when discussing the State of Emergency declared under Indira Gandhi from 1975 until 1977, when the government suspended many basic rights as a response to political and social unrest. During this time, arrest without warrant and police torture of political activists, students, and opponents of the ruling party were rampant. Yet all of the officers whom I asked about the Emergency defended it. For example, when I asked a mid-ranking army officer serving in Kashmir whether "something like the Emergency is necessary in order to maintain security," he argued, "Yes, security does not come without a price. It does not come for the weak. You have to make yourself strong." I then asked him what he thinks of the common perception that many innocent people were jailed during the Emergency, and he replied, "These were strong decisions that were supposed to be taken because security is not without a cost."

That officers express this view in response to questions about the Emergency bears special relevance to their actions, because officers in Kashmir and parts of the Northeast are currently working under Emergency laws that allow for powers similar to those that characterized the Emergency in 1975. Hence they are justifying not only a historical event, but also their own actions in the present.

Because officers believe that their primary function is to promote security, they view their violations of rights not as obstructions of justice, but as minor infringements of technical rules that at best are ill adapted to the situation. For example, a low-ranking paramilitary police officer serving in Delhi, who had been previously stationed in Kashmir, asserted:

> When you find someone is really the accused, the prime task is to arrest him. In such procedures, if there is time to follow the procedure laid down by law and human rights, then it should be [followed]. But if there is not time, our main task is to arrest the person. In such cases an arrest warrant may not be able to be generated. When you have sufficient time, then the full process should be followed.

It is not that this officer is unaware of human rights requirements or domestic law, which education could solve. And it is not that he acts with no regard for any ethical or legal goal and purely for personal gain, which perhaps punishment or normative persuasion could help mitigate. Instead, his comments suggest that he sees human rights laws as less important than other goods.

Similarly, a high-ranking paramilitary officer expressed throughout the interview his support for human rights in the abstract. But he still cautioned, "Just for the mere sake of enforcing one's rights we cannot function less," and proceeded to justify human rights violations such as torture. Like the other officers, he did not outright deny the value of any human rights protection, but rather argued about when and to what extent rights should be upheld. He asserted:

> There is no proper yardstick to judge how human rights can be enforced and how human value can be maintained. You can't always go on ensuring the human value of a person because the profession is like this.

These comments suggest that officers cease to engage seriously with human rights ideals and laws once they believe these conflict with their priorities. The paramilitary officer just quoted quipped, "Should I take the suspected person to a three-star hotel, offer him a glass of beer? No [laughing]. Human rights." He dismissed the legitimacy of rights by implying that their importance is laughable compared to that of security.

Officers' capacity to resist human rights educators' efforts to persuade them may be bolstered by their ability to understand how their priorities differ from the human rights perspective. This is exemplified in the quote that opens this chapter, wherein a low-ranking paramilitary officer distinguishes the concern for civilians that he believes characterizes NGOs from the focus on security that he asserts defines his profession. He provided this explanation in response to a report I had given him, which alleged that military officers had illegally arrested and severely beaten a man who was later found dead. The incident took place in Assam, where, as in Kashmir, Emergency laws that provide security officers with expanded policing powers are in effect. His comment in response to my question of why human rights activists criticized the action indicated that he is able to frame activists' critique as a matter of competing priorities. Again, these comments do not suggest a lack of knowledge about human rights or an absence of substantive beliefs. Rather, he is aware of human rights principles but disagrees, and is able to articulate the nature of his disagreement. A mere addition of information and principles through an education program would be unlikely to change his outlook.

Officers are so committed to the priority of security over rights that they are willing to accept consequences that they admit are highly negative. This acceptance extends to harming people who are clearly innocent, such as children. For example, a high-ranking army officer who had been stationed in Kashmir discussed the possible consequences of military activities:

> If an innocent is shot unknowingly by mistake [like] small children sometimes in a firefight. Despite our best efforts, there are one or two per year. If you make a political issue out of it, if you make it anti-army where people get a personal benefit, then the soldiers lose their motivation. They don't feel wanted. They feel, why should they work if people don't want them? Why should we leave the barracks? And then the whole state will collapse.

This officer described an action that is considered wrong, not only in the human rights system, but in most ethnical frameworks—the killing of children.

He still argued, however, that officers responsible for the death of children should not be punished. He maintained this, not because he thinks it is right to kill children, but because he believes that punishment would decrease morale and thereby compromise security.

Human Rights versus the State: Tension in Officers' Explanations

This compromise of the security of specific people—even children, as in the previous example—for the sake of national security indicates a tension in officers' explanations. They argue that they violate rights for the sake of security. However their actions compromise the personal security of those whose rights they violate. Moreover, their actions are often illegal and hence compromise law and order, further undermining the personal security of members of the public. This suggests that the terms *security* and *law and order* are often meant to express the state's interests or officers' goals, rather than the welfare of a community. For example, a mid-ranking military officer who had been stationed in Kashmir noted that there are different interpretations of what *human rights* means. I asked him to describe the different interpretations of human rights in Kashmir. He replied by switching focus to what he claimed is the primary question, that of national interest. He stated:

> What is the national aim? We should always think of the national aim. Our aim is to keep J & K [Jammu and Kashmir] integrated with India and not breaking away. If you want that, then you must maintain law and order.

This suggests that he understands "law and order" not as something that serves the local population, but rather as something that is for the sake of the state's control over the territory. This clarifies why the violation of the security of some people, even children, is not a violation of "security" as officers understand it. In this formulation, the point of security or law and order is to promote the interests of the state. This may conflict with the interests of civilians in general, and especially with the interests of particular civilians, such as those who happen to live in states experiencing conflict or those whom officers suspect of crimes.

This also helps explain officers' reasoning regarding Emergency laws. When I asked a mid-ranking State Police Service officer from Rajasthan whether it is ever acceptable to limit rights, he replied:

> Yes. Times of national emergency, internal threat. To agitate in an aggressive

form and damage public property, to cause big stress to people cannot be allowed in the name of human rights.

I then asked him whether the human rights system contains guidance regarding when rights can be limited, and he responded:

> The Indian constitution gives clauses for each right. Please read the fundamental rights. Nothing should threaten the unity and integrity of the nation. If any sect is doing something that feeds the separation, that breaks unity, doing something that makes you realize you are a Christian and I am a Hindu. Integrity means utmost faith in the system. If a common man breaks the law and nothing happens, then there is a loss of faith in the law.

This officer argued that even heightening awareness of religious identity can be grounds for punishment for the sake of security, because nothing should threaten national unity—although the comment should be understood in the context of significant religious violence in India. It is also only the civilian breaking the law who threatens its authority, rather than police, who would presumably break it only for the sake of the state's interest.

Conflict settings such as Kashmir offer officers a particularly strong defense of their position given the Emergency laws that provide legal backing to the priority they place on security over rights. Human rights professionals emphasize, however, that violations by the police and security forces are rampant throughout India and are by no means limited to areas of conflict. Interviews support this assertion, as civil police serving in regions without Emergency law prioritize security above rights to the same extent. They did not have a specific "emergency" situation to draw on in their explanations. Instead, they tend to understand their work as occurring in a kind of undeclared emergency, perceiving Indian society as chaotic and lawless.

Protections from the State by the State: Tensions in the Rights Framework

Human rights are intended to protect civilians against the state. In spite of efforts to create accountability above national governments, state actors such as police officers, bear the primary responsibility for protecting these rights. As with the way they interpret rights as based on security (see chapter 4), their rejection of rights for the sake of security is a reminder of why this is problematic.

Although human rights education programs stress the importance of reaching law enforcement officers, the latter's comments indicate that they do not act alone. As state agents, they exist within a web of expectations, commands, rewards, and punishments that typically center at best on the goals of the state, and at worst (in cases of corruption) on the private goals of individuals. Although some decisions officers make are likely within their control, their role as frontline representatives of the government at times poses inherent difficulties for their role as defenders of human rights against the government. This is especially the case when elected officials have significant influence over police officers' careers, as is the case in India. Hence basing the protection of civilians *from* the state *in* state actors is beset by inherent difficulties.

This is all the more the case given that officers perceive their role to be that of state representatives more than that of representatives of an abstract "rule of law." When I asked how police should deal with political protests, one officer reflected, "The elected government do what they want through the police." Another officer responded to my questions about police violence against protestors similarly, arguing, "As law enforcement officers, we are supposed to follow the government." He went on to say that violence should be avoided, but if people are disobeying the government, then officers are left with little choice. Another officer noted that the police must follow the orders of the government, musing that the police are like "the fingers" in relation to the brain: "When my brain tells my fingers to pick up the food to eat," he quipped, "they do so."

Although the establishment of government human rights bodies is an important achievement by human rights standards, it is fraught with these tensions. An officer who is responsible for investigating allegations of police abuse for a state human rights commission responded to my questions about a recent episode, in which police beat impoverished farmers who were protesting the government's seizure of their land. He replied, "That is not in the purview of the human rights commissions. When a factory comes, the government is bound to displace people, so the matter is not referred to us." This suggests that state human rights bodies likely address only those matters that the state considers human rights violations, which are unlikely to include state actions that are in the national interest.

This tension is compounded by the fact that officials in the National and State Human Rights Commissions who are responsible for investigating errant police behavior are themselves police officers. I asked the state human rights commission investigator about the challenges he faces in his work. He responded, "We always conduct inquiries against our fellow brothers." He reassured me that "when someone is violating the human rights of an individual, he is brought to task." However, he also admitted the difficulty in this arrangement, noting, "As government, we have to conduct the inquiry against other government servants." In spite of this officer's assertion, officers who torture are rarely "brought to task," as described in chapter 1.[1]

This lack of punishment may be partially explained by the beliefs and perceptions of the investigating officers within the National Human Rights Commission. In-depth interviews with these officials reveal that they hold many of the same views about torture articulated by officers serving in the field. They stress the incorrigibility of certain types of criminals, the pressures on officers to solve cases, and the expectations of supervisors and the public as motivating torture. They also note the ways in which officers' own human rights are violated by the conditions in which they work, and suggest that officers' exhaustion, combined with a lack of training, also contribute to torture. They acknowledge that the law against torture should be upheld, but express sympathy with officers who they suggest have few options outside the use of torture.

That the officials who are responsible for investigating and punishing officers share the latter's perceptions and empathize with their situation may deter them from punishing those who use torture. As police officers—and state representatives—they seemed to be hesitant to punish other officers whose constraints they understand so well.

Resistance to Human Rights: Competing International Norms

A premise of much scholarly work is that ideational obstacles to international human rights primarily take the form of domestic or local norms and values. This can be seen in the emphasis many researchers place on framing human rights in ways that match local culture.[2] Officers' comments reveal that they do endorse norms and values that could be construed as "local" and that oppose human rights. But they also articulate their resistance to human rights in terms that align with and explicitly reference competing international principles. They defend the use of torture by drawing from the international consensus on the importance of state security and national integrity. They point to human rights violations committed in the name of security by powerful countries such as the United States, and argue that any country would and should prioritize the nation above individual rights.

This suggests that domestic contexts are sites of contestation between competing international principles, as local actors draw from those that advance their interests and values, and use them to form an internationally recognized "legitimate" argument against those norms they reject. For example, I asked a mid-ranking police officer in Uttar Pradesh whether it is possible to maintain law and order while still respecting human rights. He replied:

> No, it is not possible to do both. In developed countries also. The United States is violating human rights in Afghanistan, dropping bombs. People are dying. But you can say that they are doing good fighting terrorism.

Similarly, the high-ranking police officer in New Delhi whose vignette opened this chapter drew from the actions of the United States as part of his defense of police "encounter" killings in India (wherein the police assassinate suspected criminals). He first discussed the need for the practice in India, and argued against the human rights and laws that restrict it. He asserted:

> I understand the concerns of civil society. But once a person has been caught red-handed and is guilty without a doubt—normally, this person is killed by police in a staged fake encounter. This used to be effective, because terrorists knew that once they were classified as terrorists, they would be killed. This kept the terrorist population under control. But once the human rights commission and the judiciary started interfering, this is done less and less, and this is helping terrorism to spread.

Shortly thereafter, I asked him to elaborate on an earlier assertion that a tension exists between police work and democratic values. He explained:

> Democratic culture says that arbitrary killing is not permissible, because no life should be taken without the opportunity to defend himself. So extrajudicial killings are not possible. Only capital punishment after trial. State violence is not possible. But dreaded criminals are so strong they need to be killed on the spot. I am quoting your president. Your president ordered Osama to be killed.

Here, the American president's decision to order the killing of an iconic international terrorist is salient for a police officer in Delhi when he justifies domestic extrajudicial killing by the police. His transition from discussing police violence in Delhi to international violence by the United States suggests the point he may be making: if assassination without trial can be justified in some cases, then there are indeed times when "inalienable" human rights must be sacrificed. He implies that if it is right for the United States, who is to say that it is not legitimate for other states with domestic problems? Hence international actions by faraway states can have meaning for how local state actors defend their own actions.

The United States is not the only country that police reference. For example, a high-ranking police officer from Punjab seemed to point to Israel's legalization of practices that are considered torture under international law.[3] He stated:

> You have to extract information from people. A little bit of pain is very important. Pain has been accepted in the entire schema of things. Like with the Palestinian issue. It was accepted at the international level that there should be some torture to get information from extremists.

It is unclear what he meant here by the "international level" in reference to the torture of Palestinians. At the least, the comment suggests that he believes this violence took place with some level of approval, or at least without significant international condemnation.

At other times, officers stop short of arguing for the legitimacy of human rights violations, but point them out in other countries to suggest their inevitability. For example, I asked a mid-ranking army officer in Kashmir why human rights organizations criticize the army. After first musing that human rights activists have a job to do and "must make a big deal of things," he stated, "There are aberrations everywhere, including among the US forces in Afghanistan." He later made this point again when describing the human rights course in which he is enrolled. He mentioned that in the course, they learn about "types of abuses in different places like America, Israel, Gaza, and India—anywhere it could be." A mid-ranking police officer made a similar point. When I asked for his view of an NGO report on police torture in India, he replied, "Everywhere this happens, not just in India only. It can happen anywhere, in the Netherlands." When I asked a high-ranking Indian Police Service officer from Madhya Pradesh about police violence in India, he compared the situation to the United States, reflecting:

> It happened in Los Angeles. Because people did not have faith in the police, there was a communal riot. Also in New Orleans, it was found that the majority of the police were in the hands of hooligans. The new chief demanded that overnight the salary of police should double and that the people who have authority should be properly trained and paid.

He seems to approve of the way New Orleans responded to the problem, by training and properly paying police. But he also points to the ubiquity of the problem of police violence, or at least its presence in the United States, as a way of explaining its presence in India. Similarly, a high-ranking Indian Police Service officer from Punjab discussed his experience in a police training program he attended in New York City. He reflected that the New York Police Department is "quite professional," and that there are "so many things to learn from the New York police." He noted, however, that there is "scope for further improvement." He continued:

> There is torture in New York also. But don't cross the boundary. There is more respect for human dignity there. . . . You can observe certain things. Suppose in India you can go raid a house and pick someone up. In the United States they only pick someone up with evidence. But when they do pick him up, they torture him also. I spent three hours in the police station. This is from firsthand experience.

This comment equivocates; he initially referred to torture in New York as something that should be improved, but quickly transitioned to suggesting that the torture is appropriate because it does not "cross the boundary." Because he defended the use of torture in other parts of the interview, he seems to use this comment to justify the practice, pointing out that the country from whence the researcher has come also uses torture.

At other times, police criticize the United States for torture, even as they defend it in their own country. They wish to point out that those who criticize others for human rights violations are themselves guilty. For example, a low-ranking police officer in Haryana asked me after the conclusion of our interview, "Some philosophers such as Gandhi say that the United States is the biggest violator of human rights. What do you think of this?" A mid-ranking police officer in Uttar Pradesh referred simultaneously to international support for and violation of human rights when he said:

> Human rights have gained a lot of importance at the international level. In the world, human rights are discussed in the context of arrest when people are kept in lock-up. America was criticized in this case in their role in Iraq when they arrested and tortured.

By referencing the ways in which the United States and other countries have violated rights on the world stage, police who are accused of torture in India can make an argument that torture is ubiquitous, and perhaps necessary and just. This is significant in that theorists typically focus their attention on how local norms may inspire resistance to human rights. Although officers' beliefs about justice and the priority of security are salient locally, police are aware of the ways in which such values and aims are internationally recognized and draw from this to explain and defend their actions.

The cross-pressures of the contemporary world become further evident in these revealing statements. Representatives of powerful countries like the United States might prefer to think of human rights violations in the "Global South" as unrelated to the actions of their own government, and as due to cultural norms, history, and resource deficiencies elsewhere. Similarly, state officials in India prefer to discuss police violations as caused by cultural and economic backwardness and committed by police in "far-flung" parts of the country. Such a framing posits competing moral orders between a liberal international community composed of rights-respecting national governments on one hand and the "local" places deep within them on the other. But police in "local" places see their violence as consistent with a normative order confirmed by the United States and other countries in their discourse and actions.

Implications for Human Rights Protection

Officers' rejection of human rights in favor of what they refer to as security or law and order presents particular problems for the spread of human rights norms. First, just as when they negotiate human rights, when officers reject rights, they do not deny violations. These officers admit the occurrence of violations and argue that they are worthwhile for the sake of more important goals. Hence this presents the same obstacle as officers' negotiations of rights for the "norm spiral," in which state agents' tactical concessions to rights should in theory trap them into compliance, when eventually activists can pressure them to close the gap between what they say and what they do.[4] In contrast, the officers in this study do not become trapped in the logic of rights by denying violations. Instead, they defend violations, either by negotiating rights as discussed in chapter 4 or by drawing on competing values and goals. In both of these responses, they draw on discourses that enjoy international legitimacy: those of liberalism and modern state authority.

Second, the officers in this study do not entirely ignore or disregard human rights arguments in favor of purely selfish aims. They instead argue in favor of goods that conflict with the rights framework. Educators and activists face not just a rejection of rights, then, but also beliefs and priorities that motivate these rejections. They need to convince officers that human rights are vital, but also that rights are more important than security, or at least that they do not conflict with security.

This challenge is similar to that faced by international activists who seek to influence elite state decision-makers. Previous research suggests that state leaders are more likely to violate international norms when they view the transgression as a way to promote another good.[5] A similar process may be at work among local-level domestic state actors in regard to torture. The police, and at times the public, view this violence as a necessary means of upholding security and justice. The existence of these competing values may make it easier for officers to defend—and perhaps for the public to support—what may otherwise be understood as morally problematic. These competing values may also make the self-interest involved in such violence more forgivable in the view of those who commit it and in the view of the public, which indicates an obstacle for human rights educators.

Third, that these officers understand rights principles and still disagree with them presents a problem for programs that are premised on the idea that violations arise primarily out of ignorance and aim to solve this through the addition of information about human rights.

Fourth, a major obstacle to rights diffusion is the normative legitimacy that officers' beliefs sometimes hold on the world stage. Officers are aware of and reference norms of state security codified in domestic law and demonstrated in the actions of countries like the United States. In this way, officers have a vast normative resource on which to draw to justify violations of human rights.

Finally, these obstacles point to a tension in the human rights framework. The protection of civilians from the state is based in the state itself. State actors work in institutions that reflect the interests and priorities of the state. They are limited (to greater or lesser degrees, depending on the country) in the extent to which they are likely to protect citizens from the state. Hence, even after a government has signed a human rights treaty, it is not just individual aberrant officers against whom human rights workers must argue, but also the interests of the state and the apparatus and norms that support those interests. This is particularly the case in national contexts where institutions meant to check state power do not have sufficient influence. In India, this tension is exacerbated by laws that limit the ability of civilians to prosecute public officials in court, along with corruption in the legal and political systems.

Just as law enforcement officers are aware of the discursive resources at their disposal, they also have ready explanations for why their judgments on rights are so different from the activists who dedicate themselves to their protection, to which I turn in the chapter that follows. Indeed, officers' responses not just to human rights messages, but also to activists themselves, reveal another obstacle for the global spread of these norms.

Chapter 7

Police Respond to Human Rights Activists

Allegations are not freedom of speech. You have a right to present your case in a way that doesn't harm other people, not bullshitting people, not humiliating others, not pulling others down. . . . In a sober way, they should come forth to the military and understand we are working in a sensitive atmosphere. Decent is not calling all the media and TV channels and throwing stones.

—*Mid-ranking army officer, Kashmir/West Bengal*

M HAS A WRY SENSE OF HUMOR. When I asked in what circumstances he believes it is appropriate for the National Human Rights Commission to prosecute officers for violations, he quipped that he cannot dictate to the commission and that they should do as they please. Then he added, "The best way to avoid fingers being pointed at you is to do nothing at all."

This proclivity to "function less" is the effect he believes human rights activists have on the security forces. M occupies a difficult post in the "disturbed" state of Kashmir. He is a major in the army and possesses the powers and burdens of police only because of the State of Emergency laws in the state. As such, he is the target of international and domestic criticism, as activists continue the fight to repeal the laws that allow the army vast discretion in the use of force against the majority Muslim population, including the right to "shoot to kill" civilians for offenses as mundane as gathering in groups of five or more.

M is also earnest. He spoke with regret of the distance his post puts between him and his family, though the warmth among his fellow officers compensates to some extent. During my year in Delhi, his family arranged a marriage for him. His new wife soon joined him in Kashmir, though he relayed that she, too, suffered from the isolation.

M spoke to me for many hours, discussing his understanding of why acts such as torture and the imprisonment of youth should be allowed. Many of these reasons rest on his understanding not just of what is right, but also of what is true. He doesn't see a legitimate movement for independence in Kashmir;

rather, he assumes that people will always disrupt the happiness of others and can be checked only by a strong security force. He believes that youth pose a particular danger to society due to their tendency to throw caution to the wind.

But at times he admitted genuine confusion. After a long discussion of Kashmiri separatists' motivations, he lamented, "What is independence? It is freedom to elect your officials, freedom to express your religion, freedom to education. . . . All these things are there in Kashmir." Then he confessed in a hoarse voice, "I don't know what it is they want."

When he tries to guess, he often does so without engaging the content of Kashmiri complaints. Rather than consider why some people object to India's rule, he views them in the same way he does human rights activists: they are likely being paid, or jealous of what others possess, or they are just fulfilling the role set out for them. In other words, neither those who object to the government nor human rights activists who protest their abuse are genuine in their complaints, and hence not legitimate.

Delegitimizing the Other

Police and military officers know that they use rights language in ways that conflict with the arguments of rights activists; indeed, they are often explicitly undermining activists' criticisms of police when they take up the discourse of rights. At times, they understand this as a legitimate difference of opinion. But more frequently, they do what people on opposing sides do so often: they delegitimize their opponents by questioning their competence and motives.

Human Rights Workers as Adversaries

Human Rights Workers as Illegitimate

Police believe they uphold justice, even if imperfectly, so what they perceive as human rights activists' "attacks" put activists on the wrong side of justice. Moreover, they believe that protecting the rights of "criminals" or "terrorists" is contrary to the purpose of justice, so they are suspicious of those who advocate on suspects' behalf. They attribute advocacy for suspects to foreign interference from countries that wish to see India fail, such as the United States or Pakistan, or to the self-interest of human rights groups which promote themselves to secure funding. At best, police believe that human rights activists may be well meaning, but lack the knowledge necessary to evaluate the situations in which police work. In other words, officers see activists as corrupt in their motivations in the worst case, or naively idealistic in the best case. Drawing on the view that these activists lack credibility, officers disregard activists' messages that conflict with their actions.

Often, officers' perceptions of activists include a mixture of these different views, all of which call the latter's legitimacy into question. For example, in response to the NGO report that criticizes the police for allegedly torturing a suspect (recall Ajay) in custody, a mid-ranking police officer in Haryana argued:

> The NGO is criticizing because they are not aware of the actual facts. They don't know the way our society thinks. They blame the police because they don't know the truth. If the police are investigating, asking questions, then the police [are] doing all this to solve the case, and if the police [are] not doing all this, then how [are] the police going to solve the case? The NGO people don't understand that the police have that right. They can question anybody. Then people start saying that the police are harassing them. Actually, not many people come forward to help the police. . . . People should cooperate. Every man should have the right facts before questioning. But there is nothing like that in our society. Many times criminals blame the police for doing wrong things to them, like rape in some cases. Then the media and NGOs all come and write things . . . which is not right.

I then asked the officer why NGOs and the media (which officers typically see as in league with each other) behave in this way. He responded:

> The mentality of the NGOs and the media is they highlight everything police do, and then the culprits blame the police for something they have not done. Say women culprits blame the police for rape when they have not raped them. . . . There is a lack of knowledge among the media people. There is small thinking. Some NGOs work for their own selfish reasons like politics, though there are some good NGOs. Article Eleven of the Universal Declaration of Human Rights says nobody can say anything against anyone unless the charges have been proved. But if a culprit says something for his own protection and blames a police officer, then the media gets hold of it. There is an absence of quality in the media. They take their cameras and run around, and it leads not to harmony but to violence. They don't care about the results.

This officer draws on the perception that NGOs and the media are uninformed, corrupt in their motivations, and highly biased against police. Given all this, the officer can argue it is not "human rights" he rejects, but the activists themselves.

Officers often draw from this range of reasons to undermine the legitimacy of activists who criticize them. A mid-ranking army officer in Kashmir reasoned:

> At least fifty to a hundred human rights organizations must be keeping an eye on J and K [Jammu and Kashmir]. So what is the infrastructure here? There will be something that is reported to them that is not verified. Last week an incident was reported. A lady came and said she was kidnapped and raped for two days by the army. So the separatists used this to say that the army is violating human rights. The whole issue was taken up by the army, and the army said the person would be punished. . . . All this sound about human rights abuse. But then she contradicted her own statements. . . . Then came the proof that she is lying. The medical exam doctor said that there had been no penetration for seventy-two hours. . . . You can get anything, and it will become an issue. Human rights organizations are doing their jobs. If they don't give their reports, people will think they are sleeping. The same is true for the separatist forces. Everyone has a job to do.

In this passage, the officer rejects the legitimacy of human rights complaints against the army in three ways. He first indicates that NGOs are not capable of attaining the facts by pointing to the complexity of the situations in which they work. He then uses the example of a woman who accuses the army of rape, and is then undermined by a medical examination stating otherwise. The "medical" testing of women who report rape in India is a highly controversial issue in itself.[1] Here, the officer uses a doctor's conclusion about the occurrence of recent intercourse as definitive "proof" that the woman had not been sexually assaulted. He draws from this medical opinion to discredit what he sees as the untrustworthy testimony of the woman herself and the NGOs that may have supported her. Lastly, he attributes a motive to NGOs to explain their actions. He suggests that they are working to promote their own interests in the same way that "separatist forces" do. In these ways, the officer can reject anything such organizations have to say.

Human Rights Workers as Biased

Over and over in interviews, law enforcement officers express resentment toward human rights activists for what they perceive as bias against the police. Officers believe that activists are aggressive, and that they aim to punish and humiliate police rather than to resolve conflicts. They assert that activists blame the police and security forces no matter who is in the wrong. For example, a low-ranking paramilitary officer stated:

> Everything has two faces. . . . NGOs always make a view in favor of civilians. They don't try to find out the views of police and the security forces before writing their opinion. The NGOs should try to find out why he has taken such actions.

Many officers express this perception that activists are uninterested in the complexity of the situation and are biased against them. One high-ranking Indian Police Service officer from Madhya Pradesh argued heatedly:

> I would like to make an important point. Human rights should not be used as a tool to protect terrorists. What rules do terrorists have to follow? They can shoot police. Shoot his family. NGOs can criticize police, but they should condemn the terrorists, too. A journalist was killed in Pakistan in the street. Now if those things are not condemned, then these high-sounding human rights groups are working for the benefit of the terrorists at the cost of the police.

This officer believes that human rights criticisms help the enemies of the police, and therefore, he suggests, the enemies of peace and justice. Indeed, officers tend to perceive any claim against the police as a claim in favor of terrorists or criminals. Clearly frustrated, this officer also asserted:

> Security and police personnel always feel that people like you, the NGOs, always see that your approach is not balanced.[2] NGOs only talk about criminals' human rights. Criminals are breaking human rights left, right, and center, and this is a great challenge working with these people. If you think about their fundamental rights, you will find yourself thinking about them in heaven.

Officers often express this feeling that activists assume the police are at fault, and hence cannot be trusted as neutral arbiters of justice.

Human Rights Workers as against Officers' Human Rights

Officers frequently call the legitimacy of human rights workers into question by criticizing them on their own terms. Law enforcers assert that activists care little for the human rights of the police and military. A mid-ranking prison official complained:

> Human rights commissions are working on just one part. They are working just for the prisoners. They are not looking at whether prison officials have human

> rights. They are not looking at the work conditions of prison officials. If human rights have been curtailed, it is only of the prisoners. They think if a prisoner has filed a complaint first, then they think the prisoner's right has been curtailed. They don't look at the conditions in which officers work.

I then asked this officer why prison officials do not complain to the Human Rights Commission about their own working conditions. He responded:

> We have to run the prison, so we don't have time to complain. And before we have done anything, the prisoners have already complained. Sometimes we think, why complain on trivial issues. And there is so much pressure of work. I have so much work. . . . Today, I was thinking that maybe I should postpone your call because I need to take my wife to the hospital since she is not well. What is human rights? It is maintaining the basic dignity of a human being. Suppose a prisoner gives a tight slap to an officer. Then what can we do? We have no weapons. We are empty handed and they are empty handed. We are tens and they are thousands.

This officer refers to human rights ideals to argue that activists undermine their own values when dealing with police. He points to his own humanity, first indirectly by suggesting that his work conditions are so difficult he cannot take his wife to the hospital, and then directly, by pointing to the value of human dignity and the way his own is violated when criminals hit officers. Similarly, an officer of the armed forces attested:

> NGOs see only one side. Have you ever heard NGOs advocating for the human rights of security? The NGOs think the security forces have no rights. But they do have rights.

Beyond the perception that activists disregard their rights, some officers suggest that human rights workers do not even see them as human. For example, a mid-ranking police officer in Kashmir expressed his wish for how a human rights advocate should behave:

> He must be patient. He should be impartial. Sometimes a police officer is right and civilians are wrong. When you attack police, you must understand that the police officer is also human. He is from the society from which you also come.

The perception that activists disregard their humanity may make police even less likely to be swayed by their pleas to respect criminal suspects.

Human Rights Workers as Uninformed

Additionally, several officers voice frustration that human rights activists lack real knowledge of the conditions under which police and security forces work and the challenges they face. For instance, a mid-ranking paramilitary officer in Kashmir drew from this reasoning to deflect criticism of the Armed Forces Special Powers Act (AFSPA). When I asked him about criticisms of the act, he lamented:

> Nobody cares. Nobody knows what are our problems. Maybe human rights violations are there. But they need to see it from both sides. There are situations that may cause these problems. . . . The main problem is identifying the persons. No one is there to assist us. Nobody comes forward to help us.

Asserting that activists do not know or care about the complex problems that lead to violations is another way in which officers reject the legitimacy of the activists, rather than reject human rights ideals in themselves.

Officers Defend Their Intentions

Police seem sensitive to the suggestion that they have bad motives or are incompetent, which is arguably implicit in claims that they violate human rights. For example, many international and local NGOs accuse the security forces of arbitrary arrests and detention of students and political activists in Kashmir.[3] When I asked a mid-ranking army officer in Kashmir about allegations that security forces arrest innocent people, he asserted:

> There are no personal enmities in force here. Nobody says I will take this guy and put him in jail. That creates so much work for you. Nobody wants to take that trouble.

When I asked him about the arrests of students during the Emergency from 1975–1977, he argued:[4]

> Nobody is such a fool that they would put an innocent person in jail. I am not denying that it may also be Indira Gandhi's rivals that were put in jail, but it may not have been only that. Media can never give the full picture.

Officers often defend their intentions by suggesting that any violence that occurs is necessary to the situation. A police officer deflected questions about police violence by asserting:

> We try to do so that such situations don't emerge. We try to talk to people and satisfy them, because if we don't control the situation, there could be bloodshed.

> To stop this from happening, just to make people move away from the place, we have to use different methods like *lathi* [a police stick used for crowd control] charge or tear gas. It is to avoid further loss. Sometimes people get beaten in the process and the media highlights it unnecessarily, although the police have no interest in it. The police work in the public interest.

Along these lines, M explained that decisions to use torture are dependent on external circumstances. When I asked him why an officer would choose not to use torture, he reflected:

> Maybe someone breaks early, or maybe you find out that he is not that bad of a person and you find he was accused because he had a rivalry with someone. We make our conscious decisions. It depends on what kind of pressure is there, the environment, the level of threat. All this racket going on.

In each of these explanations, officers reject the idea that they are motivated by an intrinsic desire to use violence or that they are incompetent. Human rights activists may not explicitly state the reasons they believe officers violate human rights. But officers believe it is implied that their intention or ability is at fault. Indeed, it is difficult to argue that officers are violating human rights and that they should be punished for doing so without implying that something in their motivation or capacity is wrong. Interviews suggest that this perception deepens police resistance to human rights appeals, as they reject what they see as attacks on their character or competence.

Rejecting the Messages by Discrediting the Messengers

Officers sometimes reject activists in the aforementioned ways, while at the same time voicing support for human rights ideals. In so doing, officers align themselves with the premise of human rights, but reject actual rights claims against the police by condemning activists for their means of pursuing such claims. For example, earlier in the interview—in fact, moments before the following excerpt begins—a mid-ranking army officer who served in Kashmir expressed support for the right to free speech, asserting that it is a fundamental right that should never be taken away. However, he rejects this right when it is used as a claim against the army. He does so by taking issue with the manner in which activists exercise the right:

> RW: You said that sometimes people who make allegations against the army must be arrested. Why isn't this a matter of freedom of speech?

OFFICER: Allegations are not freedom of speech. You have a right to present your case in a way that doesn't harm other people, not bullshitting people, not humiliating others, not pulling others down.

RW: Why shouldn't people have the freedom to make allegations?

OFFICER: You have allegations . . . deteriorating the image of the army. You are just alleging fake encounters. . . . They make allegations without evidence and deteriorate the image of the army.

RW: Why are activists making these allegations?

OFFICER: It is their duty to protect the local population. They bring forth the voice of the local people. It is their right to do this. The local people cannot. They should bring forth the problems in a decent way.

RW: What would be a decent way?

OFFICER: In a sober way, they should come forth to the military and understand we are working in a sensitive atmosphere. Decent is not calling all the media and TV channels and throwing stones.

RW: How would you advise a human rights activist to bring forth a case decently?

OFFICER: First, take the consult of the person in writing [saying] these are the allegations of the person against the army. Then you find out: why did the situation happen? Nobody has patience to find out. They just call all the media. They [NGOs] should act as intermediaries between the army and the people, not raise them against each other.

This dialogue illuminates the way in which officers understand and say they respect human rights ideals, such as freedom of speech, and human rights work, such as defending the local population in Kashmir against abuse from the armed forces. At the same time, they also reject human rights activists who act on these ideals because of how they act. In this passage, the officer seems to have a visceral reaction to the attacks of human rights activists, speaking passionately about how it is wrong for activists to "humiliate" people. He suggests that if activists would refrain from public attacks, he would respect their claims.

Paradox: Persuasion versus Behavioral Change

Officers' complaints highlight a key paradox for the human rights movement. On one hand, activists' tactics, such as "naming and shaming," may further alienate officers and make it less likely that they will embrace human rights ideals when they are taught in educational settings. On the other hand, interviews suggest that these same attacks may motivate officers to restrain their behavior because they wish to avoid negative attention.

Officers express the desire for human rights activists to recognize their humanity and good intentions, appreciate the difficulty of their work, and refrain from pursuing claims so publically and punitively. They want human rights workers to help them form better relationships with the public, rather than bring negative and divisive issues to light. They also want activists to consider their rights as on par with those of other citizens. They want activists to have sympathy with them as people, and specifically as public officials who work in difficult circumstances. For example, one relatively high-ranking police officer asserted:

> A police officer should feel that human rights are also for his defense. There should be a midway point. Human rights should not only be against the police. The police should get some sort of protection from human rights. If you are a police officer, and if accidentally without malevolent intent—if firing comes from the other side and you return it and you get an innocent, someone who maybe is innocent but was among the people firing—it is very difficult to prove in these situations. Human rights should rescue police if he doesn't have any bad intention. Police should not fear human rights. They should respect human rights, and human rights should protect police if they don't have any bad intention.

Some go further than wishing activists would recognize their humanity and rights, and express a desire for activists to help the police. For example, another high-ranking Indian Police Service officer stated, "NGOs should work with the police. They will then appreciate the difficulties of police." Another mid-ranking army officer implied that NGOs could decrease torture by cultivating civilians' trust in the armed forces, so that civilians would be more open in interrogations. When I asked him when he considers torture "necessary," he replied:

> If we are suspecting someone and he is not admitting he is wrong. They should come out. The role of NGOs come [into play] here. A better understanding between the army and civilians.

This officer seems to suggest that torture would not be as necessary if NGOs helped cultivate trust between the army and civilians. This perception that NGOs could play a valuable role in building relationships with local populations is commonplace among officers, as is their frustration at what they see as NGOs' more typical tendency to instead incite anger against the army.

Law enforcement officers feel excluded from the category of "humans" with whom human rights activists are concerned. They believe that activists have little understanding of their suffering and their challenges. They note that they experience pressure from all sides: from politicians, supervisors, and competing sections of society. They describe the conditions in which they work as inhumane, explaining that lower-ranking officers typically work mercilessly long shifts for little pay in police stations that may lack basic necessities, sometimes living in barracks and unable to see their families even on important occasions. They sometimes speak of the lack of respect and the aggression that they perceive as emanating from the public, and of the difficulties in policing communities that have little trust in them. As such, they wish that human rights activists would help the police and recognize the troubles they face, rather than focus on punishment for wrong-doing.

Yet precisely the strategies that officers decry may play an important role in human rights advocacy. The officer quoted earlier expresses anger at activists for "humiliating" the army, likely reflecting the naming and shaming campaigns of human rights organizations. That officers appear distressed over these techniques suggests that they may be effective deterrents, at least to some degree, if officers alter their behavior to avoid them.

Indeed, several officers' comments suggest that strategies that fail to socialize human rights beliefs—and that may even alienate officers—may still function as a check on their behavior. The comments of a high-ranking Indian Police Service officer illustrate this well. I asked him to describe the challenges he faces in his work. In a list that included crime and terrorism, he added, "Also in Delhi we are working under the scanner of the media. We work under their constant control and monitoring. We have to be constantly careful of our human rights index." This comment suggests that feeling the "constant scanner of the media," which is often highly critical of the police in India, has not persuaded him to internalize human rights norms. On the contrary, he lists it as a problem, alongside crime and terrorism. However, because it is a problem—because the officers wish to avoid the negative attention of the media—they may restrain their behavior in some ways. While the feeling of being watched and criticized may deepen officers' perception that human rights is a problem and perhaps exacerbate their feeling of alienation from the wider community, it may also make it more likely that officers restrain their behavior at times.

When I asked this officer to describe each problem he faces in more detail, he explained first issues within the police organization and the challenges police encounter externally, such as dealing with large protests. He next stated, "Then the judiciary and human rights," and reflected:

> Somehow there is a dilemma between democratic values and police functions. The criminals being aware of the law are very smart during investigation. The third degree used to be an effective method for getting the truth out, but because of activism of human rights and the judiciary, the police do not do this. The police have resorted to scientific means, which have not evolved well. The police of the world have not been able to figure out alternative methods to the third degree. Yes, I believe violence should be avoided, but a combination of third degree and psychological methods used to be very effective. So this is causing the criminals to be more repetitive because they know they cannot be punished. They are more check-free.

This passage reveals several points. Similar to his previous comment, it suggests that human rights activism and laws have not caused him personally to endorse human rights. On the contrary, his perception is that human rights laws are forced on the police and cause an increase in crime. At the same time, his comments suggest that he believes human rights monitoring has changed police behavior, even though he believes it has changed it negatively.

This tension is reflected especially in the comments of officers stationed in Kashmir, which has been the subject of intense scrutiny by human rights workers. One mid-ranking army officer indicates that he restrains his behavior to avoid the negative attention of human rights groups. His following comments, however, suggest that this negative attention also further alienates him from human rights groups and their messages. I asked him about allegations that excessive force is used against suspects in Jammu and Kashmir. He replied that he does not know what happens in police stations, such as "how well the arrestee is behaving, how well he is giving information when he is asked." He then asserted:

> Conditions are so difficult that we are not even able to act on our suspicions and use the powers we have. . . . Even if I have a suspicion, I will not arrest them now, because people like you will think, 'What the hell is happening in J & K [Jammu

> & Kashmir]?' But people are not arrested just like that. These people are disturbing the peace. . . . If you look at it from the angle of a human rights activist and you disown every action the military takes, then security becomes a big hassle. If you start prosecuting for actions which may in their literal forms be excesses but were done earnestly, but it looks wrong, and they are prosecuted for it, then what will that do to the morale of your men? They won't risk their lives. They won't want to act, because if something goes wrong, you will be prosecuted. You will be walking on a narrow sword where if anything goes even slightly wrong, your career is gone. Your life is gone. Why would someone want to work for an organization where you are working for the organization's interests, taking care of their interests, but they are taking care of their interests? The army must hold the hand of the soldiers. That is why the Special Powers Act is there.

The officer's opening sentence summarizes the tension between strategies that may be effective at changing officers' behavior and those that might promote the internalization of human rights beliefs. He indicated that because conditions are so "difficult" he cannot do what he believes is necessary. These difficult conditions turn out to be public opinion. This suggests that the mobilization of public outcry may be effective at curbing officers' behavior. But he sees it as a difficulty that prevents him from doing important work, decidedly not a legitimate constraint. Even as he says he curbs his behavior because of this attention, he rejects its substance. Hence his behavior may have changed, but his beliefs have not.

A similar dynamic is revealed in my conversation with a high-ranking army officer who served in Kashmir. I asked him what the main obstacle is to fighting the militancy. He responded:

> Legal problems. If you have gone into an operation and some innocent has died unintentionally. If you go in at night, it is difficult to know who is innocent. This immunity from AFSPA [Armed Forces Special Powers Act] should be there because we are serving the nation only. It is not a private army after all. . . . People make it a political issue if someone dies accidentally. The local politicians make it a political issue without really caring about the people, and after two days it goes away. The media also. The government should be backing us, not against us. This legal cover is very important because if people are questioning your every move it is difficult for the army to operate. If you start questioning the army's motivation, then this problem will not be resolved.

The officer continued to argue that activists diminish officer morale, and I asked him to give me an example. He replied:

> OFFICER: Raising small issues against the army. Having them come for court cases. They should understand that he [a soldier] is not doing it [violence] for his personal interest. He is trained to fight, kill, and destroy. This is not his job. It is the job of the police. . . . We are training our soldiers to be more humane. When you read the news, sometimes it is true, but 99 percent of the time it is not true. People are not educated. There is a lot of anger. We need to explain why the army is there. This is not happening. Sometimes even when houses are searched, there is a huge hue and cry. There is a lot of support for people in the state. If something is wrong, then go hang them, but if there is a militant threat, then there should not be [negative attention].
>
> RW: Where is this criticism coming from?
>
> OFFICER: This is part of the legal process. If the police lodge an FIR, [First Information Report][5] then it has to go to court. AFSPA doesn't give immunity on everything. Sometimes, someone is shot accidentally. Police have to understand that if you start lodging cases against your own soldiers, then they won't want to come out of the barracks.
>
> RW: What should be done? For example, if a soldier accidentally shoots someone?
>
> OFFICER: The family should be given compensation. Solve the problem. If he was the breadwinner, give someone in the family a job, such as with the government. Give the children an education. . . . If there was a violation, then lodge a case with the National Human Rights Commission, but only rarely, when you have genuine proof.
>
> RW: When should the National Human Rights Commission become involved?
>
> OFFICER: Once you have authentic proof. When you have enough evidence. Enough proof, like DNA sampling with thorough investigations. Then the call has to be made, that okay, this is a human rights violation. But for normal cases it should not be.

As the others do, this dialogue reveals a contradiction. On one hand, if they make it "difficult" for the army to operate, the cases brought by the National Human Rights Commission [NHRC] may not be as ineffectual as many activists interviewed for this study believe. The possibility that human rights claims are having an effect is further supported by his belief that the army needs to explain its presence in Kashmir, and that, according to him, the army is training its soldiers to be more humane. At the same time, he views human rights activism as an obstacle to important work and as a detriment to the army, not as a legitimate constraint. Once again, his behavior may be checked but not transformed, and his beliefs either remain the same or become more antagonistic to human rights.

Similarly, a high-ranking army officer in Kashmir sees human rights groups as a problem, suggesting limited possibilities for activists to persuade officers to internalize norms. But one comment he made suggests that officers might check their behavior precisely because of the problems human rights groups cause them. When I asked him directly how human rights groups affect his work, his response was ambivalent. He said:

> OFFICER: It doesn't make a difference to us. We are working under a tight control as the army is watching us. The human rights groups do not affect us. The fact that human rights groups watch you only make you more cautious than you would be otherwise.
>
> RW: Do they have a positive or a negative impact?
>
> OFFICER: A positive impact. You are operating in a certain manner as cautiously as you can to ensure that the tenets of the SPA [Special Powers Act] are observed. Over and above that you have a feeling that people are watching you, reporting on your operations bullet by bullet. The human rights groups help the army to work more cautiously in observance of the law.

This dialogue indicates his ambivalence. On one hand, officers have an adversarial relationship with human rights groups, and hence do not wish to concede that they are successful in their attempt to control officers' behavior. On the other hand, officers' rejection of activists does not mean that they explicitly reject human rights.

Hence this officer appears to be caught between wishing to reject the legitimacy of human rights *activists* and wishing to align himself with human rights *ideals*. He reconciles this by first claiming that the army already oversees human rights sufficiently, and by alleging that activists curb rather than change officers' behavior. This was a common refrain among police and security forces. They argue that activists do not and cannot change officers' behavior, because officers defend their behavior as necessary and right. Instead, they say that human rights activists simply make the security and police forces more cautious.

The difference between this *restraint* on behavior and persuading officers to *change* their behavior is revealed in another comment the aforementioned high-ranking army officer made, in which he compares human rights groups to a classroom monitor. When I continued to ask him what he thinks of the human rights movement, he replied:

> It's a good thing. It keeps people on their toes. People who would otherwise go berserk are kept on a leash. Like at school, you have a monitor appointed when the teacher leaves the room. Rightfully, every child should be self-disciplined, but if they are not, then there is an authority who ensures discipline.

Human rights groups in this view fill a role that should ideally be occupied either by the proper authority, presumably the army, or by the individual officers themselves. The monitor may "keep people on their toes," but is unlikely to have a deep impact. Once again, this suggests the difference between checking behavior and the possibility of real normative persuasion and change.

A similar dynamic is reflected in the comments of the same high-ranking army officer in Kashmir. I asked him why the AFSPA should remain in effect. He asserted that human rights activists, who have long worked to overturn the act, are the reason it is necessary. He argued that human rights activists make security officers' work so difficult that special laws are needed to protect them. He explained:

> An army officer under the SPA [Special Powers Act] still has to go back and forth from where he is posted to deal with a case when a human rights case is registered against him. Human rights groups get involved. The judiciary gets involved. The officer who was involved in the operation where a terrorist is killed or a journalist is killed, for five years he must constantly travel back and forth from his posting to deal with the case. If this is how it is now, imagine if we did not have the SPA?

Even as he rejects their legitimacy, this officer expresses the perception that human rights activists have the power to affect the security forces.

This is a drastically different perception from that of the human rights activists interviewed for this study. Activists often feel discouraged about the effect of their work. Many are deeply frustrated by what they see as the lack of constraints on the police and security forces. They lament that their protests typically fall on deaf ears, because the state makes it so difficult to prosecute and punish officers. Yet these officers have the impression that human rights groups can, in fact, affect them. One mid-ranking police officer in Haryana was dramatic in his language. He mentioned that human rights activists stop him from conducting interrogations in the manner he believes is necessary. When I asked how they stop him, he replied, "They have power. They have supreme power. There is a law commission. Violation of human rights is a crime. It is a pressure on the police. You can be suspended." I then asked him if anyone he knows has ever been suspended for this reason. He said, "There are many examples. In district Hisar a police officer misbehaved with a girl. The second is a fake encounter [staged assassination]. An innocent was killed. The officer was suspended."

According to international and domestic human rights organizations, it is rare for officers to be suspended or seriously punished for human rights violations.[6] But at least some officers seem to believe that human rights activists can bring negative repercussions for their actions, and they wish to avoid these consequences. As will be explored following, this suggests that practices that fail to socialize human rights beliefs may serve at times to restrain officers' behavior.

Imaginaries and Assumptions about the Other

Assuming Bad Faith

Police and human rights activists delegitimize each other in strikingly similar ways: each assumes that the other is ignorant and driven by improper motives. Police accuse activists of failing to understand the reality of police work and as being motivated by the desire for money and publicity. Activists assert that police lack knowledge of the law and are driven by the desire for money and power. The assumption of bad faith pervades.

This assumption is not baseless. For one, it is often true. As has been made clear in this book and in numerous other reports, corruption in the police force is rampant. There have also been many cases of corruption among NGOs, and police are not the only ones who doubt the sincerity of human rights workers as a result.[7] NGO workers themselves discuss corruption in the nonprofit sector with some frequency. Of course, there are many hardworking and committed activists in India. But there have also been cases of NGOs that serve as little more than means of channeling money, never intending to implement the programs they proclaim.

Imaginaries in Conflict

Yet the distrust between police and human rights workers goes well beyond the fact of corruption. After all, police are aware of corruption among their own ranks, just as the NGO workers are among theirs. It is also the deeply conflicting ways in which they understand what is good and what is true—the moral and social imaginaries that form the background to their judgments—that inspire these doubts about each other. While police would understand an activist criticizing them for knowingly torturing an innocent person, they are incredulous that they are criticized for the same violence against someone whom they believe is guilty. In their minds, human rights activists criticize them not only for their failures, but also for living up to their ideals of what a police officer should be, or for at least trying to do so. They assume as a result that activists must not understand what is true about their work—this creates a conflict of social imaginaries. Or they assume that activists must be immoral or amoral, and guess that they must criticize police out of self-interest—a conflict of moral imaginaries. In the same way, activists do not recognize officers' actions as rooted in any moral orientation because it differs so dramatically from their own.

Recall, for example, M's assertion that youth are the most dangerous element in society due to their disregard for caution, and hence his belief that imprisonment and the use of force are often called for when dealing with young people. Contrast this with the human rights movement's perception of youth as vulnerable and in need of protection, and its corresponding insistence that youth deserve special and more careful treatment. These differing social imaginaries, which inform different moral positions, make it hard for each side to recognize the other as moral at all, because their views differ not only about what is right, but also about what is true regarding people and the world. Hence activists assume that corruption and ignorance, in addition to external pressures, can be the only explanations for officers' behavior, and officers assume that activists must be similarly motivated by self-interest and lack of knowledge.

Imaginaries Collapsed

Yet there is common ground between these different imaginaries and the moral orders they support. In the views of both human rights workers and the police, punishment is paramount to justice, and someone must be sacrificed for the greater good. Activists stress that police who torture must be punished to prevent more violence, even if it means that some individuals will be held accountable for a systemic problem. Police and security officers argue that criminal suspects must be tortured to ensure that criminals overall are controlled, even if it means that some innocent or "regular" individuals suffer. Clearly, human rights activists' desire for legal accountability for police is by no means comparable to officers' use of torture. The reasoning, however, whereby individuals who are not entirely guilty must be punished to fulfill a greater good, is similar.

This commonality may be rooted in their relationship to the state. Police and human rights workers fight for different ideals and use different means, but both see the state as the mechanism by which those ideals will be realized. Moreover, they are historically tied and evolved together: both law enforcers and human rights activists sprung up along with the contemporary state, developing their ethos as it emerged. The modern state adjudicates cases by deciding on whom punishment should fall. Although other means such as those based on reconciliation exist in modern legal settings, they tend not to be the explicit focus of legal pursuits. This may help explain the shared understanding that justice requires exacting punishment.

Moreover, an alternative is not easy to discern. Could activists pursue justice without vilifying officers? Activists might point to the dangers of sympathy with police: if they qualify their condemnation, they may fear that their moral message would become blurred and fail to rally the public. Interviews with officials in the NHRC who are responsible for punishing police for using torture are a case in point. Officials sympathize with the police and security forces who violate rights, recognizing their constraints and the ways in which officers' own rights are violated. In short, the officials responsible for punishing police recognize the latter's humanity. They draw on this sympathy when they explain their hesitation in punishing police. This sympathy could be part of the reason police are so rarely punished for using torture.

Implications for Human Rights Protection

The animosity officers feel toward human rights activists poses an obstacle to the latter's ability to work with police. But improving this relationship is a complex endeavor. There is much that makes it difficult to cultivate a more generous attitude toward each other. Efforts to galvanize the public confront a tension between encouraging deliberation and successful mobilization; and efforts to change state agents are stymied by a tension between changing their beliefs and changing their behavior. Both of these tensions further complicate the relationship between activists and police.

Mobilizing the Public

It is important to any social movement to identify "who or what is to blame" for the problem they address.[8] The human rights movement has been particularly adept at painting a picture of starkly differentiated "savages, victims, and saviors," a tendency that has garnered criticism.[9]

As problematic as it may be due to the way it simplifies reality, there is a reason for this widespread tendency. It is easier to mobilize a public to rally around a well-defined cause with a clear sense of who and what are right and wrong than to compel people to action regarding an ambiguous and morally complicated situation.[10]

One researcher articulated this as a tension between the twin virtues of democracy, which he defines as deliberation and mobilization. Democracies thrive when people are tolerant, well informed, and willing to engage in dialogue with one another on important issues, and when people care enough to participate.[11] But in order to mobilize participation, it may be necessary to depict a kind of moral clarity that undermines deliberation.[12] Human rights workers likewise often mobilize public outrage against torture by vilifying perpetrators, depicting their brutality without encouraging public discussion on the complex factors that lead them to engage in it.

Changing State Agents

Activists depict perpetrators in morally unambiguous terms not only because they wish to mobilize supporters. They also do so because they wish to change perpetrators' behavior. They attempt to check state power through the threat of negative public attention and legal sanctions, which are achieved by placing blame on those who commit violations. As such, emphasizing culpability has the potential to prevent future abuse.

These interviews suggest that coercive strategies such as "naming and shaming" and legal prosecution can at times curb officers' behavior. But as both officers and human rights educators attest, the kind of communication that could occur through human rights education is undermined, because officers tend to reject educators whom they associate with the human rights movement.

As such, although human rights activism and education are typically understood as complementary efforts, they may in fact be in tension. This is problematic, because when officers alter their behavior without changing their beliefs, they do not *transform* their actions to protect human rights but merely to *curb* the degree of violations. In one officer's words, they "operate less" at times when they think they may be caught.

Obstacles to Persuasion

Some scholars argue that only when actors engage in what they call "communicative" as opposed to "rhetorical" action will they succeed in changing others' beliefs. But even if activists were to alter their strategies to better meet the conditions for normative persuasion, typically they still would not fulfill what these scholars suggest is key: genuine openness to the others' argument. This marks an important difference between communicative action, in which actors are engaging in "truth-seeking" and try to understand the other's perspective, and rhetorical action, in which actors are using arguments strategically, with the sole aim of persuading the other.[13]

Human rights activists are unlikely to be genuinely open to officers' arguments in support of torture. Activists are defined by their commitment to ideals that they believe are universal and inalienable. At best, they may adopt these attributes strategically, such as listening to officers' views as a means to persuade them to accept human rights arguments. This has the potential to better meet the conditions for normative persuasion, as officers may be more likely to be persuaded if they feel listened to and respected. However, it is still a strategy for persuasion, rather than a genuine openness to officers' position. Hence it would still fall into the category of strategic and therefore rhetorical action, and not the "truth-seeking" behavior of communicative action. If these scholars are correct, activists are still likely to fall short of changing officers' beliefs.

Activists often inadvertently violate the conditions for normative persuasion in other ways as well. Scholars suggest that communicative action is most likely to occur when dialogue takes place in a private, unpoliticized setting.[14] But the use of the public political sphere to raise outcry against the police and security forces is a key strategy for activists. In addition, scholars assert that actors are more likely to engage in communicative action, and hence be persuaded, when there is an absence of coercion.[15] Human rights activists, however, do everything possible to use the law to coerce officers to uphold human rights. Moreover, persuasion is most likely when the listeners respect the speakers and see them as insiders, whereas officers identify human rights activists as a primary "out-group" to the police and security forces. The belief that the speaker is unbiased is also critical.[16] As demonstrated, officers believe activists are highly biased against them.

Reasons Not to Meet the Conditions for Normative Persuasion

There may be an important place for actions that violate the conditions for normative persuasion, as suggested by officers' comments. Human rights activists may provide an important deterrent to violations through engaging in negative publicity and legal action that state actors wish to avoid. In addition, while some scholars assert that internalization is key to human rights norm diffusion, others argue that it is not necessary.[17] According to Frank Schimmelfennig, it is not essential to change the beliefs of state actors in order to induce their compliance with norms. Instead, he argues that even though "rhetorical action" is unlikely to change beliefs, it may still be sufficient to change behavior.[18]

Human rights activists are prime examples of rhetorical actors. The goal of persuasion rather than understanding is constitutive of the identity and work of those who serve as advocates of any position. They also behave like rhetorical actors in their use of public shaming. According to Schimmelfennig, "social influence" is effective because people "want to be recognized as legitimate" and are "sensitive to social disapproval and respect."[19] As a result, shaming, which is the "public exposure of illegitimate goals and behaviors," is among the most effective tactic of rhetorical actors.[20] If this is correct, then human rights activists' failure to meet the conditions of normative persuasion is unproblematic. Activists aim for behavioral compliance and should continue to pursue it regardless of whether they succeed at changing officers' beliefs. But even if changing beliefs is not always necessary, it may be especially so in contexts that lack strong mechanisms to coerce compliance.

Shaming and Persuading in Context

A context such as India where the state does not typically punish officers for the use of extrajudicial violence, makes efforts both to change behavior and to change beliefs especially challenging, but also especially important. If the state regularly punished offenders and the public joined in condemnation of torture, then activists would not carry such singular responsibility for providing a deterrent to violence. They could focus more on persuading police by communicating human rights ideals without coercion.

This, however, is not the case. As a result, negative attention and adversarial legal action by human rights groups are among the only ways that officers' behavior might be checked. In this sense, where a norm is contested and not well enforced by the state, strategies that violate the conditions for normative persuasion are all the more important. The state's reluctance to punish officers who torture means that activists' efforts to hold officers accountable are all the more crucial.

But in such a context it is also particularly important to change state agents' beliefs, precisely because there are not strong mechanisms to coerce them through law. Hence the absence of strong state mechanisms to discipline police makes it especially important to change officers' behavior and also their beliefs. Moreover, neither approach addresses the complex circumstances that lead officers to believe that it is in their interest and at times necessary to use torture and other forms of violence.

Shaming and Persuading in Tension

The foregoing suggests that neither communicative nor rhetorical efforts alone are sufficient. Typically, this is considered unproblematic: scholars see these different approaches as complementary, or at least as having a neutral effect on each other.[21] For example, Hawkins asserts of social learning, a process similar to communicative action, that "it is difficult to separate" it from rhetorical action, and that "actors are likely to utilize and respond to both tactics."[22]

The interviews with police call this into question. First, the interviews suggest that if officers are successfully "named and shamed," it is not because there is a demonstrable gap between professed values and behavior. Rather, they seem to constrain their behavior (if at all) only to avoid what they view as illegitimate harassment.

This means that rhetorical techniques like "naming and shaming" are not only dissimilar from normative persuasion, but may actually undermine it. Officers say they constrain their behavior to avoid negative attention, but this negative attention undermines the possibility of persuading them to change their beliefs. Conversely, human rights advocates who remain genuinely open to officers' beliefs and concerns stand a chance of persuading officers of the validity of their position, but are less likely to pose the kind of threat that may actually constrain police behavior.

This is a paradox: the same strategies that may decrease the likelihood that officers will *internalize* human rights norms (for example, "naming and shaming," legal prosecution) may still provide an important *external* check on officers' behavior. This failure of internalization, however, means that officers only curb their behavior rather than transform it to actively protect human rights.

Moreover, although "naming and shaming" is a standard strategy for activists, a debate rages among scholars about whether activism of this type is effective. Some scholars demonstrate through case studies how pressure on governments can be successful.[23] Others use quantitative methods to examine the relationship between activism and repression, and suggest that the former is effective within certain scope conditions, such as when a country is transitioning to democracy after political upheaval or when a government is dependent on its relationship with stronger states.[24] Indeed, there are myriad factors that scholars argue make human rights treaties and accompanying activism more effective, such as economic development, linkages between an international and domestic network, and the existence of robust democratic institutions.[25]

Other scholars assert that these scope conditions reveal the limitations of standard techniques such as "naming and shaming," and that more conciliatory means of dealing with perpetrators are needed. They argue that the human rights movement should focus on obtaining desired outcomes rather than to upholding principles of justice. These scholars attest that powerful spoilers in government and cultural diversity will undermine rights efforts without this tolerant approach.[26] Moreover, rights efforts can backfire, such as when the quest to hold perpetrators accountable disrupts stabilization and reconciliation.[27] A number of studies support this assertion that "naming and shaming" and other forms of monitoring are ineffective, and even have a negative impact on rights protection.[28]

Scholars have suggested several reasons for this disagreement, to which the findings in this book contribute another. For one, researchers point to methodological differences. They point out that qualitative studies focus on subtle gains that are not visible in large-scale quantitative measures, for example, or focus too narrowly on a particular kind of right and fail to see increased repression of other rights. This may explain why qualitative studies tend to be more optimistic about rights efforts. The moral orientation of researchers may also be relevant, with some scholars loathe to call ineffective an effort that might save some lives, while others take a more utilitarian stance.[29]

This book suggests an additional reason for the ambivalence found in such studies: the effects of human rights efforts are themselves ambivalent. "Naming and shaming," in this case seems to both constrain officers' behavior in the short term, by making them more cautious about what they do, and stoke their antipathy to rights and alienate them to human rights messengers and messages in the long term.

Such tensions may be endemic to human rights efforts. This is in part because changing beliefs and behavior in any setting is challenging. But the complexities of human rights efforts present particular ethical and practical dilemmas. In the final chapter, I turn to these dilemmas and how a way forward might be found.

Conclusion

Dilemmas and Possibilities

ACCORDING TO CHARLES TAYLOR, whether or not we live up to it, we live our lives by a moral measure. We cannot help but orient ourselves to our understanding of what is good, judging our actions in part by how close we feel we come to it. In the contemporary West, the rich variety of moral sources that have inspired people throughout history have been forgotten, Taylor and others argue, leading to a narrowing of our moral imaginations.[1]

The implications of this forgetting are twofold. First, we fail to recognize our own moral orientation as a vision of the good life. We come to see it as neutral and use technical, rational language to discuss it. One example of this is the widespread tendency to describe the realization of particular ideals of childhood, marriage, and personal development as "healthy" rather than "good."[2] Second, as psychologists Jonathan Haidt and Jesse Graham have pointed out, we also fail to recognize moral sources that compete with our own.[3] Seeing our own orientation as an objective measure of natural phenomena, we view other ways of thinking morally as inaccurate and irrational.

Human rights has become the dominant frame for social justice worldwide."[4] Based largely in secular organizations such as the United Nations and NGOs, rights activists at times frame their work in technical-rational terms, basing their authority in their knowledge rather than in faith in a moral vision.[5] Often the language they use collapses liberal ideals with objective fact, claiming, for example, to promote the "full development of the human personality" as if alternative conceptions of how to live a good life fail to develop the person in the same way that a lack of nutrients compromise growth.[6] As I discuss in what follows, there are sometimes strategic reasons to intentionally obfuscate the ethical premise of human rights by using technical-rational language. But the movement tends not to recognize competing visions of the good as ethical at all; there are only human rights and human rights violations.

Social scientists further the sense that human rights reflect a neutral view of reality rather than a particular ethical stance. They do so by drawing on the conceptual categories of the rights movement and using them to collect information, the legitimacy of which is bolstered by the authority that research possesses in the contemporary world.[7] This is most evident in the standardization and quantification of phenomena through "indicators," whereby diverse experiences are coded in the categories of rights discourse and understood to provide an objective measure of the world.[8]

This book is no exception; each time I refer to a "human rights violation" or "violators" I am applying an ethical construction of phenomena as if it were a neutral description of reality. Such elision is difficult to avoid in a world where, as Mark Goodale has pointed out, it is as necessary to protect human rights as it is to question them.[9] This is because however imperfectly they accomplish this task, rights are a means of reducing suffering.

Indeed, relativism is no solution to myopia. The broadening of our vision does not require a relativistic stance in which we suspend all judgment. The effort to understand the ethical lives of others does not entail giving up our own. It can rather accompany a strong rejection of another's ethical claims. Tolerance without engagement can lead to a stance in which diverse views are tolerated but poorly understood, which can weaken the public's ability to deliberate about substantive questions.

Ironically, liberal societies may at times inadvertently fail to recognize diversity precisely because of the demand to tolerate it. One way to avoid seeming intolerant is to assert that an ethical vision is universal and therefore does not diminish any other way of life. The human rights movement's insistence that human rights principles can be found within every cultural and religious tradition is one example. If human rights are universal, then those who advocate for them can affirm an ethics without seeming intolerant of others; in other words, without seeming illiberal.

But it is possible to affirm a moral vision while still acknowledging its particularity. Richard Rorty claims as much in his call for liberals to understand the injunction to prevent suffering as contingent and particular, but no less worth committing to for that reason.[10] Although Taylor urges us to pay attention to the moral sources that move us and seeks to broaden our vocabulary for describing these sources, Rorty suggests that we consider our "final vocabulary" of moral life a creative act. But whether we consider the good to be a call to which we respond or an act of experimental creativity, understanding it as a moral vision rather than a neutral lens on the world can strengthen our commitment to it. Moreover, genuine interest in the moral visions of others does not weaken our own; after all, the existence of competing perceptions does not mean they are all equal.

Thus this book occupies a delicate position, describing the spread of the liberal moral order while at the same time helping to spread this order by taking on its language and aims. I am not neutral in regard to the fierce moral battles in which police and human rights activists engage. As Paul Brass, a political scientist of violence in North India, writes:

> When the search for categories, constructs, and contexts is central to the political struggle, the scholar's own concepts and the scholar himself cannot stand apart from and outside them.[11]

As such, this book occupies a curious position of both studying and attempting to support the diffusion of the modern moral order. I do not unequivocally embrace the liberal project, and moreover, I agree with critiques that its advance has often served the interests of power more than justice.[12] As postcolonial scholars have especially pointed out, in practice the liberal West has caused tremendous suffering. Furthermore, some of the most prominent movements in support of ostensibly "Western" liberal ideals have been those that oppose Western power. The Indian independence movement is a prime example.[13] On torture and related violence, however, I believe (the formal position of) liberalism is on the right side. It certainly does not stand there alone; traditions from the world's major religions as well as many conservative political traditions oppose torture.[14] But the human rights movement is among the most prominent and systematic efforts to prevent it.

At the same time, this is a work of scholarship, not of advocacy, and in keeping with that purpose, my aim has been not to persuade but to understand. I strive to illuminate how the officers, so often maligned in the public eye, understand and judge their own behavior. Although it is not possible to eschew all frames and dwell always in the complexity of irreducible events and individuals, it is my hope that this book will deepen understanding of people who are often seen as little more than obstacles to what is right.

This aim is, however, rife with dilemmas. In his work on Japanese war criminals, Dawes articulates with particular elegance the paradox of understanding brutality. He writes, "Conceptualizing perpetrators as people we can understand is a moral affront, and refusing to conceptualize perpetrators as people we can understand is a moral affront. In other words, we must and must not demonize them."[15] He quotes the director of the monumental Holocaust documentary *Shoah*, who confessed, "There is an absolute obscenity in the very project of understanding."[16]

Dawes recounts several reasons why there may be a moral imperative to condemn and even to recoil in horror rather than to understand. Recognizing the humanity of perpetrators and seeking to understand their acts risk collapsing crucial moral distinctions. By naming what they do as evil, we commit ourselves to maintaining those distinctions and to actions that promote the good and resist what is wrong. The condemnation of evil can both clarify and energize this effort, while trying to understand it can come "perilously close" to excusing it.[17] Moreover, putting that which perhaps *should* "defy comprehension" into relatable terms can obscure its true horror. Dawes recalls the anger generated by Hannah Arendt's identification of Adolf Eichmann as thoughtless and banal rather than evil. He quotes Saul Bellow, who writes, "The best and purest human beings, from the beginning of time, have understood that life is sacred. To deny that understanding is not banality. There was a conspiracy against the sacredness of life."[18]

This raises the question of whether there is in fact a universal human morality that is violated by officers' support of torture. The human rights movement is premised on this assertion, but must it be so? It may be possible to instead see alternative ways of thinking about justice as rational and genuinely held ethical convictions, but *still ethically wrong*. This is necessary if our commitment to protecting life is not to be based on an empirical question of whether the best people throughout history have in fact held this commitment: it makes it enough that we hold it.

It also opens the possibility of seeking to understand without losing the capacity to condemn. I share with authors such as Dawes the conviction that such an effort is worthwhile. He pursues his book on Japanese war criminals because in spite of the dangers of the endeavor, he feels that to recognize the others' humanity and to seek to understand them has implications both for our own ethical position in the world and for preventing brutality.[19] We run the risk of becoming inhumane in our rejection of others' humanity, Dawes writes, and moreover, when we view brutality as inexplicable, we weaken the possibility of stopping it. And so I base this book on two premises: that the effort to understand those who seem to be utterly unlike us is its own good and that this understanding may help reduce the harm caused both by these "others" and by their alienation from advocates of liberalism.

This effort to understand support for brutality without accepting it becomes all the more important given its pervasiveness. Long believed to be a specter of the distant past or repressive governments, torture has entered the public lexicon of democracies. This was made clear by American acts of torture at places such as Guantanamo Bay and Abu Ghraib. And support for this violence did not end when the administration changed. In 2015, for example, the moderator of the Republican primary debate in the United States asked a candidate whether if elected he would bring back the practice of "waterboarding" detainees. It is striking that such a question is considered legitimate in a liberal democracy. Even more striking is that the candidate believed that the politically savvy response would be affirmative; he replied, "What we do in order to get the information that we need is our business."[20] And still more alarming is that his calculation may have been accurate, as his response won him resounding applause.

Police in India and presidential candidates in the United States have different reasons for endorsing torture. This book concerns the former, and an effort to understand one will not substitute for efforts to understand the unique predicament and views of others. But that such questions can be asked and so answered in public by political contenders in the United States is a reminder that uneducated police in "far-flung" parts of rural India are not the only ones who endorse torture. Hence refusing to understand these beliefs constitutes a refusal to engage with central debates of modern democracies and with the citizens who hold these views.

Understanding Violence

The conclusions arising from this project help to illuminate the complex relationship among beliefs, norms, and structures, and how these in combination inform law enforcers' responses to human rights messages. This book has also showed that resistance to human rights is not a matter of "bad" local beliefs resisting "good" international norms, and revealed instead the high degree of normative competition at both the local and international level as well as how this ethical diversity provides a resource for those who oppose human rights. Finally, the book has detailed the paradoxical ways in which law enforcers respond to activists themselves. I review each of these conclusions next, before turning to their implications for education and activism to prevent torture and the complex dilemmas to which these efforts lead.

Beliefs, Norms, and Structures

The police interviewed for this book draw from a distinct set of beliefs about what is true and what is good wherein their key distinctions do not concern whether to use torture, but rather center on the reasons for using it. Police see certain reasons for torture as consistent with their moral identities and reject other motivations for torture as immoral. These distinctions are based in part on their views of human nature and justice. While the human rights movement is inspired by the belief that all human beings are equal in their right to protection, these officers believe that there are different types of people who deserve and require different treatment and that justice depends upon their receiving it. In their minds, respecting the basic rights of a "hardened criminal" as one would the rights of an innocent person would undermine justice, not uphold it. If a police officer acts to uphold justice rather than for personal gain, officers believe that this is a good and legitimate use of violence.

But officers' beliefs do not exist in isolation from their lives. To some extent, differential treatment based on assessments of guilt and innocence or type of criminal is inherent in the law and law enforcement work. And police across the world share these officers' assessments that not all people deserve or can feasibly receive equal treatment if law and order—and justice—are to be maintained.[21]

Yet the officers in this study work in an environment that exacerbates these beliefs—and their potential to cause harm. First, corruption and inefficiency in the legal system undermine the legitimacy of the rule of law. These weaknesses give officers reason to believe that in order to uphold justice, it is necessary to violate the law more often than they believe they would in a better system. Second, this same corruption and inefficiency in addition to legal protections for public officials mean that officers are unlikely to be held accountable when they act on these views. The chaos they perceive in society, their perceived lack of capacity to contain it nonviolently, and the direct challenges to their authority from a public with whom they hold little legitimacy compound their perception that it is sometimes right to use illegal violence.

As much as it provides a rationale for violence, this environment inhibits officers' ability to live by their conceptions of justice. Police lament that they must use violence against people who do not truly "deserve" it due to a weak criminal justice system and multiple pressures. Hence, although they justify extrajudicial violence by restricting it to certain categories of people, they acknowledge that such distinctions break down in practice. But because their conceptions of justice include the belief that torture and other forms of violence are sometimes defensible, they are able to see these infractions as an imperfect implementation of their principles rather than as outright violations.

Finally, although officers differentiate between what they see as illegitimate reasons to use torture (that which serves their self-interest) and what they see as legitimate reasons to use torture (that which serves the public good), in practice both are likely involved in any particular act. Police may be pressured by supervisors and the public to close a case quickly with torture, and they may also receive a bribe to do so. Although no officers admitted emotional motivations for torture, it is possible that they may be angry or enjoy a sense of power. But in addition to these reasons, they may also believe that such violence is necessary to maintain order and justice. The existence of the latter reason may help officers to live with the first three. In these ways, the conditions in which officers work, their self-interest, and their beliefs about justice are always in interaction, and together contribute to high rates of torture.

Responses to Human Rights Messages

When these police officers learn the human rights framework, they use it to contest the very principles that educators and activists most hope to spread. The officers master the language and logic of contemporary liberalism, and then they adapt it to their own conceptions of justice, drawing from it to make rights-based arguments for torture.

These microdynamics of police resistance to human rights reveal how the vocabulary of a political theory can be stretched to express a multitude of different conclusions about the good. In theory, the principles of "natural" or "human" rights are at odds with a Hobbesian view of the state as always legitimate in its exercise of power. In practice, though, police draw from a Hobbesian view of human nature and the social contract and articulate it in the language of human rights. Norms do not simply "diffuse," then, but change as actors with different interests and beliefs interpret them, and even use them to contest the principles those norms are meant to protect.

Normative Competition: Not Global versus Local

This resistance to human rights is not primarily a conflict between "global" and "local" norms, wherein liberal norms originate in the North/West and must contend with local cultural opposition in the South. Although resistance to human rights is often depicted in this way, officers' statements belie this claim.[22] When they explicitly reject rights, it is not in favor of "local" beliefs as they are typically understood. Indeed, the officers mostly agree with educators who insist that human rights are consistent with Indian religious, cultural, and political traditions. But this is trumped by what they see as the purpose of their profession as law enforcers: to uphold security and order.

Moreover, if there was a time when state officials in the Global South rejected human rights because of their perceived "Western" character, that time seems to have passed. Police view their actions as in keeping with the stance of Western countries such as the United States. Indeed, they reference the use of torture by the United States to support their own behavior. An internationally shared language of modern state security is available to local police to justify their violation of human rights.

Responses to Human Rights Activists

Although they hold different beliefs about what is true and good, in some ways activists and police have more in common than they realize. Both are concerned by what they perceive as pervasive lawlessness in Indian society due in part to political corruption that allows perpetrators to go unpunished. Both feel strongly that the best way to realize justice is through stricter punishments for perpetrators, even if this means punishing people who do not bear singular responsibility for their crimes. This is informed by the shared belief that people will behave well only with strict punishments to fear. In this way, their views of human nature converge.

They have different views, however, of *who* threatens justice. Human rights activists view state actors as perpetrators of injustice, whereas police and security officers apply this judgment to criminals, terrorists, and anyone who they perceive as against the national interest. (They both view politicians as contributing to the lawlessness they wish to abate, but both feel powerless to control politicians.) Both are focused on stricter punishments for the supposed offenders to counteract an environment they feel is chaotic, arbitrary, and unjust. Police thusly justify their violence against suspects, and human rights activists call for police to be punished. In the end, each feels that to empathize with those who do wrong—whether they are criminal suspects or the police who torture them—is too costly.

The views and strategies of human rights activists differ significantly from those of law enforcement officers in regard to *how* stricter punishments should be obtained. Activists typically aim to prosecute police in court. They work to overturn laws that protect police from lawsuits so that torture victims can press charges, rallying the public by "naming and shaming" officers they suspect of torture. This desire for due process to apply to police is a far cry from the use of torture and extrajudicial killing. In spite of what one constable in this study remarked, bringing someone to court is not in fact "a kind of torture."

There is still a cost to the adversarial relationship that exists between the police and many activists, however. Police feel alienated from the human rights community and also from the public at large. Officers are convinced that the people who advocate for them to treat others humanely fail to recognize their own humanity and care little about the ways in which officers' rights are violated. And police feel attacked for actions that they believe are right, or at least necessary. As such, they reject activists and their messages, at times vehemently expressing their resentment.

Yet without activists' efforts, there would be few external checks on officers' behavior because the state rarely punishes police for torture. Officers seem sensitive to the negative publicity generated by human rights activism and dread the prospect of human rights commission investigations and lengthy court cases. As such, they sometimes speak of being more careful in their behavior in order to avoid such outcomes.

This presents a paradox. Strategies that might make police more open to the messages of human rights activists and educators, such as listening to police and recognizing their humanity, may be disrupted by negative media campaigns and aggressive court cases. But these coercive strategies may provide a crucial external restraint on police behavior that would otherwise be absent.

Human rights educators and activists face a dilemma, then, because they typically hope to do more than compel police through punishments. Human rights workers hope to create a "culture of human rights" as the *World Programme in Human Rights Education Plan of Action* attests, in which police have internalized these norms.[23] In essence, the human rights movement aims to change not only what police do, but also what they believe. Although these goals are typically seen as mutually reinforcing, there is a tension between them.

A Way Forward for Human Rights Education

Many activists understandably see human rights education (HRE) as a chance to engage in activism with the police, providing them with information to "raise awareness" or convincing them that what they do is wrong and that they will be punished.[24] But the value of education lies in that which activism cannot accomplish. HRE offers educators a rare occasion to work with police in precisely the way activists do not. Rather than simply disseminating information or allocating blame, educators can instead seek to understand and address the complexity of the circumstances in which police work and why they believe violence is the right or only way to respond to those circumstances. This involves entering into dialogue with police, listening to their views and experiences, connecting their messages to officers' actual interests and beliefs, and framing their messages in these terms.

In fact, a long tradition of progressive education holds that such engagement is precisely what distinguishes educational projects. Theorists such as John Dewey insist that true education is always an act of communication, not a mere transmission of information. For Dewey, when one communicates, "one shares in what another has thought and felt and in so far, meagerly or amply, has his own attitude modified."[25] This effect is not only on the student, but also on the teacher. Dewey continues:

> Nor is the one who communicates left unaffected. Try the experiment of communicating, with fullness and accuracy, some experience to another, especially if it be somewhat complicated, and you will find your own attitude toward your experience changing. . . . The experience has to be formulated in order to be communicated. To formulate requires getting outside of it, seeing it as another would see it, considering what points of contact it has with the life of another so that it may be got into such form that he can appreciate its meaning. Except in dealing with commonplaces and catch phrases one has to assimilate, imaginatively, something of another's experience in order to tell him intelligently of one's own experience.[26]

In order to "assimilate" police officers' experience, educators must first listen to it. Then to allow themselves to be changed by what they hear is a difficult task for educators who are teaching precisely because of their commitment to abolishing the violence the police describe. Although such receptivity may be particularly challenging for instructors of HRE due to the strength of their ethical commitment, it is also particularly important. HRE is especially meant to avoid what critical educational theorist Paulo Freire called the "banking" method of education wherein the teacher "deposits" knowledge into students. Instead, scholars and practitioners of HRE insist that it should cultivate human rights "through" education, which entails listening to the perspectives of students and taking those perspectives seriously. Such engagement can compel educators to develop responses to the difficulties raised by the police, and in this way strengthen the discourse of human rights.

Moreover, prior research on police reform supports this strategy. David Bayley notes, for example, that reformers must take care to work with rather than against law enforcers, which involves including them in developing solutions.[27] Other researchers too note that HRE for police is only worthwhile when it is based on extensive knowledge of officers' circumstances and views.[28] Theory on normative persuasion also supports this approach. Scholars argue that a speaker will be most persuasive if she or he is genuinely open to the listeners' views and frames his or her messages in those terms.[29] The speaker will also be more persuasive if she or he is an authoritative member of the listeners' group, suggesting that it is preferable to partner with trainers who have experience in the police and military.

Indeed, although it could clarify and enrich the public conversation to recognize human rights as an ethical vision rather than a neutral reflection of reality, this does not mean that ethical language is always the most strategic way to persuade someone to change their behavior. Although the law enforcers I interviewed care little about whether they "protect human rights," many are personally invested in being professional, capable police officers. Given the deep differences in conceptions of human nature and justice held by these officers and human rights workers, the (deceptively) neutral language of "capacity building," "professionalization," and "scientific" policing may be more effective, even though (and in part because) such language obscures its ethical premise.

And although educators can try to convince police to make different choices in response to their circumstances, there is still more they can do. What they learn from police about the structural factors that give rise to torture can inform activism to change those structures. Decades of reform efforts in India have proven that obstacles such as political resistance undermine such change. But engaging in these efforts, including explicit attempts to improve the working conditions of police, can increase the legitimacy of the human rights movement in the eyes of officers as well as move (however slowly) toward lasting structural change.

Transcending Principle? Political and Ethical Dilemmas

A focus on aiding and understanding the police may seem impractical and unethical. Practically, there is the possibility that a shift away from accountability and punishment will remove the only restraint there is on police behavior. As I have argued, though, it may in fact be quite practical to focus at least in part on officers' concerns and circumstances. Other studies of violent state officials suggest this as well. In his study of New Delhi prison wardens' (warders' in British English) resistance to human rights reforms, Tomas Martin attests:

> Understanding the warders' opposition to human rights as dynamic bargaining means that they are, in fact, not locked in a zero-sum game. Warders might be more willing to buy into the human rights reform if, as knowledgeable and able actors, they found that it was in line with their efforts to push their work in a direction they opted for. They might not insist on beating the prisoners if the complexities of their work situation were reduced and they were assured that reform initiatives would take a direction that also addressed their pressing problems.[30]

Some programs do take such an approach. For example, a European Union–funded Prevention of Torture program designed by faculty at the University of Sydney for police in Nepal and Sri Lanka helps officers to map the constraints and pressures that lead to torture, and works with them to create solutions that do not involve the use of violence. Researchers Danielle Celermajer and Kiran Grewal, who designed the program, stress that the attention to context is crucial to the success of any such effort.[31] Such a model might be built upon to make officers' own beliefs and concerns the starting point. Trainers can position the abandonment of torture as in keeping with what police believe is good, helpful, and necessary.

Still, this may seem to some concerned human rights advocates and scholars like an unethical abandonment of principles of justice. Indeed, this maps on to a contentious debate among human rights researchers, who disagree on whether human rights activists should continue to pursue justice by attempting to hold violators accountable or whether they should make strategic concessions such as granting amnesties.[32] This difference of opinion has been described as a contest between scholars who prioritize upholding principles of justice, on the one hand, and on the other hand, scholars who favor the pragmatism of working with those in power, however "dirty" their hands may be.[33]

But whether something is a violation of principle depends upon the principle in question. More specifically, the importance of upholding a code of justice such as human rights depends upon whether one understands codification as desirable in regard to ethics. Charles Taylor worries that although it has the potential to protect people from abuse, the "code fetishism . . . of modern liberal society is potentially very damaging."[34] He wonders, "could one, by transcending/amending/re-interpreting the code, move us all vertically?"[35] Taylor's hope is that by aspiring to forgiveness, humility, and understanding, by "renounc[ing] the right conferred by suffering, the right of the innocent to punish the guilty," we might reduce violence more effectively *and* more ethically than if we retain the rights of victims to punish perpetrators.[36] He says of those such as the Dalai Lama, whom he sees as having achieved such a move, that, "their power lies not in suppressing the madness of violent categorization, but in transfiguring it in the name of a new kind of common world."[37] Thus human rights activists face the same question as scholars who approach the topic of brutality. Should they forego punitive action for the sake of understanding and to form a "common world" that includes concern for the well-being of violent state officials?

Other researchers on state violence resolve this question by drawing on the democratic theorist Chantal Mouffe, who articulates a model of democracy in which opponents respect each other as worthy adversaries rather than decry each other as enemies. Mouffe contends that rather than idealize a "deliberative" democracy as articulated by Jürgen Habermas, where citizens deliberate together to arrive at a rational consensus, democracy should be understood as inherently agonistic. By this she means that deep disagreement is inevitable and salutary for democracy, and the aim should be not to quiet such clashes but to channel them into democratic politics.[38] Steffen Jensen and Andrew Jefferson draw on this model to suggest that human rights workers should "agonize together" with state officials over the complex place of violence in the latter's work rather than simply insist that it should have no place.[39]

Such mutual agonizing, wherein the right solution is not taken as settled, could indeed be precisely what is required for progress to be made. But evoking a theorist of democratic politics highlights the difficulty of this suggestion. Mouffe writes that *interpretations* of liberal democratic ideals such as liberty and equality are forever unsettled, but that people can respect each other as adherents to those shared ideals as they continue to argue over their proper realization.[40] But police who engage in torture violate key tenets of liberal democracy, leaving an uncertain basis for mutual respect between them and human rights advocates.

This lack of a common political orientation suggests that human rights activists' concern for violent state officials' welfare must be based on something that transcends politics but is truer to their own philosophy: human rights activists can be concerned for and respect officers by virtue of their humanity. Are the drawbacks to human rights workers' punitive approach significant enough, though, to outweigh its potential benefits? The answer to this question is complicated by several tensions.

First, the human rights movement is premised on that which transcends all politics, a common human predicament that admits no exceptions. But the movement must realize these ideals in political and legal systems that operate based on categorization and exclusion, the identification of guilt and its punishment. Human rights workers are caught in the same circumstances as police in this sense, and likely fear that they would make little progress were they to abandon the tools of justice at their disposal.

This tension between ethics and law may be inevitable in a world where moral visions must be safeguarded by legal means, and this is precisely what concerns Taylor. He regrets the translation of ethics into codes upheld by bureaucracies and institutions. He fears that this has replaced what was radical about early Christian thought, which he sees as antecedent to liberalism. According to Taylor, what is lost is a "gut" response of love for the other human beings in our midst, to whom we attend as particular beings in particular situations.[41]

Second, a tension exists between acknowledging the systemic problems that give rise to torture and holding individuals accountable for their actions. Although police believe that torture is often the *right* thing to do, they also stress that they are caught in a system in which they are left with few choices.

Officials at the National Human Rights Commission (NHRC) asked me to remember this when I write about police. And police themselves did as well, pleading with me to show readers that the police officer is "also a man." Or as one officer said when I asked at the close of the interview if there is anything else I should understand:

> I would like you to understand the ground reality of police. Their work conditions . . . the emotional and physical security they possess. . . . A hungry, tired, and dissatisfied individual cannot be expected to deliver fruit, fragrance, and joy.

Officials in the NHRC seemed keenly aware of this ground reality. And this awareness—combined with a shared conception of justice—may make them less likely to hold police accountable when they are accused of torture. They know all too well the pressures and expectations with which a police officer lives, and given this, it becomes less surprising that they typically award monetary compensation to the victim of police torture rather than discipline or prosecute the offending officer.

Fearing precisely this outcome, human rights activists stress that the conditions in which police work cannot be accepted as an excuse for torture: police must be punished when they use torture, they emphasize, regardless of whatever deplorable conditions contributed to the act. Otherwise, they aver, police will never have an incentive to refrain from torture, and the practice will continue unabated. Hence recognizing the systemic roots of torture—and perhaps, compassion for the police caught in this system—is in tension with holding individuals responsible for it. In theory these goals do not necessarily conflict, but in practice they often do.

The third and related tension is between accountability and persuasion, as discussed earlier. As activists point out, a reform strategy without a means of enforcing the attempted reforms is unlikely to be effective. At the same time, holding police accountable could increase their adversarial relationship to human rights activists and their messages, as such accountability often involves public shaming as well as legal action.

Even if activism is alienating to officers, however, does that make it dehumanizing? At the most basic level, Taylor is concerned with the way righteous efforts to redress wrongs can themselves become violent. Although the human rights movement may neglect perpetrators' welfare, it is unlikely to develop into a revolutionary force that exerts violence against them. Indeed, its decidedly legalistic character is what Taylor and other critics lament as a weak solution to this threat.[42]

Compromises seem inevitable in this realm of irreconcilable tensions. Activists committed to the struggle against torture would lose an important tool to constrain this violence if they relinquished the coercive capacity of the law and the tactics that mobilize the public to demand it. At the same time, to effect the deeper change within the people who make up the state, they must go beyond the law and find common ground with those who have harmed others. Although police insist that "those who violate the rights of others should not themselves have human rights," activists should make clear that their stance toward police is radically different.

A clearer division of labor between educators and activists may offer one way forward. Although educators could focus on understanding and connecting with police as well as helping them to navigate the structures within which they work, outside of education settings activists could continue to "name and shame" and pursue legal prosecution. These tactics may deepen officers' resistance to human rights beliefs, but still provide a crucial external check on officers' behavior in contexts where the state does not fulfill this function.

In essence, educators could play the "good cop" to police, committed to helping them navigate their dilemmas, while activists play "bad cop," holding police accountable for violations and, ideally, effecting deeper structural change so that the state to a greater extent polices itself.

In addition, the more officers are held accountable, the easier it will be for educators to argue that it is in officers' interests to refrain from torture. Educators can frame their lessons as a means to help police avoid the negative publicity of activists. It is important, though, that officers of all ranks are held responsible rather than only the lower-ranking police who may commit the violence.

This approach combines "traditional" human rights strategies focused on accountability with "pragmatic" methods that work in partnership with the police. However, I see this compromise not as one between principle and pragmatism, but between competing principles, of justice and its transcendence. The approach has as its ultimate aim the (at least partial) transcendence of punitive measures in the long term, while in the short term seeks to provide a disincentive for torture. Indeed, this need for a disincentive is why coercive strategies like "naming and shaming," however ethically ambiguous and limited in their effectiveness, are still likely crucial in the struggle to reduce violence.

This compromise responds to but does not resolve the tensions at the heart of human rights work. Uneasiness still remains between human rights as an aspirational ethics and as legal tools, between recognizing the complex structural factors that lead to torture and holding individuals responsible for their actions, and between the educational aim of opening officers' minds to human rights messages and activists' efforts to coerce their compliance.

Moreover, these tensions are only part of the reason that human rights activists' and educators' work is so difficult. They face not only these quandaries but also unresponsive states, distracted publics, and daily confrontations with brutality, admirably facing cruelty from which most of us in other lines of work, most days, are able to look away. The lack of perfect means to do such work does not undermine the worthiness of doing it.

Indeed, none of the foregoing is intended to diminish the noble efforts and genuine accomplishments of human rights workers, nor is it an attempt to provide directives for them to follow. Ultimately, all educators, activists, and organizations will draw on their own rich and varied experience to deliberate and perhaps even agonize[43] over the best way to resolve the tensions highlighted in this book. It is my aim to inform and encourage such deliberations by illuminating how police understand the violence they commit and how they respond to efforts to prevent this violence. In short, the foregoing reveals how it is so that a person may engage in acts of brutality and at the same time remain, as the police repeatedly reminded me, "also a man."

Notes

Introduction

1. Asian Human Rights Commission, "India: Police Torture of Young Man Part of Investigation."

2. First Information Report, which by law police are required to register when a complaint is made.

3. Allen, *Talking to Strangers.*

4. A "norm" is that which constitutes or regulates appropriate behavior for actors with a particular identity, e.g. Katzenstein, *The Culture of National Security.*

5. Simmons, *Mobilizing for Human Rights*; Risse *et al., The Persistent Power of Human Rights*; Finnemore and Sikkink, "International Norm Dynamics and Political Change."

6. Taylor, *A Secular Age*; Asad, *Formations of the Secular*; MacIntyre, *After Virtue.*

7. Meyer et al., "World Society and the Nation-State"; Ramirez et al., "The Worldwide Rise of Human Rights Education"; Russell and Suárez, "Symbol and Substance"; Krucken and Dori, *World Society.*

8. As will be explored in Chapter 5, there is a rich anthropological literature on how activists translate norms into local idioms, e.g. Merry, *Human Rights and Gender Violence*; Goodale, *Surrendering to Utopia*; Bajaj, *Schooling for Social Change.*

9. Taylor, *Modern Social Imaginaries*, 3.

10. Merry, *Human Rights and Gender Violence.*

11. See, for example, Hafner-Burton, *Making Human Rights a Reality.*

12. See, for example, Simmons, *Mobilizing for Human Rights*; Hafner-Burton, *Making Human Rights a Reality.*

13. Jensen and Jefferson, *State Violence and Human Rights.*

14. Ibid., 11.

15. Ibid.; See, for example, contributions to their edited volume such as Martin, "Taking the Snake Out of the Basket," 139–157.

16. Mutua, *Human Rights.*

17. Dawes, *Evil Men*, 37.

18. Benford & Snow, "Framing Processes and Social Movements," 611–639.

19. All but two of the officers I interviewed are male.

20. See Appendix A for more details on the officers.

21. United Nations General Assembly, *Code of Conduct*.

22. See Appendix A for more information on distinctions between civil police, military, and paramilitary officers.

23. Human Rights Watch, *Broken System*.

24. Taylor, *Sources of the Self*, 27. Taylor argues that "the horizons within which we live our lives and which make sense of them" inevitably include "strong qualitative discriminations."

25. Sutton and Levinson, *Policy as Practice*, 2.

26. Dewey, *Democracy and Education*, 4.

27. Suárez, "Education Professionals and the Construction of Human Rights Education."

28. Risse et al., *The Persistent Power of Human Rights*.

29. Ramirez, "The Worldwide Rise of Human Rights Education," 35–52.

30. Taylor, *Sources of the Self*.

31. Ibid., 58.

32. Taylor, *A Secular Age*, 23.

33. Ibid., 6.

34. Ibid., 8.

Chapter 1

1. Celermajer and Grewal, "Preventing Human Rights Violations"; Nowak, "On the Prevention of Torture."

2. Office of the United Nations High Commissioner for Human Rights, "Plan of Action," 2006.

3. Celermajer, "The Ritualization of Human Rights Education and Training."

4. Office of the United Nations High Commissioner for Human Rights, "Human Rights Education and Training."

5. United Nations General Assembly, Resolution 66/137; Amnesty International, *Annual Report*; Tibbitts, "Evolution of Human Rights Education Models."

6. Reardon, *Human Rights Learning*.

7. Bajaj, *Schooling for Change*; Bajaj, "Human Rights Education."

8. Tibbitts, "Understanding What We Do"; Tibbitts, "Evolution of Human Rights Education Models."

9. Political scientists do not typically analyze HRE as a mechanism for the diffusion of human rights norms, even though many social constructivists insist that it is important for state agents to internalize new norms, and furthermore analyze other persuasive techniques such as the way activists frame and communicate new norms in their campaigns.

10. Bajaj, *Schooling for Social Change*.

11. Russell and Suárez, "Symbol and Substance."

12. Ibid.

13. Ramirez et al., "The Worldwide Rise of Human Rights Education"; Russell and Suárez, "Symbol and Substance."

14. Bajaj, *Schooling for Social Change.*

15. See for example Schulz et al., *ICCS 2009 International Report*; Gaudelli and Fernekes, "Teaching about Global Human Rights for Global Citizenship"; Stellmacher and Sommer, "Human Rights Education."

16. Mejias, "Politics, Power and Protest."

17. See for example Steiner-Khamsi, "Cross-National Policy Borrowing"; Steiner-Khamsi and Stolpe, "Decentralization and Recentralization Reform in Mongolia,"; Vavrus and Bartlett,"Comparative Pedagogies and Epistemological Diversity"; Anderson-Levitt, "A World Culture of Schooling?"

18. Office of the United Nations High Commissioner for Human Rights, "Plan of Action," 2012; Meyer et al., "World Society and the Nation-State."

19. Office of the United Nations High Commissioner for Human Rights, "Human Rights and Law Enforcement," 15.

20. Donnelly, *Universal Human Rights in Theory and Practice.*

21. Ibid., 34.

22. Das and Palmiotto, "International Human Rights Standards."

23. Office of the United Nations High Commissioner for Human Rights, "Human Rights Education and Training"; Office of the United Nations High Commissioner for Human Rights, "Plan of Action," 2012.

24. Celermajer and Grewal, "Preventing Human Rights Violations 'From the Inside.'"

25. Ibid.

26. Ibid.; Kaufman, "Human Rights Education for Law Enforcement," 278–295; DuBois, "Human Rights Education for the Police."

27. Martin, "Taking the Snake out of the Basket"; Jefferson, "Prison Officer Training and Practice"; Celermajer and Grewal, "Preventing Human Rights Violations 'From the Inside.'"

28. Jensen, "The Vision of the State."

29. Celermajer and Grewal, "Preventing Human Rights Violations 'From the Inside.'"

30. Das and Verma, "Teaching Police Officers Human Rights."

31. Ibid., 42.

32. Donovan and Vlais, *VicHealth Review of Communication Components of Social Marketing/Public Education Campaigns Focusing on Violence against Women*, 197–198.

33. Tibbitts, "Understanding What We Do," 159–171; Tibbitts, "Evolution of Human Rights Education Models," 18–41.

34. See also Bayley, *Democratizing the Police Abroad*; Celermajer and Grewal, "Preventing Human Rights Violations 'From the Inside.'"

35. Tibbitts, "Evolution of Human Rights Education Models," 33.

36. Bajaj, "Human Rights Education," 481–508.

37. For a more extensive review, see Bajaj, *Schooling for Social Change*; Bajaj and Wahl, "Between the Local and the Global."

38. Interviews with NHRC and BPRD staff, 2012.

39. Asian Centre for Human Rights, *Torture in India*; Nag and Prasad, *Police Complaints Authorities*; United States Department of State, *Country Reports on Human Rights Practices: India*; Human Rights Watch, *Broken System.*

40. Nag and Prasad, *Police Complaints Authorities*; Personal interviews with the staff of the Human Rights Law Network, New Delhi, 2012.

41. Asian Centre for Human Rights, *Torture in India.*

42. According to a Wikileaks-released cable, as reported in Burke, "WikiLeaks Cables: India accused of systematic use of torture in Kashmir."

43. Government of India, Armed Forces Special Powers Act.

44. For example, see Sharma, "J-K, NHRC Spar over Jurisdiction."

45. Personal interviews with human rights activists and NHRC officials, 2011–2012.

46. See, for example, Human Rights Watch, *World Report*, 328–333; Amnesty International, *Annual Report*; Nag and Prasad, *Police Complaints Authorities.*

47. Asian Centre for Human Rights, *Torture in India*; Human Rights Watch, *Broken System*; personal interviews with New Delhi-based human rights professionals, 2012.

48. United States Department of Justice, *Memorandum for Alberto R. Gonzales*, 1.

49. The Prevention of Torture Bill, 2010. Lok Sabha, Bill no. 58, Section 3i.

50. Jauregui, "Dirty Anthropology," 130.

51. Ibid., 131.

52. Kalhan et al., "Colonial Continuities"; Banerjea, *Criminal Justice in India Series.*

53. Nag and Prasad, *Police Complaints Authorities*; Prakash Singh vs. Union of India; Commonwealth Human Rights Initiative, *Feudal Forces.*

54. Human Rights Watch, *Broken System.*

55. Dugan, "Corruption Concerns All Generations of Indian Voters."

56. Medcalf, "India Poll 2013."

57. See, for example, Yardley, "Protests Awaken a Goliath in India."

58. Aam Aadmi Party, "Mission Vistaar"; see also The Economist, "India;'s Left-Leaning, Anti-Graft Party Made a Stunning Debut."

59. *New York Times*, "Dangerous Corruption in India."

60. Government of India Department of Justice, Ministry of Law and Justice. *Report of the Working Group for the Twelfth Five-Year Plan (2012–2017)*, 2.

61. *Report of the Working Group for the Twelfth Five-Year Plan* (*2012–2017*), presented at the end of 2010.

62. See, for example, Commonwealth Human Rights Initiative, *Feudal Forces*; Human Rights Watch, *Broken System.*

63. For government reviews, see, for example, "The Padmanabhaiah Committee on Police Reforms"; for NGOs, see Daruwala and Doube, *Police Accountability.*

64. According to a statement by Union Home Minister P. Chidambaram reported in numerous newspapers. See Press Trust of India, "Police Force Understaffed: Over 3 Lakh Vacancies."

65. Personal interviews with police reform advocates, 2011–2012. These NGOs include among others the Commonwealth Human Rights Initiative, Asian Centre for Human Rights, and the South Asian Human Rights Documentation Centre.

66. Commonwealth Human Rights Initiative, *Feudal Forces*; Human Rights Watch, *Broken System*.

67. See, for example, Yardley, "Urging Action, Report on Brutal Rape Condemns India's Treatment of Women." The issue of police neglect of crimes against women is significant and extensive. This study focuses, however, on police violence against criminal suspects. Although there may also be a gendered aspect to how police treat criminal suspects, it is beyond the scope of the current study.

68. Commonwealth Human Rights Initiative, *Feudal Forces*.

69. Ibid.

70. Personal interviews with police reform advocates, 2011–2012. This included New Delhi–based staff of the Commonwealth Human Rights Initiative, the Human Rights Law Network, the South Asian Human Rights Documentation Centre, and the South Asian Centre for Human Rights.

71. Personal interviews with police reform experts, 2011–2012; Lokaneeta, Transnational Torture, 133; Daruwala and Doube, *Police Accountability*; Dhillon, Police and Politics in India; Verma, The Indian Police; Campion, "Authority, Accountability, and Representation."

72. Jaugerui, "Beatings, Beacons, and Big Men"; Tankebe, "Public Cooperation with the Police in Ghana."

73. Jaugerui, "Beatings, Beacons, and Big Men."

74. Personal interviews with police reform advocates, 2011–2012; Commonwealth Human Rights Initiative, Police Organisation in India.

75. Commonwealth Human Rights Initiative, *Feudal Forces*; Human Rights Watch, *Broken System*.

76. Jauregui, "Beatings, Beacons, and Big Men"; personal interviews with police officials such as at the Bureau of Police Research and Development and National Human Rights Commission, 2011–2012.

77. Jauregui, "Introduction to Cultures of Legitimacy and Postcolonial Policing"; Personal interviews with police reform advocates, 2011–2012; Brass, Theft of an Idol.

78. Lokaneeta, *Transnational Torture*, 1–; Baxi, *The Crisis of the Indian Legal System*, 85.

79. Baxi, *The Crisis of the Indian Legal System*, 85. Quoted in Lokaneeta, *Transnational Torture*, 135.

80. Jauregui, "Beatings, Beacons, and Big Men."

81. Jauregui, "Introduction to Cultures of Legitimacy and Postcolonial Policing"; Cohn, "Anthropological Notes on Law and Disputes in North India."

82. Rejali, *Torture and Democracy.*

83. Conrad et al., "Political Institutions, Plausible Deniability, and the Decision to Hide Torture."

84. Lokaneeta, *Transnational Torture.*

85. Waddington et al., "Singing the Same Tune?"

86. Ibid.

87. Goldstein, *Outlawed*; see Martin, "Taking the Snake out of the Basket," for research in New Delhi.

88. Goldstein, *Outlawed*; Wilson, *The Politics of Truth and Reconciliation.*

89. Zimbardo, *The Lucifer Effect*; Milgram, *Obedience to Authority.*

90. Dawes, *Evil Men*; Huggins et al., *Violence Workers.*

91. Dawes, *Evil Men*; Browning, *Ordinary Men*; Haritos-Fatouros, "The Official Torturer."

92. Haritous-Faritous, "The Official Torturer."

93. Conroy, *Unspeakable Acts, Ordinary People: The Dynamics of Torture.*

94. Dawes, *Evil Men*; Browning, *Ordinary Men.*

95. Huggins et al., *Violence Workers.*

96. Dawes, *Evil Men,* 57.

97. Dawes, *Evil Men.*

98. Payne, *Unsettling Accounts*; Dawes, *Evil Men.*

99. Miller et al., "Torture and Public Opinion."

100. Jessberger, "Bad Torture—Good Torture."

101. Chan, "Police Stress and Occupational Culture," 148.

102. Sklansky, "Seeing Blue," 21; Muir, *Police.*

103. Westley, *Violence and the Police*; Skolnick and Fyfe, *Above the Law*; Waddington, "Police (Canteen) Sub-culture."

104. Dempsey and Forst, *An Introduction to Policing,* 220; Caldero and Crank, *Police Ethics.*

105. Skolnick and Fyfe, *Above the Law,* 91.

106. Ibid., 93.

107. Ibid., 92.

108. O'Neill et al, *Police Occupational Culture*; Hills, "Lost in Translation."

109. Waddington, "Police (Canteen) Sub-Culture"; Baker, "Conflict in African Police Culture; Hills, "Lost in Translation"; Liska and Yu, "Specifying and Testing the Threat Hypothesis."

110. Muir, *Police.*

111. Terrill et al., "Police Culture and Coercion"; Waddington, "Police (Canteen) Sub-Culture."

112. Waddington, "Police (Canteen) Sub-Culture."

113. Celermajer and Grewal, "Preventing Human Rights Violations 'From the Inside.'"

Chapter 2

A limited portion of this chapter is adapted from Wahl, R. (2014). "Justice, Context, and Violence: How Police Explain Torture."

1. Union Home Minister P Chidambaram as quoted by media reports. See for example "Chidambaram's Ode to the 'Most Reviled' Police Constable," *Rediff News*.

2. National Police Commission of India, *Commission Report 1*, 16.

3. Personal interviews with police reformers, New Delhi 2012; Jauregui, "Beatings, Beacons, and Big Men"; Jauregui, "If the Constable Could Speak."

4. See, for example, *Bhagavad Gita* 2.47, "You have control over doing your respective duty only, but no control or claim over the results. The fruits of work should not be your motive."

5. The bill was passed by the Lok Sabha, the lower house of the legislature, but has yet to be passed by the Rajya Sabha, the upper house of the legislature.

6. The Prevention of Torture Bill, no. 58, United Nations Convention Against Torture, on April 19, 2010; Asian Centre for Human Rights, *Torture in India.*

7. Niezen, "The Law's Legal Anthropology."

8. Taylor, *Modern Social Imaginaries*, 7.

9. Moyn, *The Last Utopia.*

10. Baxi, *Human Rights in a Post-Human World.*

11. Badiou, *Ethics*; Fagan, "Human Rights."

12. For example, the United Nations "Universal Declaration of Human Rights" (1948) begins: "Whereas recognition of the *inherent dignity and of the equal and inalienable rights* of all members of the human family is the foundation of freedom, justice and peace in the world . . ."

13. Baxi, *The Future of Human Rights.*

14. Rorty, *Contingency, Irony, ad Solidarity.*

15. Ruggie, "What Makes the World Hang Together"; Finnemore and Sikkink, "International Norm Dynamics and Political Change"; Katzenstein, *The Culture of National Security*; Wendt, "Constructing International Politics"; Adler, "Seasons of Peace."

16. Finnemore and Sikkink, "International Norm Dynamics and Political Change"; Payne, "Persuasion, Frames and Norm Construction."

17. Hawkins, "Explaining Costly International Institutions"; Keck and Sikkink, "Transnational Advocacy Networks in International and Regional Politics."

18. Taylor, *Sources of the Self*; Bernstein, *Torture and Dignity.*

19. Shklar, *Ordinary Vices*, 43–44. Rorty, *Contingency, Irony, and Solidarity*, 146.

20. Hawkins, "Explaining Costly International Institutions"; Finnemore and Sikkink, "International Norm Dynamics and Political Change."

21. The Prevention of Torture Bill, no. 58; Asian Centre for Human Rights, *Torture in India.* Human rights activists criticize the law for narrowing the definition of *torture*

and placing other restrictions on litigation such as the requirement that the case be filed within six months of the offense occurring.

22. Statement of the Government of India as recorded by the United Nations Human Rights Council (2008) in the *Report of the Working Group on the Universal Periodic Review: India*. In the most recent report (2012) India reiterated that its current laws support the principles of CAT, and noted that in 2010 the Lok Sabha ("people's" or lower house of the legislature) had passed the Prevention of Torture Bill that would allow for CAT ratification, but that the Rajya Sabha (upper house of the legislature) had not yet passed the bill.

23. Human rights groups in India routinely lobby the state to ratify CAT. In the most recent *United Nations Human Rights Council Report of the Working Group on the Universal Periodic Review: India* (2012), countries such as Sweden, Turkey, Australia, Canada, and the Czech Republic urged India to ratify CAT.

24. As suggested by the aforementioned statements to the United Nations and actions such as advancing the Prevention of Torture Bill through the lower house of the legislature.

25. See, for example, Finnemore and Sikkink, "International Norm Dynamics and Political Change"; Risse et al., *The Power of Human Rights*; Checkel, "International Institutions and Socialization"; Simmons, *Mobilizing for Human Rights*.

26. See, for example, Finnemore and Sikkink, "International Norm Dynamics and Political Change"; Risse et al., *The Power of Human Rights*; Checkel, "International Institutions and Socialization in Europe."

27. Risse et al., *The Power of Human Rights*.

28. Checkel, "Why Comply?"; Cortell and Davis, "Understanding the Domestic Impact of International Norms."

29. Schimmelfennig, *The EU, NATO and the Integration of Europe*, 219.

30. Risse et al., *The Persistent Power of Human Rights*.

Chapter 3

A limited portion of this chapter is adapted from Rachel Wahl, "Justice, Context, and Violence: How Police Explain Torture," *Law and Society Review* 48.4 (2014): 807–836.

1. Law Commission of India, "Law Commission Reports"; Commonwealth Human Rights Initiative, *Feudal Forces*.

2. Law Commission of India, "Law Commission Reports"; Commonwealth Human Rights Initiative, *Feudal Forces*.

3. University of Minnesota Human Rights Library, The Terrorist and Disruptive Activities (Prevention) Act.

4. See, for example, Human Rights Watch, *India: Stop Executions*; Human Rights Watch, *India Human Rights Press Backgrounder*; Commonwealth Human Rights Initiative, *Terror Assured Lawless Law*.

5. Personal interviews with human rights activists and criminal justice experts in New Delhi, as discussed in the text. Assertions about public perceptions of the justice

system are based on anecdotal evidence, such as the commonplace nature of this assumption in daily interactions during fieldwork.

6. Human Rights Watch, *Broken System.*

7. The narco-analysis test is itself highly controversial. See for example Lokaneeta, 'The Aditi Sharma case and the implications for human rights in India.

8. Langbein, *Torture and the Law of Proof.*

9. Lokaneeta, *Transnational Torture*; Wisnewski and Emerick, *The Ethics of Torture.*

10. Nag and Prasad, "Police Complaints Authorities"; National Police Commission, "National Police Commission Reports"; Personal interviews, e.g. Asian Centre for Human Rights staff, 2011.

11. For example, Huggins et al., *Violence Workers.*

12. Montgomery, "Imposing Rights? A Case Study of Child Prostitution in Thailand."

13. Taylor, *Sources of the Self.*

14. For example, protests against the police broke out across India following the gruesome rape and murder of a young woman in New Delhi on December 16, 2011. These protests have continued to gain momentum in response to subsequent rapes that became public. Protestors have issued a demand for the Delhi Police commissioner to step down. The protestors' complaint is that police are unresponsive to violence against women and are too soft on rape suspects. The suspects in the now infamous December 16 case have alleged that they have been tortured in jail, and one has died while incarcerated. These allegations of police violence have not gained attention in the current protests. For examples of coverage see Yardley, "Urging Action, Report on Brutal Rape Condemns India's Treatment of Women"; Gulf News, "India Rape: Protests Across Delhi Against Police Laxity"; New Delhi Television Limited (NDTV), "Delhi Gang Rape Protests."

15. Niezen, "*The Law's Legal Anthropology.*"

16. Schaffer and Smith, *Human Rights and Narrated Lives.*

17. Merry, "Transnational Human Rights and Local Activism."

18. Keck and Sikkink, "Transnational Advocacy Networks in International and Regional Politics"; Klotz, "Transnational Activism and Global Transformations"; Payne, "Persuasion, Frames and Norm Construction"; Finnemore and Sikkink, "International Norm Dynamics and Political Change."

19. Tyler and Huo, *Trust in the Law.*

20. Tyler and Blader, "Can Businesses Effectively Regulate Employee Conduct?"; Tyler, "Promoting Employee Policy Adherence and Rule Following in Work Settings."

21. Tyler, Callahan, and Frost, "Armed and Dangerous(?)."

22. Martin, "Taking the Snake Out of the Basket."

23. Jensen and Jefferson, eds., *State Violence and Human Rights*; Martin, "Taking the Snake Out of the Basket."

24. Waddington et al., "Singing the Same Tune? International Continuities and Discontinuities in How Police Talk about Using Force."

25. Finnemore and Sikkink, "International Norm Dynamics and Political Change"; Wendt, "Constructing International Politics."

26. Snyder and Vinjamuri, "Trials and Errors."

Chapter 4

1. Spivak, Outside in the Teaching Machine, 47; see also Brown, "Suffering Rights as Paradoxes."

2. Hobbes, *Leviathan*; Locke, *Two Treatises of Government.*

3. Locke, *Two Treatises of Government*; Rousseau, *On the Social Contract.*

4. Taylor, *Sources of the Self*, 58.

5. Taylor, *Modern Social Imaginaries*, 4–5.

6. See, for example, Ignatieff et al., *Human Rights as Politics and Idolatry*, 53.

7. Taylor, *Modern Social Imaginaries*, 8.

8. Onazi, "Towards a Subaltern Theory of Human Rights"; Baxi, *The Future of Human Rights*; Baxi et al., "Legacies of Common Law"; Santos, *Towards a New Legal Common Sense.*

9. Bob, *Marketing of Rebellion*; Merry, "Transnational Human Rights and Local Activism," 38–51; Hertel, *Unexpected Power.*

10. Hafner-Burton and Ron, "Seeing Double."

11. Baxi et al., "Legacies of Common Law."

12. Risse et al., *The Power of Human Rights*; March and Olsen, "The Institutional Dynamics of International Political Orders"; Finnemore and Sikkink, "International Norm Dynamics and Political Change"; Katzenstein, *The Culture of National Security.*

13. Risse et al., *The Power of Human Rights*; Risse et al., *The Persistent Power of Human Rights*; Simmons, *Mobilizing for Human Rights.*

14. For an example of such reports, see Human Rights Watch, *Broken System.*

15. Anand, "Chidambaram: Poor Conditions 'Dehumanize' Police."

16. Schimmelfennig, *The EU, NATO, and the Integration of Europe.*

17. Acharya, "How Ideas Spread."

18. Bullock and Johnson, "The Impact of the Human Rights Act 1998 on Policing in England and Wales," 630.

19. Merry, "Transnational Human Rights and Local Activism."

20. Stewart, "Syncretism and Its Synonyms."

21. Berry, "Developing Women."

22. Merry, "Transnational Human Rights and Local Activism."

23. Ibid.

24. Ibid., 44.

25. Meyer, et al., "World Society and the Nation-State."

26. Merry, "Human Rights, Gender, and New Social Movements."

27. Allen, *The Rise and Fall of Human Rights.* Allen uses the term *cynical* to refer to the ironic approach of Palestinian civilians to human rights, but here I am employing the term's more standard meaning to refer to her description of state officials' superficial acquiescence to human rights.

28. Vavrus and Bartlett, "Comparative Pedagogies and Epistemological Diversity."

29. Merry, "Transnational Human Rights and Local Activism," 40.

30. Wilson, *The Politics of Truth and Reconciliation.*

31. Hornberger, "My Police—Your Police"; Hornberger, *Policing and Human Rights.*

32. Martin, "Taking the Snake out of the Basket."

33. Wilson, *Human Rights, Culture, and Context.*

34. Goldstein, *Outlawed*, 26.

35. Hills, "Lost in Translation."

36. Ibid., 753

37. As I discuss elsewhere, this does not mean that police always protect the rights of children and other vulnerable groups. Wahl, "The Trouble with Frames."

38. Laverty, "Learning Our Concepts," 37.

39. Bajaj, "Human Rights Education."

40. Tibbitts, "Evolution of Human Rights Education Models."

41. Ibid.

42. United Nations General Assembly, Resolution 66/137; Amnesty International, *Annual Report: India*; Tibbitts, "Evolution of Human Rights Education Models."

43. Reardon, "Human Rights Learning."

44. Howe and Covell, "Miseducating Children about Their Rights."

45. Mobley, "Two Liberalisms," 6–34; Locke, *Two Treatises of Government;* Hobbes, *Leviathan*

46. Dunn, *The Political Thought of John Locke*, 83.

47. Hobbes, *Leviathan.*

48. Locke, *Two Treatises of Government*; Rousseau, *On the Social Contract.*

49. Wallach, "Constitutive Paradoxes of Human Rights."

Chapter 5

A portion of this chapter is adapted from Rachel Wahl, "Policing, Values, and Violence: Human Rights Education with Law Enforcers in India." Special Issue on Human Rights Education and Training: Taking Stock of Theory and Practice. *Oxford Journal of Human Rights Practice* 5.2 (2013): 220–242.

1. Sharma, *Hindu Narratives on Human Rights*; Shweder et al., "The 'Big Three' of Morality"; Mitra, "Human Rights in Hinduism."

2. Charlesworth et al., "Feminist Approaches to International Law."

3. Sen, "Human Rights and the Westernizing Illusion"; Juergensmeyer, "Hindu Nationalism and Human Rights."

4. Merry, "Human Rights Law and the Demonization of Culture (and Anthropology along the Way)"; Merry, "Transnational Human Rights and Local Activism."

5. For example, United Nations, *The Challenge of Human Rights and Cultural Diversity.*

6. Merry, "Transnational Human Rights and Local Activism"; Keck and Sikkink, *Activists Beyond Borders.*

7. See, for example, The International Center for Religion and Diplomacy at http://icrd.org/.

8. Mitra, "Human Rights in Hinduism."

9. The addition of the honorific "ji" at the end of a name signifies respect.

10. Taylor, *A Secular Age.*

11. Das and Verma, "Teaching Police Officers Human Rights"; Dempsey and Forst, *An Introduction to Policing*; Crank and Caldero, *Police Ethics: The Corruption of Noble Cause.*

12. Baxi, *Human Rights in a Post-Human World.*

13. Ibid.; Guha, *Dominance without Hegemony.*

14. Shweder, "The 'Big Three' of Morality (Autonomy, Community, Divinity) and the 'Big Three' Explanations of Suffering."

15. Petro, *Crafting Democracy.*

16. Finnemore and Sikkink, "International Norm Dynamics and Political Change"; Merry, "Transnational Human Rights and Local Activism."

Chapter 6

1. Asian Centre for Human Rights, "Torture in India"; Personal interviews with human rights professionals in New Delhi, 2011–2012.

2. Merry, "Transnational Human Rights and Local Activism"; Keck and Sikkink, *Activists Beyond Borders*; Checkel, "Norms, Institutions, and National Identity in Contemporary Europe."

3. In 1987, Israel legalized practices that under international law constitute torture. The High Court of Justice ruled in 1999 that "moderate physical pressure" should not be used routinely, but did not rule out its use entirely. Hajjar, "International Humanitarian Law and 'Wars on Terror,'" 27.

4. Risse et al., *The Persistent Power of Human Rights.*

5. Dolan, "Unthinkable and Tragic."

Chapter 7

1. The standard medical response to rape victims in India is commonly thought to retraumatize and intimidate women. Doctors often conduct intrusive physical examinations to determine if a woman has been "raped," defined by whether intercourse recently occurred. Human Rights Watch, 2010.

2. I was conscious throughout the interviews not to align myself with human rights activists and, instead, presented myself as wishing to learn from the police and security forces. Sometimes, though, officers saw me as someone associated with the human rights community and seemed to view the interview as a chance to be heard by a community they feel fails to understand them.

3. South Asia Human Rights Documentation Centre, "Ignoring the Disappeared of Kashmir with Impunity"; Human Rights Watch, "India: Investigate Unmarked Graves in Jammu and Kashmir."

4. As discussed in previous chapters, between 1975 and 1977 India operated under State of Emergency laws that suspended many democratic freedoms. Among other violations, the police routinely arrested and tortured political activists including students

thought to be involved with political activities, according to the Shah Commission (a government body later convened to investigate allegations of such violations under the Emergency).

5. Police are required to file this to register a case.

6. Personal interviews with human rights professionals, 2011–2012; Asian Centre for Human Rights, "Torture in India."

7. For example, as documented by the BBC program, "India: The Truth about NGOs."

8. Benford and Snow, "Framing Processes and Social Movements," 615.

9. Mutua, *Human Rights*, 10.

10. Benford and Snow, "Framing Processes and Social Movements"; Smith and Schaffer, *Human Rights and Narrated Lives.*

11. The notion of deliberative democracy is supported by a rich body of literature in political theory. See, for example, Habermas on communicative action in the public sphere and Fishkin on deliberation.

12. Shields, *The Democratic Virtues of the Christian Right.*

13. Risse, "Let's Argue! Communicative Action in World Politics"; Checkel, "Why Comply? Social Learning and European Identity Change"; Schimmelfennig, *The EU, NATO, and the Integration of Europe*; Habermas, *The Theory of Communicative Action, Vol. 2: Lifeworld and System: A Critique of Functionalist Reason.*

14. Checkel, "Why Comply? Social Learning and European Identity Change."

15. Ibid.

16. Ibid.

17. Risse et al., *The Power of Human Rights.*

18. Schimmelfennig, *The EU, NATO, and the Integration of Europe.*

19. Ibid., 218.

20. Ibid., 219.

21. Risse et al., *The Power of Human Rights.*

22. Hawkins, "Explaining Costly International Institutions," 784.

23. Sikkink, "Human Rights, Principled Issue Networks, and Sovereignty in Latin America"; Finnemore and Sikkink, "International Norm Dynamics and Political Change"; Risse et al., *The Power of Human Rights*; Risse et al., *The Persistent Power of Human Rights.*

24. Simmons, *Mobilizing for Human Rights.*

25. Ibid.; Risse et al., *The Persistent Power of Human Rights.*

26. Snyder, "Harnessing the Power of Mass Movements, Religion, and Reform Parties to the Cause of Human Rights"; Hopgood, *The Endtimes of Human Rights.*

27. Snyder and Vinjamuri, "Trials and Errors."

28. Hafner-Burton, "Sticks and Stones"; Conrad and Demeritt, "Unintended Consequences."

29. Hafner-Burton and Ron, "Seeing Double."

Conclusion

1. Taylor, *Sources of the Self*; Taylor, *A Secular Age*; See MacIntyre, *After Virtue* for another insightful discussion of this theme.

2. The National Healthy Marriage Resource Center, which stresses that it is "evidence based," is one of numerous examples of this tendency to use the language of science to articulate a normative vision.

3. Haidt and Graham, "When Morality Opposes Justice."

4. Ignatieff et al., *Human Rights as Politics and Idolatry*, 53.

5. Barnett and Finnemore, *Rules for the World*.

6. United Nations General Assembly, *Universal Declaration of Human Rights*, Article 26(2).

7. Niezen, "The Law's Legal Anthropology."

8. Merry, "Human Rights Monitoring and the Question of Indicators."

9. Goodale, "Human Rights after the Post-Cold War."

10. Rorty, *Contingency, Irony, and Solidarity*.

11. Brass, *Theft of an Idol*, 5.

12. Inayatullah and Blaney, "Liberal Fundamentals"; Inayatullah and Blaney, "The Dark Heart of Kindness."

13. Baxi, *Human Rights in a Post-Human World*; Guha, *Dominance without Hegemony*.

14. Taylor, "Modes of Secularism," 31–53; For example, as Taylor writes, the Buddhist emphasis on compassion coincides with liberal mandates to protect people, though each relies on different philosophical positions regarding the nature and causes of suffering.

15. Dawes, *Evil Men*, 34.

16. Ibid., 30.

17. Ibid., 35.

18. Ibid., 37.

19. Ibid., 34.

20. Presidential hopeful Ben Carson at the first Republican primary debate for the 2016 election on August 6, 2015. The full text of the debate is accessible at http://time.com/3988276/republican-debate-primetime-transcript-full-text/

21. Dempsey and Forst, *An Introduction to Policing*; Caldero and Crank, *Police Ethics*.

22. As noted, for example, by Acharya, "How Ideas Spread"; for other theorists contesting this assumption see Finnemore and Jurkovich, "Getting a Seat at the Table"; Sikkink, "Latin American Countries as Norm Protagonists of the Idea of International Human Rights."

23. United Nations, *The United Nations World Programme in Human Rights Education Plan of Action*.

24. Personal interviews with human rights educators, New Delhi, 2012.

25. Dewey, *Democracy and Education*, 4.

26. Ibid.

27. Bayley, *Democratizing the Police Abroad.*

28. Celermajer and Grewal, "Preventing Human Rights Violations 'From the Inside.'"

29. Checkel, "Why Comply? Social Learning and European Identity Change"; Risse, "Let's Argue! Communicative Action in World Politics"; Keck and Sikkink, *Activists beyond Borders.*

30. Martin, "Taking the Snake Out of the Basket," 154.

31. Celermajer and Grewal, "Preventing Human Rights Violations 'From the Inside.'"

32. See the forthcoming volume *Human Rights Futures* for a description of this debate and for contributors on both sides of it. For examples of the former position, see Sikkink and Simmons. For examples of the latter position, see Snyder and Vinjamuri.

33. Snyder, "Empowering Rights through Mass Movements, Religion, and Reform Parties."

34. Taylor, *A Secular Age*, 707.

35. Ibid.

36. Ibid., 709.

37. Ibid., 710.

38. Mouffe, "Deliberative Democracy or Agonistic Pluralism," 16.

39. Jensen and Jefferson, *State Violence and Human Rights*, 15.

40. Mouffe, "Deliberative Democracy or Agonistic Pluralism," 15.

41. Taylor, *A Secular Age*, 742.

42. See, for example, Badiou, *Ethics.*

43. As per Jensen and Jefferson, *State Violence and Human Rights*, 20, drawing on Mouffe, "Deliberative Democracy or Agonistic Pluralism."

Bibliography

Aam Aadmi Party. "Mission Vistaar." Last accessed February 6, 2016, at: www.aamaadmiparty.org/mission-vistaar.

Ab Tak Chhappan. Directed by Shimit Amin. K Sera Sera and Varma Corporation, 2004.

Acharya, Amitav. "How Ideas Spread: Whose Norms Matter? Norm Localization and Institutional Change in Asian Regionalism." *International Organization* 58.2 (2004): 239–275.

Adler, Emanuel. "Seasons of Peace: Progress in Postwar International Security." In *Progress in Postwar International Relations*, Emanuel Adler and Beverly Crawford (Eds.), 128–173. New York: Columbia University Press, 1991.

Allen, Danielle. *Talking to Strangers: Anxieties of Citizenship since Brown v. Board of Education.* Chicago: University of Chicago Press.

Allen, Lori. *The Rise and Fall of Human Rights: Cynicism and Politics in Occupied Palestine.* Stanford, CA: Stanford University Press, 2013.

Amnesty International. *Annual Report: India.* 2012. Accessible at: www.amnesty.org/en/region/india/report-2012.

Anderson-Levitt, Kathryn. "A World Culture of Schooling?" In *Local Meanings, Global Schooling: Anthropology and World Culture Theory*, Kathryn Anderson-Levitt (Ed.), 1–26. New York: Palgrave Macmillan, 2003.

Asian Centre for Human Rights. *Torture in India.* November 21, 2011. Last accessed February 23, 2013, at: www.achrweb.org/reports.htm.

Asian Human Rights Commission. "INDIA: Police Torture of Young Man Part of 'Investigation.' " Last modified February 26, 2007: www.humanrights.asia/news/urgent-appeals/UA-065-2007.

Badiou, Alain. *Ethics: An Essay on the Understanding of Evil.* London: Verso, 2001.

Bajaj, Monisha. "Human Rights Education: Ideology, Location, and Approaches." *Human Rights Quarterly* 33 (2011): 481–508.

Bajaj, Monisha. *Schooling for Social Change: The Rise and Impact of Human Rights Education in India.* London: Bloomsbury Publishing, 2012.

Bajaj, Monisha, and Rachel Wahl. "Between the Local and the Global: Vernacularizing Human Rights Education in India." In *Global Perspectives on Human Rights Educa-*

tion, Monisha Bajaj (Ed.), 123–141. Philadelphia: University of Pennsylvania Press, forthcoming.

Baker, Bruce. "Conflict and African Police Culture: The Cases of Uganda, Rwanda, and Sierra Leone." In *Police Occupational Culture: New Debates and Directions*, Megan O'Neill, Monique Marks, and Anne-Marie Singh (Eds.), 321–348. Sociology of Crime, Law and Deviance Vol. 8. Oxford: Elsevier, 2007.

Banerjea, D. (Ed.). *Chandisgarh, Part II*, Criminal Justice in India Series Vol. 17: Lucknow, India: Allied Publishers Private Limited.

Barnett, Michael, and Martha Finnemore. *Rules for the World: International Organizations in Global Politics*. Ithaca, NY: Cornell University Press, 2004.

Baxi, Upendra. *The Crisis of the Indian Legal System. Alternatives in Development: Law*. Vikas Publishing House Pvt Ltd., 1982.

Baxi, Upendra. *The Future of Human Rights*. New Delhi: Oxford University Press, 2002.

Baxi, Upendra. *Human Rights in a Post-Human World*. New York: Oxford University Press, 2009.

Baxi, Pratiksha, Shirin M. Rai, and Shaheen Sardar Ali. 2006. "Legacies of Common Law: 'Crimes of Honour' in India and Pakistan." In "The Politics of Rights: Dilemmas for Feminist Praxis," Andrea Cornwall and Maxine Molyneux (Eds.). Special Issue, *Third World Quarterly* 27.7 (2006):1239–1253.

Bayley, David H. *Democratizing the Police Abroad: What to Do and How to Do It*. United States Department of Justice, Office of Justice Programs, National Institute of Justice, 2001.

Benford, Robert D., and David A. Snow. "Framing Processes and Social Movements: An Overview and Assessment." *Annual Review of Sociology* 26 (2000): 611–639.

Bernstein, J. M. *Torture and Dignity: An Essay on Moral Injury*. Chicago: University of Chicago Press, 2015.

Berry, Kim. "Developing Women: The Traffic in Ideas about Women and Their Needs in Kangra, India." In *Regional Modernities: The Cultural Politics of Development in India*, K. Sivaramakrishnan and Arun Agrawal (Eds.), 75–98. Stanford, CA: Stanford University Press, 2003.

Bob, Clifford. *The Marketing of Rebellion: Insurgents, Media, and International Activism*. Cambridge: Cambridge University Press, 2005.

Brass, Paul R. *Theft of an Idol: Text and Context in the Representation of Collective Violence*. Princeton: Princeton University Press, 1997.

Browning, Christopher. *Ordinary Men: Reserve Police Battalion 101 and the Final Solution in Poland*. New York, Harper Perennial, 1998.

Bullock, Karen, and Paul Johnson. "The Impact of the Human Rights Act 1998 on Policing in England and Wales." *British Journal of Criminology* 52.3 (2012): 630–650.

Burke, Jason. "WikiLeaks Cables: India Accused of Systematic Use of Torture in Kashmir." *The Guardian*, December 16, 2010. Accessible at: www.guardian.co.uk/world/2010/dec/16/wikileaks-cables-indian-torture-kashmir.

Caldero, Michael, and John P. Crank. *Police Ethics: The Corruption of Noble Cause*. Atlanta: Elsivier, 2010.

Campion, David A. "Authority, Accountability, and Representation: The United Provinces Police and Dilemmas of the Colonial Policeman in British India, 1902–1939." *Historical Research* 76.192 (2003): 217–237.

Celermajer, Danielle. "The Ritualization of Human Rights Education and Training: The Fallacy of the Potency of Knowing." *Journal of Human Rights.* Forthcoming.

Celermajer, Danielle, and Kiran Grewal. "Preventing Human Rights Violations 'From the Inside': Enhancing the Role of Human Rights Education in Security Sector Reform." *Journal of Human Rights Practice* 5.2 (2013): 243–266.

Chan, Janet. "Police Stress and Occupational Culture." In *Police Occupational Culture: New Debates and Directions*, Megan O'Neill, Monique Marks, and Anne-Marie Singh (Eds.), 129–152. Sociology of Crime, Law and Deviance Vol. 8. Oxford: Elsevier, 2007.

Charlesworth, Hilary, Christine Chinkin, and Shelley Wright. "Feminist Approaches to International Law." *The American Journal of International Law* 85.4 (1991): 613–645.

Checkel, Jeffrey T. "International Institutions and Socialization in Europe: Introduction and Framework." *International Organization* 59.4 (2005): 801–826.

Checkel, Jeffrey T. "Norms, Institutions, and National Identity in Contemporary Europe." *International Studies Quarterly* 43.1 (1999): 84–114.

Checkel, Jeffrey T. "Why Comply? Social Learning and European Identity Change." *International Organization* 55.3 (2001): 553–588.

"Chidambaram's ode to the 'most reviled' police constable." *Rediff News.* October 5, 2009. Accessible at: http://news.rediff.com/report/2009/oct/05/chidambarams-ode-to-the-most-reviled-police-constable.htm.

Cohn, Bernard S. "Anthropological Notes on Law and Disputes in North India." In *An Anthropologist among the Historians and Other Essays*, Bernard S. Cohn (Ed.), 575–631. New Delhi: Oxford University Press, 1987 [1965].

Commonwealth Human Rights Initiative, *Police Organisation in India*, 2008. Last accessed January 20, 2016, at: www.humanrightsinitiative.org/publications/police/police_organisation_in_india_english.pdf.

Commonwealth Human Rights Initiative, *Feudal Forces: Reform Delayed (Moving from Force to Service in South Asian Policing)*, 2010.

Commonwealth Human Rights Initiative, "Terror-Assured Lawless Law." *CHRI News*, 2013. Last accessed January 23, 2016, at: www.humanrightsinitiative.org/publications/nl/articles/india/terror_assured_lawless_law.pdf.

Conrad, Courtenay R., Daniel W. Hill, Jr., and Will H. Moore. "Political Institutions, Plausible Deniability, and the Decision to Hide Torture." Working paper, July 9, 2014. Accessible at: http://myweb.fsu.edu/dwh06c/pages/documents/ConHilMooTortType2July14.pdf.

Conrad, Courtenay R., and Jacqueline H. R. DeMeritt. "Unintended Consequences: The Effect of Advocacy to End Torture on Empowerment Rights Violations." In *Examining Torture: Empirical Studies of State Repression*, Tracy Lightcap and James P. Pfiffner (Eds.), 159–183. New York: Palgrave MacMillan, 2014.

Conroy, John. *Unspeakable Acts, Ordinary People: The Dynamics of Torture*. Berkeley, CA: University of California Press, 2000.

Cortell, Andrew P., and James W. Davis Jr. "Understanding the Domestic Impact of International Norms: A Research Agenda." *International Studies Review* 2.1 (2000): 65–87.

Daruwala, Maja, and Clare Doube, (Eds.). *Police Accountability: Too Important to Neglect, Too Urgent to Delay*. New Delhi: Commonwealth Human Rights Initiative, 2005. Last accessed January 24, 2015, at: www.humanrightsinitiative.org/publications/chogm/chogm_2005/chogm_2005_full_report.pdf.

Das, Dilip K., and Michael J. Palmiotto. "International Human Rights Standards: Guidelines for the World's Police Officers." *Police Quarterly* 5.2 (2002): 206–221.

Das, Dilip K., and Arvind Verma. "Teaching Police Officers Human Rights." *The International Journal of Human Rights* 6.2 (2010): 35–48.

Dawes, James. *Evil Men*. Cambridge: Harvard University Press, 2013.

Dempsey, John S., and Linda S. Forst, *An Introduction to Policing* (6th ed.). Stamford, CT: Cengage Learning, 2011.

Department. Directed by Ram Gopal Varma. Dreamforce Enterprise, 2012.

Dewey, John. *Democracy and Education: An Introduction to the Philosophy of Education*. Los Angeles: Indo-European Publishing, 2010.

Dhillon, Kirpal. *Police and Politics in India: Colonial Concepts, Democratic Compulsions*. New Delhi: Manohar, 2005.

Dolan, Thomas M. "Unthinkable and Tragic." *International Organization* 67.1 (2013): 37–63.

Donnelly, Jack. *Universal Human Rights in Theory and Practice*. Ithaca, NY: Cornell University Press, 2003.

Donovan, Robert J., and Rodney Vlais. *VicHealth Review of Communication Components of Social Marketing/Public Education Campaigns Focusing on Violence against Women*. Melbourne: Victorian Health Promotion Foundation, 2005.

Drori, Gili S., John W. Meyer, and Hokyu Hwang. "Global Organization: Rationalization and Actorhood as Dominant Scripts." *Research in the Sociology of Organizations* 27 (2009): 17–44.

Dubois, Marc. "Human Rights Education for the Police." *In Human Rights Education for the 21st Century*, George Andreopolous and Richard Claude (Eds.), 310–333. Philadelphia: University of Pennsylvania Press, 1997.

Dugan, Andrew. "Corruption Concerns All Generations of Indian Voters." Gallup, 2014. Last accessed February 5, 2016, at: www.gallup.com/poll/168488/corruption-concerns-generations-indian-voters.aspx.

Dunn, John. *The Political Thought of John Locke: An Historical Account of the Argument of the 'Two Treatises of Government*. Cambridge: Cambridge University Press, 1969.

Fagan, Andrew. Human Rights. *Internet Encyclopedia of Philosophy: A Peer-Reviewed Academic Resource*. Accessible at: www.iep.utm.edu/hum-rts/.

Finnemore, Martha, and Kathryn Sikkink. "International Norm Dynamics and Political Change." *International Organization* 52.4 (1998): 887–917.

Finnemore, Martha, and Michelle Jurkovich. "Getting a Seat at the Table: The Origins of Universal Participation and Modern Multilateral Conferences." *Global Governance* 20.3 (2014): 361–373.

Gaudelli, William, and William R. Fernekes. "Teaching about Global Human Rights for Global Citizenship." *The Social Studies* 95.1 (2004): 16–26.

Goldstein, Daniel. *Outlawed: Between Security and Rights in a Bolivian City* (*The Cultures and Practice of Violence*). Durham, NC: Duke University Press, 2012.

Goodale, Mark. *Surrendering to Utopia: An Anthropology of Human Rights*. Stanford, CA: Stanford University Press, 2009.

Goodale, Mark. "Human Rights After the Post-Cold War." In *Human Rights at the Crossroads*, Mark Goodale (Ed.). New York: Oxford University Press, 2013.

Government of India. Armed Forces Special Powers Act. September 11, 1958.

Government of India Department of Justice, Ministry of Law and Justice. *Report of the Working Group for the Twelfth Five-Year Plan (2012–2017)*. September 2011. Accessible at: http://planningcommission.gov.in/aboutus/committee/wrkgrp12/wg_law.pdf.

Guha, Ranajit. *Dominance without Hegemony: History and Power in Colonial India*. Cambridge: Harvard University Press, 1997.

Habermas, Jürgen. *Lifeworld and System: A Critique of Functionalist Reason*, Reason and the Rationalization of Society Vol. 2. Boston: Beacon Press, 1987.

Hafner-Burton, Emilie M. *Making Human Rights a Reality*. Princeton: Princeton University Press, 2013.

Hafner-Burton, Emilie M. "Sticks and Stones: Naming and Shaming the Human Rights Enforcement Problem." *International Organization* 62.4 (2008): 689–716.

Hafner-Burton, Emilie M., and James Ron. "Seeing Double: Human Rights Impact through Qualitative and Quantitative Eyes." *World Politics* 61.2 (2009): 360–401.

Haidt, Jonathan, and Jesse Graham. "When Morality Opposes Justice: Conservatives Have Moral Intuitions That Liberals May Not Recognize." *Social Justice Research* 20.1 (2007): 98-116.

Hajjar, Lisa. "International Humanitarian Law and 'Wars on Terror': A Comparative Analysis of Israeli and American Doctrines and Policies." *Journal of Palestine Studies* 36.1 (2006): 21–42.

Haritos-Fatouros, Mika. "The Official Torturer: A Learning Model for Obedience to the Authority of Violence." *Journal of Applied Social Psychology* 18.13 (1988): 1107–1120.

Hawkins, Darren. "Explaining Costly International Institutions: Persuasion and Enforceable Human Rights Norms." *International Studies Quarterly* 48.4 (2004): 779–804.

Hertel, Shareen. *Unexpected Power: Conflict and Change among Transnational Activists*. Ithaca, NY: Cornell University Press, 2006.

Hills, Alice. "Lost in Translation: Why Nigeria's Police Don't Implement Democratic Reforms." *International Affairs* 88.4 (2012): 739–753.

Hobbes, Thomas. *Leviathan*. New York: Penguin Classics, 1982.

Hopgood, Stephen. *The Endtimes of Human Rights*. Ithaca, NY: Cornell University Press, 2013.

Hornberger, Julia. "'My Police—Your Police.' The Informal Privatisation of the Police in the Inner City of Johannesburg." *African Studies* 63.2 (2004): 213–230.

Hornberger, Julia. *Policing and Human Rights. The Meaning of Violence and Justice in the Everyday Policing of Johannesburg*. Law, Development and Globalisation Series. London: Routledge, 2011.

Howe, R. Brian, and Katherine Covell. "Miseducating Children about Their Rights." *Education, Citizenship and Social Justice* 5.2 (2010): 91–102.

Huggins, Martha K., Mike Haritos-Fatouros, and Philip G. Zimbardo. *Violence Workers: Police Torturers and Murders Reconstruct Brazilian Atrocities*. Berkeley, CA: University of California Press, 2002.

Human Rights Watch, India Human Rights Press Backgrounder. 2001. Last accessed January 23, 2016, at: https://www.hrw.org/legacy/backgrounder/asia/india-bck1121.htm.

Human Rights Watch. *Broken System: Dysfunction, Abuse, and Impunity in the Indian Police*. August 4, 2009. Accessible at: www.hrw.org/en/reports/2009/08/04/broken-system-0.

Human Rights Watch. "India: Investigate Unmarked Graves in Jammu and Kashmir." August 24, 2011. Accessible at: www.hrw.org/news/2011/08/24/india-investigate-unmarked-graves-jammu-and-kashmir.

Human Rights Watch. *World Report*. 2012. Accessible at: https://www.hrw.org/video-photos/interactive/2012/01/19/world-report-2012.

Human Rights Watch. *India: Stop Executions*. 2013. Last accessed January 23, 2016, at: www.hrw.org/news/2013/08/21/india-stop-executions.

Ignatieff, Michael. *Human Rights as Politics and Idolatry*. Princeton: Princeton University Press, 2003.

Inayatullah, Naeem, and David L. Blaney. "Liberal Fundamentals: Invisible, Invasive, Artful, and Bloody Hands." *Journal of International Relations and Development* 15.2 (2012): 290–315.

Inayatullah, Naeem, and David L. Blaney. "The Dark Heart of Kindness: The Social Construction of Deflection." *International Studies Perspectives* 13.2 (2012): 164–175.

"India Rape: Protests across Delhi against Police Laxity." *Gulf News*. July 25, 2016. Accessible at: http://gulfnews.com/news/asia/india/india-rape-protests-across-delhi-against-police-laxity-1.1172982.

"India: The Truth About NGOs." BBC video. December 28, 2011. Accessible at: www.bbc.co.uk/programmes/p00mmn3s.

Jauregui, Beatrice. "Beatings, Beacons, and Big Men: Police Disempowerment and Delegitimation in India." *Law and Social Inquiry* 38.3 (2013): 643–669.

Jauregui, Beatrice. "Dirty Anthropology: Epistemologies of Violence and Ethical Entanglements in Police Ethnography." In *Policing and Contemporary Government*, William Garriott (Ed.), 125–156. New York: Palgrave Macmillan, 2013.

Jaureguie, Beatrice. "If the Constable Could Speak: Notes on a Continuing Failure to Secure the Masses and Reform the Police in India." *India in Transition*. Center for the

Advanced Study of India, December 7, 2009. Accessible at: https://casi.sas.upenn.edu/iit/Jauregui.

Jauregui, Beatrice. "Introduction to Cultures of Legitimacy and Postcolonial Policing." *Law and Social Inquiry* 38.3 (2013): 547–552.

Jefferson, Andrew M. "Prison Officer Training and Practice in Nigeria Contention: Contradiction and Re-Imagining Reform Strategies." *Punishment and Society* 9.3 (2007): 253–269.

Jensen, Steffen. "The Vision of the State: Audiences, Enchantments, and Policing in South Africa." In *State Violence and Human Rights: State Officials in the South*, Steffen Jensen and Andrew Jefferson (Eds.), 60–78. New York: Routledge, 2009.

Jensen, Steffen, and Andrew Jefferson. (Eds.). *State Violence and Human Rights: State Officials in the South*. New York: Routledge, 2009.

Jessberger, Florian. "Bad Torture—Good Torture: What International Criminal Lawyers May Learn from the Recent Trial of Police Officers in Germany." *Journal of International Criminal Justice* 3 (2005): 1059–1073.

Juergensmeyer, Mark. "Hindu Nationalism and Human Rights." In *Religious Diversity and Human Rights*, Irene Bloom, J. Paul Martin, and Wayne L. Proudfoot (Eds.), 243–261. New York, Columbia University Press, 1996.

Katzenstein, Peter J. *The Culture of National Security: Norms and Identity in World Politics*. New York: Columbia University Press, 1996.

Kaufman, Edy. "Human Rights Education for Law Enforcement." In *Human Rights Education for the 21st Century*, George Andreopolous, and Richard Claude (Eds.), 278–295. Philadelphia: University of Pennsylvania Press, 1997.

Keck, Margaret E., and Kathryn Sikkink, *Activists beyond Borders: Advocacy Networks in International Politics*. Ithaca, NY: Cornell University Press, 1998.

Keck, Margaret E., and Kathryn Sikkink. "Transnational Advocacy Networks in International and Regional Politics." *International Social Science Journal* 51.159 (1999): 89–101.

Klotz, Audie. "Transnational Activism and Global Transformations: The Anti-Apartheid and Abolitionist Experiences." *European Journal of International Relations* 8.1 (2002): 49–76.

Langbein, John H. *Torture and the Law of Proof: Europe and England in the Ancient Regime*. Chicago: The University of Chicago Press, 2006.

Laverty, Megan J. "Learning Our Concepts." *Journal of Philosophy of Education* 43.1 (2009): 27–40.

Law Commission of India. "Law Commission Reports." Last modified August 25, 2015. Accessible at: http://lawcommissionofindia.nic.in/.

Liska, Allen E., and Yu, Jiang. "Specifying and Testing the Threat Hypothesis: Police Use of Deadly Force." In *Social Threat and Social Control,* Allen E. Liska, (Ed.), 53–68. Albany, NY: State University of New York, 1992.

Locke, John. *Two Treatises of Government*. Cambridge Texts in the History of Political Thought, Peter Laslett (Ed.). Cambridge: Cambridge University Press, 1988.

Lokaneeta, Jinee. *Transnational Torture: Law, Violence, and State Power in the United States and India*. New York: New York University Press, 2011.

Lokaneeta, Jinee. "The Aditi Sharma case and the implications for human rights in India." *Human Rights in Postcolonial India* (2016): 95.

MacIntyre, Alasdair. *After Virtue: A Study in Moral Theory*. Notre Dame, IN: University of Notre Dame Press, 1981.

March, James G., and Johan P. Olsen. "The Institutional Dynamics of International Political Orders." *International Organization* 52.4 (1998): 943–969.

Martin, Tomas. "Taking the Snake out of the Basket: Indian Prison Warders' Opposition to Human Rights Reform." In *State Violence and Human Rights: State Officials in the South*, Steffen Jensen and Andrew Jefferson (Eds.), 139–157. New York: Routledge-Cavendish, 2009.

Medcalf, Rory. "India Poll 2013." Lowy Institute for International Policy, 2013. Last accessed February 5, 2016, at: www.lowyinstitute.org/publications/india-poll-2013.

Mejias, Sam. "Politics, Power and Protest: Rights-Based Education Policy and the Limits of Human Rights Education." In *Human Rights Education: Theory, Research, Praxis*, Monisha Bajaj (Ed.), 142–161. Philadelphia: University of Pennsylvania Press, forthcoming.

Merry, Sally E. *Human Rights and Gender Violence: Translating International Law into Local Justice*. Chicago: University of Chicago Press, 2006.

Merry, Sally E. "Transnational Human Rights and Local Activism: Mapping the Middle." *American Anthropologist* 108.1 (2006): 38–51.

Merry, Sally Engle. "Human Rights Monitoring and the Question of Indicators." In *Human Rights at the Crossroads*, Mark Goodale (Ed.), 140–150. New York: Oxford University Press, 2013.

Meyer, John W., John Boli, George M. Thomas, and Francisco O. Ramirez. "World Society and the Nation?State." *American Journal of Sociology* 103.1 (1997): 144–181.

Milgram, Stanley. *Obedience to Authority: An Experimental View*. New York: Harper Perennial, 1974.

Miller, Peter, Paule Gronke, and Darius Rejali. "Torture and Public Opinion: The Partisan Dimension." In *Examining Torture: Empirical Studies of State Repression*, Tracy Lightcap and James P. Pfiffner (Eds.). New York: Palgrave Macmillan, 2014.

Mitra, Kana. "Human Rights in Hinduism." In *Human Rights in Religious Traditions*, Arlene Swindler (Ed.). New York: The Pilgrim Press, 1982.

Mobley, Van A. "Two Liberalisms: The Contrasting Visions of Hobbes and Locke." *Humanitas* 9.1 (1996): 6–34.

Montgomery, Heather. "Imposing Rights? A Case Study of Child Prostitution in Thailand." *Culture and Rights: Anthropological Perspectives* (2001): 80–101.

Mouffe, Chantal. "Deliberative Democracy or Agonistic Pluralism?" *Dialogue International Edition* 07–08 (1998): 9–21.

Moyn, Samuel. *The Last Utopia: Human Rights in History*. Cambridge: Harvard University Press, 2012.

Muir, William. *Police: Streetcorner Politicians*. Chicago: University of Chicago Press, 1977.

Mutua, Makua. *Human Rights: A Political and Cultural Critique*. Philadelphia: University of Pennsylvania Press, 2002.

Nag, Diya, and Devika Prasad. *Police Complaints Authorities: Reform Resisted*. New Delhi: Commonwealth Human Rights Initiative, 2011.

National Police Commission of India. *National Police Commission Reports* 1–8. 1979–1981. Last accessed May 12, 2013, at: http://bprd.nic.in/searchdetail.asp?lid=407.

New York Times. "Dangerous Corruption in India." July 12, 2015. Last accessed February 5, 2016, at: www.nytimes.com/2015/07/13/opinion/dangerous-corruption-in-india.html.

Niezen, Ronald. "The Law's Legal Anthropology." In *Human Rights at the Crossroads*, Mark Goodale (Ed.), 185–197. New York: Oxford University Press, 2013.

Nowak, Manfred. "On the Prevention of Torture." In *An End to Torture: Strategies for Its Eradication*, Bertil Dunér (Ed.), 247–251. London: Zed Books, 1998.

Office of the United Nations High Commissioner for Human Rights. "Human Rights Education and Training." United Nations Human Rights. Last accessed August 27, 2015, at: www.ohchr.org/EN/Issues/Education/Training/Pages/HREducationTrainingIndex.aspx.

Office of the United Nations High Commissioner for Human Rights. "Plan of Action: World Programme for Human Rights Education." New York: United Nations, 2006. Accessible at: www.ohchr.org/Documents/Publications/PActionEducationen.pdf.

Office of the United Nations High Commissioner for Human Rights. "Plan of Action: World Programme for Human Rights Education." New York: United Nations, 2012. Accessible at: www.ohchr.org/Documents/Publications/WPHRE_Phase_2_en.pdf.

Onazi, Oche. "Towards a Subaltern Theory of Human Rights." *Global Jurist* 9.2 (2009): 1–25.

O'Neill, Megan, Monique Marks, and Anne-Marie Singh. (Eds.). *Police Occupational Culture: New Debates and Directions*. Sociology of Crime, Law and Deviance Vol. 8. Oxford: Elsevier, 2007.

Payne, Leigh A. *Unsettling Accounts: Neither Truth Nor Reconciliation in Confessions of State Violence*. Durham, NC: Duke University Press, 2007.

Payne, Rodger A. "Persuasion, Frames and Norm Construction." *European Journal of International Relations* 7.1 (2001): 37–61.

Petro, Nicolai N. *Crafting Democracy: How Novgorod Has Coped with Rapid Social Change*. Ithaca, NY: Cornell University Press, 2004.

Prakash Singh v. Union of India (Supreme Court of India September 22, 2006). Accessible at: www.humanrightsinitiative. org/index.php?option=com_content&view=article&catid=91%3Ashiva&id=743%3Asupreme-court-judgment-of-22-september-2006-and-subsequent-orders&Itemid=98.

Press Trust of India. "Police Force Understaffed, over 3 Lakh Vacancies: PC." *Deccan Herald*, November 26, 2010. Accessible at: www.deccanherald.com/content/115958/F.

Ramirez, Francisco O., David Suárez, and John W. Meyer. "The Worldwide Rise of Human Rights Education." In *School Knowledge in Comparative and Historical Perspective: Changing Curricula in Primary and Secondary Education*, Aaron Benavot and Cecilia Braslovsky (Eds.), 35–52. Comparative Education Research Center. Hong Kong: Springer, 2007.

Reardon, Betty. "Human Rights Learning: Pedagogies and Politics of Peace." Paper for the UNESCO Chair for Peace Education Master Conference at the University of Puerto Rico, April 15, 2009. Last accessed February 5, 2016 at: www.pdhre.org/HRLreardon.pdf.

Rejali, Darius. *Torture and Democracy*. Princeton: Princeton University Press, 2007.

Risse, Thomas. "Let's Argue! Communicative Action in World Politics." *International Organization* 54.1 (2000): 1–39.

Risse, Thomas, Stephen C. Roppe, and Kathryn Sikkink. *The Power of Human Rights: International Norms and Domestic Change*. Cambridge: Cambridge University Press, 1999.

Risse, Thomas, Stephen C. Roppe, and Kathryn Sikkink. *The Persistent Power of Human Rights: From Commitment to Compliance*. Cambridge: Cambridge University Press, 2013.

Rorty, Richard. *Contingency, Irony, and Solidarity*. Cambridge: Cambridge University Press, 1989.

Rousseau, Jean-Jacques. "On the Social Contract." In *Basic Political Writings*, Donald A. Cress (Ed.), 141. Cambridge, Hackett Publishing, 1987.

Ruggie, John Gerard. "What Makes the World Hang Together? Neo-Utilitarianism and the Social Constructivist Challenge: *International Organization* 52.04 (1998): 855–885.

Russell, Garnett, and David Suárez. "Symbol and Substance: Human Rights Education as an Emergent Global Institution." In *Human Rights Education: Theory, Research, Praxis*, Monisha Bajaj (Ed.), 19–45. In. Philadelphia: University of Pennsylvania Press, forthcoming.

Santos, Boaventura de Sousa. *Towards a New Legal Common Sense: Law, Globalization and Emancipation*. Cambridge: Cambridge University Press, 2002.

Schaffer, Kay, and Sidonie Smith. *Human Rights and Narrated Lives: The Ethics of Recognition*. New York: Palgrave Macmillan, 2004.

Schimmelfennig, Frank. *The EU, NATO, and the Integration of Europe: Rules and Rhetoric*. Cambridge: Cambridge University Press, 2003.

Shklar, Judith N. *Ordinary Vices*. Cambridge: Belknap Press, 1985.

Schulz, Wolfram, John Ainley, Julian Fraillon, David Kerr, and Bruno Losito. *ICCS 2009 International Report: Civic Knowledge, Attitudes, and Engagement among Lower-Secondary School Students in 38 Countries*. Amsterdam: IEA, 2010.

Sen, Amartya. "Human Rights and the Westernizing Illusion." *Harvard International Review* 20.3 (1998): 40–43.

Sharma, Arvind. *Hindu Narratives on Human Rights*. Santa Barbara, CA: ABC-CLIO, 2010.

Sharma, Tanu. "J-K, NHRC Spar over Jurisdiction." *Indian Express*, January 17, 2011. Accessible at: http://indianexpress.com/article/news-archive/web/jk-nhrc-spar-over-jurisdiction/.

Shields, Jon A. *The Democratic Virtues of the Christian Right*. Princeton: Princeton University Press, 2009.

Shweder, Richard, Nancy C. Much, Manamohan Mahapatra, and Lawrence Park. "The 'Big Three' of Morality (Autonomy, Community, Divinity) and the 'Big Three' Explanations of Suffering." In *Morality and Health,* Allan M. Brandt and Paul Rozin (Eds.), 119–169. New York: Routledge, 1997.

Sikkink, Kathryn. "Human Rights, Principled Issue Networks, and Sovereignty in Latin America." *International Organization* 47.3 (1993): 411–441.

Sikkink, Kathryn. "Latin American Countries as Norm Protagonists of the Idea of International Human Rights." *Global Governance* 20.3 (2014): 389–404.

Simmons, Beth A. *Mobilizing for Human Rights: International Law in Domestic Politics*. Cambridge: Cambridge University Press, 2009.

Sklansky, David A. "Seeing Blue: Police Reform, Occupational Culture, and Cognitive Burn-In." In *Police Occupational Culture: New Debates and Directions*, Megan O'Neill, Monique Marks, and Anne-Marie Singh (Eds.), 19–46. Sociology of Crime, Law and Deviance Vol. 8. Oxford: Elsevier, 2007.

Skolnick, Jerome H., and James J. Fyfe. *Above the Law: Police and the Excessive Use of Force*. New York: Free Press, 1994.

Snyder, Jack. "Empowering Rights through Mass Movements, Religion, and Reform Parties." In *Human Rights Futures*, Stephen Hopgood, Leslie Vinjamuri, and Jack Snyder (Eds.). Cambridge and New York: Cambridge University Press, forthcoming in 2017)

Snyder, Jack, and Leslie Vinjamuri. "Trials and Errors: Principle and Pragmatism in Strategies of International Justice." *International Security* 28.3 (2003): 5–44.

Snyder, Jack, and Leslie Vinjamuri. (Eds). *Human Rights Futures*. (Under review.)

Spivak, Gayatri Chakravorty. *Outside in the Teaching Machine*. New York: Routledge, 2012.

South Asia Human Rights Documentation Centre. "Ignoring the Disappeared of Kashmir with Impunity." *Economic and Political Weekly* 47.45 (2012): 20–24.

Steiner-Khamsi, Gita, and Ines Stolpe. "Decentralization and Recentralization Reform in Mongolia: Tracing the Swing of the Pendulum." *Comparative Education* 40.1 (2004): 29–53.

Steiner-Khamsi, Gita. "Cross-National Policy Borrowing: Understanding Reception and Translation." *Asia Pacific Journal of Education* 34.2 (2014): 153–167.

Stellmacher, Jost, and Gert Sommer. "Human Rights Education: An Evaluation of University of Seminars." *Social Psychology* 39.1 (2008): 70–80.

Stewart, Charles. "Syncretism and Its Synonyms: Reflections on Cultural Mixture." *Diacritics* 29.3 (1999): 40–62.

Suárez, David. "Education Professionals and the Construction of Human Rights Education." *Comparative Education Review* 118.3: 253–280.

Sutton, Margaret, and Bradley A. Levinson. *Policy as Practice: Toward a Comparative Sociocultural Analysis of Educational Policy*. Westport, CT: Ablex Press, 2001.

Tankebe, Justice. "Public Cooperation with the Police in Ghana: Does Procedural Fairness Matter? *Criminology* 47.4 (2009): 1265–1293.

Taylor, Charles. *Sources of the Self: The Making of the Modern Identity*. Cambridge: Cambridge University Press, 1989.

Taylor, Charles. *Modern Social Imaginaries*. Durham, NC: Duke University Press, 2004.

Taylor, Charles. *A Secular Age*. Cambridge: The Belknap Press of Harvard University Press, 2008.

Taylor, Charles. "Modes of Secularism." In *Secularism and Its Critics*, R. Bhargava (Ed.). Delhi: Oxford University Press, 1998.

Terrill, William, Eugene A. Paoline III, and Peter K. Manning. "Police Culture and Coercion." *Criminology* 41.4 (2003): 1003–1034.

Tibbitts, Felisa. "Understanding What We Do: Emerging Models for Human Rights Education." *International Review of Education* 48.3 (2002): 159–171.

Tibbitts, Felisa. "Evolution of Human Rights Education Models." In *Human Rights Education: Theory, Research, Praxis*, Monisha Bajaj (Ed.). Philadelphia: University of Pennsylvania Press, forthcoming.

Tyler, Tom R. "Promoting Employee Policy Adherence and Rule Following in Work Settings: The Value of Self-Regulatory Approaches." *Brooklyn Law Review* 70 (2004): 1287–1312.

Tyler, Tom R., and Yuen Huo. *Trust in the Law: Encouraging Public Cooperation with the Police and Courts*. New York: Russell Sage Foundation, 2002.

Tyler, Tom R., Patrick E. Callahan, and Jeffrey Frost. "Armed and Dangerous (?): Motivating Rule Adherence among Agents of Social Control." *Law & Society Review* 41.2 (2007): 457–492.

United Nations General Assembly. The Prevention of Torture Bill. Lok Sabha, 58, Section 3i. United Nations Convention Against Torture. April 19, 2010. Accessible at: www.prsindia.org/uploads/media/Torture/prevention%20of%20torture%20bill%202010.pdf.

United Nations General Assembly, Resolution 34/169. "Code of Conduct for Law Enforcement Officials." December 17, 1979. Accessible at: www.un.org/disarmament/convarms/ATTPrepCom/Background%20documents/CodeofConductforlawEnfOfficials-E.pdf.

United Nations General Assembly, Resolution 66/137. "United Nations Declaration on Human RightsEducation and Training." December 19, 2011. Accessible at: www.ohchr.org/EN/Issues/Education/Training/Compilation/Pages/UnitedNationsDeclarationonHumanRightsEducationandTraining(2011).aspx.

United Nations General Assembly, Article 26(2). "Universal Declaration of Human Rights." December 10, 1948.

United Nations. *The Challenge of Human Rights and Cultural Diversity*. United Nations Department of Public Information, 1995.

United Nations. *The United Nations World Programme in Human Rights Education Plan of Action*. New York and Geneva: United Nations, 2006.

United Nations. *The Universal Declaration of Human Rights.* December 10, 1948. Accessible at: www.un.org/en/documents/udhr/.

United States Department of Justice, Office of Legal Counsel. *Memorandum for Alberto R. Gonzales, Counsel to the President.* August 1, 2002. Accessible at: www.pbs.org/wgbh/pages/frontline/torture/themes/redefining.html.

United States Department of State. *Country Reports on Human Rights Practices: India.* 2011. Last accessed February 23, 2013, at: www.state.gov/j/drl/rls/hrrpt/humanrightsreport/index.htm?dlid=186463.

University of Minnesota Human Rights Library. *The Terrorist and Disruptive Activities (Prevention) Act, 1987.* Last accessed January 23, 2016, at: www1.umn.edu/humanrts/research/terroristpreventionact-1987.html.

Vavrus, Frances, and Lesley Bartlett. "Comparative Pedagogies and Epistemological Diversity: Social and Materials Contexts of Teaching in Tanzania." In "The Local and the Global in Reforming Teaching and Teacher Education." Special Issue, *Comparative Education Review* 56.4 (2012): 634–658.

Verma, Arvind. *The Indian Police: A Critical Evaluation.* New Delhi: Regency Publications, 2005.

Waddington, P. A. J. "Police (Canteen) Sub-Culture: An Appreciation. *British Journal of Criminology* 39.2 (1999): 287–309.

Waddington, P. A. J., Otto Adang, David Baker, Christopher Birkbeck, Thomas Feltes, Luis Gerardo Gabaldón, Eduardo Paes Machado, and Philip Stenning. "Singing the Same Tune? International Continuities and Discontinuities in How Police Talk about Using Force." *Crime, Law and Social Change* 52.2 (2009): 111–138.

Wahl, R. "Justice, Context, and Violence: How Police Explain Torture." *Law and Society Review.* 48.4 (2014): 807–836.

Wendt, Alexander. "Constructing International Politics." *International Security* (1995): 71–81.

Westley, William A. *Violence and the Police: A Sociological Study of Law, Custom, and Morality.* Cambridge: MIT Press, 1970.

Wilson, Richard. *The Politics of Truth and Reconciliation: Legitimizing the Post-Apartheid State.* Cambridge: Cambridge University Press, 2001.

Wisnewski, J. Jeremy, and R. David Emerick. *The Ethics of Torture.* Bloomsbury Publishing, 2009.

Yardley, Jim. "Protests Awaken a Goliath in India." *New York Times.* October 29, 2011. Last accessed February 5, 2016, at: www.nytimes.com/2011/10/30/world/asia/indias-middle-class-appears-to-shed-political-apathy.html.

Yardley, Jim. "Urging Action, Report on Brutal Rape Condemns India's Treatment of Women." *New York Times.* January 23, 2013. Accessible at: www.nytimes.com/2013/01/24/world/asia/report-in-india-rape-case-condemns-nations-treatment-of-women.html?_r=0.

Zanjeer. Directed by Prakash Mehra. Prakash Mehra Productions, 1973.

Zimbardo, Philip. *The Lucifer Effect: Understanding How Good People Turn Evil.* New York: Random House, 2008.

Index

Stanford Studies in Human Rights

Mark Goodale, editor

Bodies of Truth: Law, Memory, and Emancipation in Post-Apartheid South Africa
Rita Kesselring
2016

Rights After Wrongs: Local Knowledge and Human Rights in Zimbabwe
Shannon Morreira
2016

If God Were a Human Rights Activist
Boaventura de Sousa Santos
2015

Digging for the Disappeared: Forensic Science after Atrocity
Adam Rosenblatt
2015

The Rise and Fall of Human Rights: Cynicism and Politics in Occupied Palestine
Lori Allen
2013

Campaigning for Justice: Human Rights Advocacy in Practice
Jo Becker
2012

In the Wake of Neoliberalism: Citizenship and Human Rights in Argentina
Karen Ann Faulk
2012

Values in Translation: Human Rights and the Culture of the World Bank
Galit A. Sarfaty
2012

Disquieting Gifts: Humanitarianism in New Delhi
Erica Bornstein
2012

Stones of Hope: How African Activists Reclaim Human Rights to Challenge Global Poverty
Edited by Lucie E. White and Jeremy Perelman
2011

Judging War, Judging History: Behind Truth and Reconciliation
Pierre Hazan
2010

Localizing Transitional Justice: Interventions and Priorities after Mass Violence
Edited by Rosalind Shaw and Lars Waldorf, with Pierre Hazan
2010

Surrendering to Utopia: An Anthropology of Human Rights
Mark Goodale
2009

Human Rights for the 21st Century: Sovereignty, Civil Society, Culture
Helen M. Stacy
2009

Human Rights Matters: Local Politics and National Human Rights Institutions
Julie A. Mertus
2009